MANAGING FOR RESULTS

Effective Resource Allocation for Public Libraries

Sandra Nelson
Ellen Altman
Diane Mayo

for the Public Library Association

AMERICAN LIBRARY ASSOCIATION

Chicago and London 2000

While extensive effort has gone into ensuring the reliability of information appearing in this book, the publisher makes no warranty, express or implied, as to the accuracy or reliability of the information, and does not assume and hereby disclaims any liability to any person for any loss or damage caused by errors or omissions in this publication.

Project manager: Joan A. Grygel

Cover: Baugher Design

Text design: Dianne M. Rooney

Composition: the dotted i in Stempel Schneidler and Univers using QuarkXpress 4.04 on a Macintosh

Printed on 50-pound white offset, a pH-neutral stock, and bound in 10-point coated cover stock by Data Reproductions

The paper used in this publication meets the minimum requirements of American National Standard for Information Sciences—Permanence of Paper for Printed Library Materials, ANSI Z39.48-1992. ∞

Library of Congress Cataloging-in-Publication Data

Nelson, Sandra S.
    Managing for results : effective resource allocation for public libraries / Sandra Nelson, Ellen Altman, and Diane Mayo for the Public Library Association.
        p.   cm.
    Includes index.
    ISBN 0-8389-3498-6 (alk. paper)
    1. Public libraries—Administration.   2. Public libraries—United States—Administration.   3. Resource allocation.   I. Altman, Ellen. II. Mayo, Diane, 1950– .   III. Public Library Association. IV. Title.
    Z678.N45   1999
    025.1'974—DC21   99-33130

Printed in the United States of America.

04 03   5 4 3 2

Contents

Figures

Instructions and Workforms

Acknowledgments

anaging for Results: Effective Resource Allocation for Public Libraries is the third in a series of PLA books dedicated to helping public librarians map out the futures of their libraries. *Planning for Results: A Public Library Transformation Process* and *Wired for the Future: Developing Your Library Technology Plan,* the first two books in the series, have served public librarians well. Thanks to the authors, Sandra Nelson, Ellen Altman, and Diane Mayo, we are certain this latest addition will prove as helpful as its predecessors.

As with most Public Library Association projects, this book is a product of the hard work and dedication of several persons. We thank the authors and contributors for their time, expertise, and contributions to this publication. We are also grateful to the PLA Resource Allocation Committee members Ron Dubberly, Marilyn Boria, Susan Kent, Gordon Conable, Anne Menzies, Mary Dempsey, Ruth Foley Metz, Regina Minudri, and Samuel Morrison for their thorough and constructive suggestions and to the chair of that committee, June Garcia. PLA is fortunate to be represented by such dedicated and knowledgeable leaders.

Harriet Henderson
PLA President 1999–2000

Greta K. Southard
PLA Executive Director

Introduction

In 1998, the Public Library Association published *Planning for Results: A Public Library Transformation Process* to provide a framework to help library managers make choices from among an ever-increasing number of possible priorities.[1] *Planning for Results* helps library managers, library staff, library boards, and community residents work together to identify community needs, select services to meet those needs, determine how to measure the effectiveness of the selected services, and allocate the resources required to implement those services.

Managing for Results: Effective Resource Allocation for Public Libraries is a companion volume to *Planning for Results*. A key element in *Planning for Results* is the identification of thirteen service responses. A service response is defined as "what a library does for, or offers to, the public in an effort to meet a set of well-defined community needs. . . . [Service responses] represent the gathering and deployment of specific critical resources to produce a specific public benefit or result."[2] *Managing for Results* provides library staff and managers with the tools they need to gather information about current resource allocation and to make decisions about deploying or redeploying resources to accomplish the desired results.

The thirteen service responses in *Planning for Results* are

Basic Literacy A library that offers Basic Literacy service addresses the need to read and to perform other essential daily tasks.

Business and Career Information A library that offers Business and Career Information service addresses a need for information related to business, careers, work, entrepreneurship, personal finances, and obtaining employment.

Commons A library that provides a Commons environment helps address the need of people to meet and interact with others in

1

their community and to participate in public discourse about community issues.

Community Referral   A library that offers Community Referral addresses the need for information related to services provided by community agencies and organizations.

Consumer Information   A library that provides Consumer Information service addresses the need for information to make informed consumer decisions and to help community residents become more self-sufficient.

Cultural Awareness   A library that offers Cultural Awareness service helps satisfy the desire of community residents to gain an understanding of their own cultural heritage and the cultural heritage of others.

Current Topics and Titles   A library that provides Current Topics and Titles helps to fulfill community residents' appetite for information about popular cultural and social trends and their desire for satisfying recreational experiences.

Formal Learning Support   A library that offers Formal Learning Support helps students who are enrolled in a formal program of education or who are pursuing their education through a program of home-schooling to attain their educational goals.

General Information   A library that offers General Information helps meet the need for information and answers to questions on a broad array of topics related to work, school, and personal life.

Government Information   The library that offers Government Information service helps satisfy the need for information about elected officials and governmental agencies that enables people to participate in the democratic process.

Information Literacy   A library that provides Information Literacy service helps address the need for skills related to finding, evaluating, and using information effectively.

Lifelong Learning   A library that provides Lifelong Learning service helps address the desire for self-directed personal growth and development opportunities.

Local History and Genealogy   A library that offers Local History and Genealogy service addresses the desire of community residents to know and better understand personal or community heritage.[3]

Planning for Results also includes a process to help library planners develop other service responses if their community has special needs or if they are serving a unique client group.

The service responses a library selects and the goals, objectives, and activities that are derived from those responses become the library's plan. *Managing for Results* is about turning plans into realities—about implementing the library's service priorities. That means that to use this book effectively, you must already have decided what you want to accomplish.

Every Library Has Some Sort of Plan

As a companion volume to *Planning for Results,* most of the examples given in *Managing for Results* are based on the *Planning for Results* service responses, described previously. However, *Managing for Results* can also be used to help allocate resources to accomplish results identified through any other planning model your library chooses to use.

While many libraries have used *Planning for Results* as the model for their planning efforts, other libraries have participated in city or county strategic planning processes. Some libraries choose to develop annual goals and objectives for the library as a whole rather than developing a multiyear plan. Others develop goals and objectives for individual units or for specific programs or services. Even libraries that do not go through any kind of formal planning process have implicit plans that are reflected in their budgets. In fact, no matter what planning process a library uses, the budget identifies the actual priorities that will be addressed during the fiscal year.

Using the budget process as the primary planning tool presents two main problems. The first is that it is easy to let the available resources determine what services will be provided rather than building the service program on identified community needs. In other words, the tail often wags the dog. The second problem in using the budget as a planning tool is that it makes it very easy to continue existing programs and fairly difficult to reallocate existing resources.

What should you do if your library has no current plan? Must you complete the whole planning process before you can use any of the tools in this book? Absolutely not. *Managing for Results* has been organized to help you make resource decisions whatever your environment might be. However, it is worth repeating that this book is about *implementing* services and not about determining priorities and identifying desired outcomes. *Before you can decide how to allocate your resources you must know what you want to accomplish.* Any process used to determine the library's desired outcomes can serve as the starting point for the resource allocation process described in this book.

Wired for the Future

In 1999, the Public Library Association published *Wired for the Future: Developing Your Library Technology Plan* to help libraries identify their technology options and select from among those options the best technology infrastructure and products to support the library's service goals.[4] *Wired for the Future* is fully compatible with *Planning for Results;* indeed, the library service priorities serve as a starting point for the technology planning process just as they do in *Managing for Results.* Obviously, *Wired for the Future* addresses technology resource-allocation issues. How then does it relate to *Managing for Results,* which also includes a chapter on allocating resources for technology?

Actually, the two books overlap very little. *Wired for the Future* helps library managers make decisions about establishing a technological infrastructure and selecting the products and services that support their identified service outcomes. If you have not yet developed a basic technology infrastructure in the library or if you suspect that the library infrastructure needs to be significantly changed or upgraded, you should use *Wired for the Future* as the basis for decision making. If, on the other hand, the library's basic technology infrastructure is in place and your resource allocation concerns are focused on the availability and use of hardware, software, and online resources, then *Managing for Results* has many of the tools you will need.

Other Uses for This Book

The discussion so far has focused on ways library managers might use the information in this book to implement the outcomes in a full-scale library service plan. However, that is by no means the only use for the processes presented here and the data you gather using those processes. The following list is just a sampling of ways the tools in the book might be used by library managers.

- Develop project budgets
- Gather information to use when developing zero-based budgets
- Provide justification for grant applications
- Review internal data collection efforts
- Organize data about existing resource allocation in more meaningful ways
- Determine the effectiveness of specific services or programs

All of these possible applications have one of two things in common: They focus on using information to make resource allocation decisions that lead to specific results or on measuring the effectiveness of previous resource allocation decisions. In other words, they all deal with helping library managers determine what resources will be required to achieve their desired outcomes.

Some Basic Definitions

Before you begin to read this book and use it to make resource decisions, it will be helpful if you understand how some basic terms have been used. Every public library is a little different. One library uses the term *branches,* another uses the term *agencies,* and a third refers to both branches and departments as *units.* Some libraries have *central* libraries; others have *main* libraries. There are libraries that report to authority boards and libraries that are units of the government entity that funds them. These differences can cause confusion among readers because each reader expects to see his or her reality reflected in the terms and examples used. A list of terms and their meanings *in this book* follows.

Library Terms

branch   A separate facility from the central library

central library   The largest library facility, normally in a downtown area; referred to as the "main" library in some places

department   A unit within a single facility that is normally a central library

library   The entire organizational entity and its units

manager   A generic term that refers to the staff member or members who are responsible for resource allocation in a particular area; in some libraries the "manager" is actually a team of staff members

team   A group of staff members brought together to work on a specific project or program; often includes members from different departments and with different job classifications

unit   A term used to refer to library departments and branches, if any

Other Terms

allocate   To set apart or designate for a specific purpose

allocation   That which has been set apart or designated

case study   Fictional example from a midsized public library

resource   The unit of allocation in each area:

collection: the basic unit of allocation is money, for example, the materials budget

staffing: the basic unit of allocation is staff time, for example, full-time equivalent (FTE)

facility: the basic unit of allocation is square feet of space

technology: the basic unit of allocation is money, for example, the budget for equipment and infrastructure

Using the Materials in This Book Effectively

Resource allocation is a complex activity that requires balancing a number of factors and, in the end, is always a matter of judgment. There are no absolutes in this area—no right or wrong answers. In other words, this is never going to be easy. However, the process can be made easier if you have accurate information upon which to base decisions.

Managing for Results provides a flexible process for helping library managers get the information needed to make resource decisions. The book has been divided into five chapters. The first chapter includes a discussion of a variety of issues that have an impact on every aspect of resource allocation in public libraries today. The remaining four chapters focus on specific library resources: staff, collections, facilities, and technology. Each of these four chapters has been divided into two parts: first, a discussion of the issues relating to the allocation of the resource under review; second, a variety of workforms intended to help library staff members gather the data they need to make the resource allocation decisions required to achieve the library's service priorities. The workforms are reproducible.

Deciding What Data to Collect

It is extremely unlikely that any library will ever collect all of the data described in this book or use all of the workforms included here, nor is it easy to think of a situation in which that would be desirable. Just as every library has different priorities, so will every library need different information to make resource decisions. Virtually every library already has some current data that can be used. The key is to determine what additional information should be collected and analyzed before staff can make informed decisions.

The underlying assumption in this book is that you will gather only the information that you plan to use for a specific purpose in the immediate future. We are all far too busy to gather data because it might be useful sometime. Actually, given the rapidly changing environment in which we are working, if data isn't used fairly quickly it becomes useless.

To underline the fact that you will be collecting only certain specific pieces of information, this book has been designed to be used like the *Choose Your Own Adventure* titles published by Bantam Books. In those books, you are offered several choices at each decision point in the story. Once you make your choice, you move to another part of the book to pick up the narrative from the point of your choice.

Decisions Are Based on Activities

You will also select from the information in this book those parts that are most relevant to your current situation. You will base your choices on the *outcomes* the library is trying to achieve. Specifically, you will work from the activities you have selected to accomplish those outcomes. The activities you select should be directly related to intended outcomes (goals) and the way you plan to measure progress toward meeting those outcomes (objectives).

The activities in a library plan form the actual blueprint from which the library will implement its goals and objectives. Because activities are very specific, it is easier to use them as the basis for determining resource needs than to use the more general goals or objectives. If *Planning for Results* was used as the model to develop the library plan, the activities for the current planning cycle are probably listed on the *Planning for Results* Activities for This Planning Cycle Workform. (For your convenience, that workform is reproduced in appendix A.) If you used another planning model or if you are working from a project plan, you will need to develop a list of the activities required to accomplish the intended outcomes to serve as the basis for data collection and analysis. If you wish, you may want to use the workform in appendix A to record your activities, although it is not necessary.

Analyzing Activities

The first step toward using the information and processes in this book is to review your list of activities to determine what types of resources are required to accomplish each. Some activities are clearly staff intensive, while others have a greater impact on materials allocations or technology or facilities. For example, activities intended to help a library achieve goals and objectives related to the Commons service response (the need of people to meet and interact) are going have serious facility implications. It is equally clear that activities intended to support the goals and objectives related to the Information Literacy service response are going to be affected by and have an impact on technology resources.

However, it is important not to make quick decisions about the resource implications of activities. You will want to look carefully at the impact of your activities on all resources and not just on the most obvious resources. Very few activities affect only one type of resource. For example, you may think that the activities relating to the Current Topics and Titles service response would deal primarily with the library's collections. However, collection development activities have significant staffing implications, including the additional staff time needed to acquire, catalog, and process the materials; the additional time required to shelve more materials; added time at the circulation desk to handle the increased workload; and, perhaps, increased staff time required to deliver materials from one unit to another. There may also be facility and technology issues to consider as well.

You might find it helpful to create a table like the one illustrated in figure 1 to help review the activities. Figure 1 includes a scale to rank the

FIGURE 1
Analyzing Activities

List the activities. For each, rank the impact the activity will have on each of the four resources using the scale below.

1 = Critical resource to accomplish activity
2 = Important resource to accomplish activity
3 = Resource will be affected by the activity but not significantly
4 = Resource will not be affected by the activity

Activity	Staff	Collection	Facility	Technology

impact of an activity on each of the resources. One activity might be "to set up a homework help Web page." Using the scale in figure 1, staff and technology could be ranked as "1" (critical resource to accomplish activity). Collection might be ranked as "2" or "3," depending on the kinds of materials support the library staff decides to provide for the information on the Web page. The facility would probably be ranked as "4" (resource will not be affected by the activity). If the activity under review was "to purchase additional preschool materials," collection would probably be ranked "1." Staffing would probably be ranked "2"; facility would be ranked "2" or "3," depending on the specific circumstances of the library. Technology would be ranked "4."

Clearly such rankings are judgment calls. The rankings will differ in each library and in each library unit depending upon local conditions. In fact, you may prefer to use a completely different ranking scale or another review process altogether. The process used is not important. What is important is that you develop a clear understanding of the kinds of resources required to accomplish each activity and the extent to which those resources will be affected by the activity.

When you have completed reviewing the resource implications of each of the activities in the current planning cycle, you are undoubtedly going to discover that all four major resource areas will be affected. At first glance, it is difficult to see how knowing this is going to help you decide what information is needed to make informed decisions. However, if you look more carefully at the results of the review, it will probably become apparent that some resources are going be affected more significantly by the activities than others. It may be that five or six of the activities will have a major impact on staffing, while only two or three will have a significant impact on the facility. That suggests that the place to start collecting data is in the staffing area.

Remember, too, that different staff members can be involved in collecting different types of data. Perhaps the activities that affect the youth librarians are collection-intensive. They, then, could be asked to review the collection chapter of this book to select the data that would help them allocate collection resources. At the same time, adult services staff might find that the activities they will be assigned have a heavy technology emphasis. Those staff members might be encouraged to review the technology chapter.

One Step at a Time

What you want to avoid is running off in all directions at once. There is no point in trying to do everything at the same time. It will be far more effective for you and your colleagues to focus attention on one or two resource areas, decide what information is needed in those areas, gather and analyze that data, and then make decisions based on what you learn. This process of gathering and analyzing data will be a continuing one. One analogy might be to the situation in which a woman makes a New Year's resolution to begin an exercise program. If she starts out on January 1 by walking five miles and then on January 2 she again tries to walk five miles, by January 3 she is going to be tired and stiff. She is probably going to quit walking "until the stiffness goes away" and, for one reason or another, may not start again until it's time for the next set of New Year's resolutions. If, on the other hand, she starts slowly and walks for ten minutes three times during the first week, for fifteen minutes three times during the second week, and then gradually increases her walking time to thirty minutes three or four times a week, she is far more likely to sustain the exercise program.

It is the same with the processes suggested in this book. If library managers decide to gather a wide variety of data in all four resource areas, they may or may not get information they can use. However, they are very likely to become so frustrated by the increased data collection workload and so overwhelmed by data that they give up on the whole thing. On the other hand, if those same managers begin to use the processes suggested in this book carefully and gradually, they will find that the data they gather can be very useful. That, in turn, may lead to a new management approach in which data is collected when needed and used to help make and justify resource allocation decisions.

A Word about Workforms

As noted earlier, four chapters in this book focus on specific resources: staff, collections, facilities, and technology. The second part of each of those chapters includes a number of workforms intended to help library managers gather the data they need to make resource decisions. The workforms for each chapter are quite different, reflecting the unique nature of each type of resource. For a summary listing of the workforms in a chapter, see the first figure in that chapter.

Staff workforms begin with the letter *S,* and the eighteen workforms are grouped into five main categories. The five categories of workforms in this chapter are interrelated to a degree, and some workforms will require data collected through the use of other workforms within the chapter. However, you should select from among the workforms within each category those that seem most applicable to your library.

Collection workforms begin with the letter *C.* Although the seventeen collection workforms are grouped in six categories, each workform stands alone. You can choose to use as many or as few of the workforms as you wish based on the activities in the library's plan that will affect collection resources.

Facilities workforms begin with the letter *F.* This group of six workforms is fairly generic. Because each library facility is unique, it would be virtually impossible to develop detailed workforms that would have any value for specific buildings and furniture. The first part of the facilities chapter includes a number of more open-ended questions that managers might consider when evaluating their unit's current facilities.

Technology workforms begin with letter *T.* These fifteen workforms are different from the others in that they were designed to be used in sequence. That is, the data gathered on one set of workforms is required to complete the next set of workforms.

It is important to review *all* of the workforms in each chapter carefully before deciding what data to collect. Each of the resource chapters contains considerably more information about the workforms, including a summary list of the workforms and their purposes along with discussions of the major issues to consider in deciding which workforms to use. In addition, instructions are included with each workform, and general instructions preceding each group of workforms cover common elements of that set. These instructions include

factors to consider before completing the workform

step-by-step directions

suggested sources of data

factors to consider when reviewing the data collected

All of the workforms are intended to be examples. You might find it useful to create similar forms with your spreadsheet program rather than simply photocopying the workforms presented here. For example, because the workforms in this book are constrained by the size of the book pages, you may find that the data collected for your situation may not fit on those pages. Creating a spreadsheet will allow you to add columns and enlarge their width, add rows as needed, and modify the format to suit your situation. Spreadsheet programs also have the capability to do many of the arithmetical calculations called for in the instructions. Furthermore, you can easily copy a spreadsheet format to create summary sheets for the entire library system.

When Asking Staff to Complete Forms

All of the workforms in this book were field tested by public librarians. One of the most important things learned during the field tests had nothing to do with the workforms at all. It had to do with the kinds of information staff members need to effectively complete the workforms. Each workform includes full instructions for gathering the data requested. In some field-test libraries, staff members were simply given the workforms and asked to fill in the blanks in accordance with the instructions. In other field-test libraries, staff members were given copies of chapter 1 and the chapter pertinent to the subject of the workforms to be completed. These people were asked to read those chapters before beginning to collect data. In every instance, the staff members who had a context for the data collection were more comfortable with the workforms and collected more-appropriate data. Remember, the data to be collected pertains to specific activities. Staff members must have enough information about the processes recommended in *Managing for Results* to be able to identify the appropriate activities before data collection can even begin.

When working with the processes in this book in a real-world environment and not in a field-test environment, it is clear that communication is going to be critical. All staff members must know why the data is being collected. They will have to reach agreement on the resources to review and the relation of those resources to the activities in the library service plan or project plan. They will have to discuss the data once it is collected to reach consensus on the meaning of the data. Finally, they will have to work together to implement the changes in resource allocation that result from this thorough review. Chapter 1 includes information on these issues and more.

NOTES

1. Ethel Himmel and William James Wilson, *Planning for Results: A Public Library Transformation Process* (Chicago: American Library Assn., 1998).

2. Himmel and Wilson, 54.

3. Himmel and Wilson, Workform M1–M2.

4. Diane Mayo and Sandra S. Nelson, *Wired for the Future: Developing Your Library Technology Plan* (Chicago: American Library Assn., 1999).

Chapter 1

Results Require Resources

If your library is typical, you and your colleagues collect a lot of data about a wide variety of services and programs. However, when it is time to make decisions, you probably never seem to have exactly the information you think you need to make the best decision. When you start to search for that elusive piece of information that will make all things clear, you find that the library is actually collecting far more data than you (or anyone else) realized. In fact, you probably discover that most people are not sure why they are collecting the data or what to do with it after they have gathered it.

Instead of finding information that clarifies your thinking and leads logically to a decision point, you realize that you are awash in a flood of unrelated and unanalyzed "facts" of one sort or another. The information you need might be included in that mass—in fact it probably is—but you have no easy way of finding it, and you certainly don't have the time or energy to analyze all the data the library collects to find the pieces that are pertinent to your problem. So, in the end, you do what you have done before: You make the best decision you can based on your general understanding of the problem, and you promise yourself that someday soon you will get a handle on all of the data gathering in the library—or at least that part of the library that is your responsibility.

For most of us, that "someday soon" never comes. *Managing for Results* offers the tools and encouragement you need to turn "someday" into "now." It has been designed to help you first decide what data to collect and then to organize that data into meaningful information, information that can be used to make decisions about how to allocate library resources effectively. That is, after all, the primary reason we should collect data about library services and programs in the first place.

Resource Allocation Issues

In *Managing for Results,* library resources have been divided into four general categories: staff, collections, facilities, and technology. The issues surrounding the resources in each category are quite different and are identified and discussed at the beginning of each of the chapters. There are, however, some underlying issues that have an impact on every aspect of resource allocation in public libraries in this time of rapid and continuous change.

Communication Is Essential

When beginning to consider allocating and reallocating resources in a changing environment, the first thing to remember is that communication is the key element in creating an organization that is flexible and responsive to change.

> In 1993, The Wyatt Company asked CEOs in 531 U.S. organizations that had recently undergone major restructuring to identify one thing they would change about their restructuring effort. Overwhelmingly they said they would like to alter the way they communicated with their employees about the change effort.[1]

It is very difficult to change an organization by fiat. Change doesn't happen because managers want it to. Change occurs when staff at all levels understand the reasons for the change and the benefits that are expected to result from the change and then incorporate the change into the way they do their jobs. Achieving staff understanding and cooperation requires consistent, ongoing communication from top management down through the organization and then back up from staff at all levels to top management. Now, more than ever before, library managers, library staff members, library board members, and community stakeholders need to work together to ensure that their lines of communication are open and clear, for together they are engaged in redesigning every aspect of library service.

Libraries Are Being Transformed

Libraries of all types are literally being transformed from stand-alone, print-based organizations to multimedia organizations electronically linked to other libraries and to hundreds of thousands of other institutions, organizations, and individuals as well. In public libraries this transformation started slowly with the introduction of microforms, films, and records and picked up steam with the advent of video and audiotapes. Next came the CD-ROM electronic reference resources and then, suddenly, there was the World Wide Web offering access to the vast resources of the Internet.

When you think about the typical public library of the early 1980s and compare that with the typical public library today, you get an idea of the magnitude of the changes that have occurred in our profession.

These changes have not necessarily affected the outcomes we are trying to achieve in our libraries, but they have certainly given us powerful new tools to achieve those outcomes. Because we have these tools, we are all learning to do things differently. Reference librarians are becoming cybrarians; children's librarians use print, video, audio, and electronic resources to introduce children to books and learning; librarians providing services to clients with special needs have access to a wide array of resources modified to specifically serve each client group; and technical services staff members work in an increasingly automated environment. In addition, a significant and growing portion of our business comes through offsite access to our resources via the Internet. It is more and more difficult to do things "the way we always have."

Meanwhile, managers are trying to balance the costs of installing and using all of these new electronic resources while maintaining more traditional and still heavily used services and programs. This is truly an interesting time to be a librarian—and many library managers have come to understand why "may you live in interesting times" was once considered a powerful curse in China.

Managers Must Make Hard Choices

Most library managers have never had all of the resources they require to meet all of the needs in the communities they serve. Good managers learn early in their careers that to provide quality library services they must make informed choices from among a wide range of competing priorities. Furthermore, they soon discover that those choices rarely involve selecting a very important priority over a relatively unimportant priority. Often the priorities under review are quite different but equally valid and equally important.

Making these choices wasn't easy twenty years ago, and it has become more challenging every year since. However, while choosing is difficult, not choosing is fatal. Library managers who continue to do business the same way they did last year and the year before are jeopardizing the very existence of the library itself.

Change Isn't Just about New Programs and Services

The thirteen service responses in *Planning for Results* are not intended to be considered solely as new or add-on services. Actually, taken together they probably represent many, if not all, of the services your library currently provides. What the service responses do is offer a mechanism for library planners to identify the most important community needs and review the current library programs and services in relation to those needs. Although this review occasionally results in a new program or service, far more often it results in increased or decreased emphasis on programs or services currently provided.

This *new* versus *changed* emphases is an important distinction to make. All too often in the past, library managers have thought about planning only in terms of new or expanded services that would require additional resources. If the new resources were not available for whatever reason, the proposed new services were often delayed or dropped altogether. Library managers have rarely thought about planning as a process of *re*allocating resources. In fact, many would agree with the library director who said, "I can't reallocate my resources. I don't have enough as it is."

As noted earlier, libraries of all types are being transformed as a result of the new technologies and the changing needs of their clients. The service responses, used in conjunction with the rest of the process described in *Planning for Results,* provide a mechanism for determining which of the services the library currently offers or might choose to offer best meet the unique needs of your community. The process then suggests a framework to help you ensure that those services are offered in the most effective way possible. This is a continuation of the key theme in earlier planning documents published by the Public Library Association: Public libraries are more effective when they focus their resources on meeting the most important needs in the community rather than trying to do everything for everyone.[2]

Managing for Results continues to build and expand on this theme of focusing resources to achieve excellence. However, in *Managing for Results* there is an strong emphasis on the fact that library managers can and should look at how they are *currently* doing business, as well as what they want to do in the future. Further, the assumption is that given the rapidly changing environment in which libraries operate, almost every library could use some of its resources more effectively.

The Difference between Effectiveness and Efficiency Is More Important Than Ever

Efficiency can be defined as "doing something right," and *effectiveness* can be defined as "doing the right thing." It is not only possible but common for libraries to do something very well that they shouldn't be doing at all.

For example, a branch library staff might have established an efficient process for maintaining and updating the vertical files. They might have divided the responsibility by subject areas, developed finding aids to help people identify and locate the files they need, and scheduled time for regular filing and refiling. They might even have scheduled regular weeding of the vertical files (although that isn't as likely). However, the fact that they are efficiently managing the vertical files in no way addresses the fundamental question of why a branch library would keep vertical files at all when thousands, perhaps millions, of articles are available relatively inexpensively on CD-ROM or online. It isn't just a question of the number of articles available; the electronic resources are fully indexed for easy access. When you consider the amount of staff time required to maintain vertical files, the relatively limited resources available through vertical files, and the difficulty of retrieving information from vertical files, it seems clear that vertical files are not the most effective way to provide access to ephemeral information.

Pareto's Law

One hundred years ago Vilfredo Pareto, an Italian economist and sociologist, formulated what has come to be known as the 80/20 Rule:

> In most endeavors, eighty percent of your results come from twenty percent of your efforts.

It is important to note that the 80/20 Rule talks about achieving results. You can't determine how effective your organization is until you know what you want to accomplish. Let's look at an example of Pareto's Law in a library we'll call the Anytown Public Library.

CASE STUDY PART 1

The Anytown Public Library serves a community that includes a large number of families with young children. The community is made up primarily of lower- and middle-class families, and in most families both parents work. The library completed a planning process last year and decided that one priority should be lifelong learning, specifically introducing young children to the love of books and reading. The progress made toward meeting this priority would be measured in three ways:

> the number of individual children under the age of seven who participate in one or more library-sponsored programs
>
> the increase in circulation of easy books and picture books
>
> the opinion of parents obtained through focus groups about the importance of the library in introducing their children to the love of books and reading

The library has two full-time staff members who work in the children's area. Their activities include working with students who come in after school and planning and presenting four story programs a week in the library. They also plan and present special puppet shows during the major holidays throughout the year and manage a summer reading program targeted for grade school children. In addition, they select materials and maintain the juvenile collections. The budget for juvenile materials was not increased last year, and the staff made no significant changes in the kinds of materials purchased. During the past year the staff developed a homework help Web page for grade school students. Almost all staff work is done in the library, although they visit some classrooms each spring to promote the summer reading program.

Does the staff do these things well? Probably. Are the staff members being effective; that is, will their activities result in the progress they hope to make? Probably not. The vast proportion of staff time and energy is expended on programs inside the library for children who can get to the library. However, in most families in Anytown both parents work during the day and can't bring their children to the library. As a result, the number of individual children reached will be relatively small. The major new program developed during the past year focused on homework help, a very different priority from creating a love of books and reading. Even the summer reading program, the program most likely to introduce children to books and reading, is targeted for older children who can read. It also is held in the library and therefore restricted to children who can get to the library. The materials budget was not increased, and no extra resources were allocated to purchase easy books and picture books.

How can the library restructure these services to be more effective in terms of the intended outcomes and ensure that a greater proportion of staff efforts will go into achieving the results identified as desirable? The answer is simple in theory but difficult in practice. All staff members involved, management staff as well as front-line staff, first have to develop a list of activities likely to achieve the desired outcomes. Then they need to look critically at the way resources are currently allocated. Finally, they have to make the changes in staff time, materials budget, use of technology, etc., required to accomplish the activities that will lead to the desired results.

The first intended outcome was that the number of individual children under the age of nine who participate in one or more library programs would increase. To make progress toward this result, the staff will have to take more programs to children outside the library, working with day-care centers, Head Start programs, and grades 1 through 3 in the public schools. They might also present a series of evening or weekend story programs in the library specifically targeted at families with young children. To plan and present these new programs, it is likely that several of the in-library daytime story programs will have to be discontinued. One or two of the puppet shows might be continued with performances scheduled in day-care centers, schools, etc. The summer reading program could be expanded to include a "read-to-me" component targeted at preschool children. The library could enter into a partnership with the recreation department to do some joint programming in recreational facilities over the summer. The library might develop a "dial-a-story" program that parents and children could access any time. Finally, the staff might choose to develop a Web page for parents of young children with links to child development sites, recommended book lists, and suggestions for connecting children and books.

The second intended outcome was to increase the circulation of easy books and picture books. While there are a number of factors that affect circulation, the most important is the availability of new materials. Therefore, to increase circulation, the library could allocate additional resources to purchase new easy books and picture books. If that can't happen, the staff could reallocate their collection budget to emphasize this area, understanding that such a decision means that other parts of the collection will get proportionately fewer resources.

The third intended outcome was to obtain the opinion of parents through focus groups about the importance of the library in introducing their children to the love of books and reading. The early childhood Web page is one tool that might help achieve this result. Other possibilities include short recommended reading lists distributed through day-care centers and Head Start programs, presentations at grade school PTAs, etc.

There Are No Guarantees

All of us would like assurances that the decisions we make are the right ones and that the programs and services we offer will accomplish what we hope. However, experienced library managers know that there are no guarantees. While planning generally leads to better results than not planning, the best plan in the world can deal only with possibilities and intentions. The minute a plan stops being an idea and starts being an actual service or program, it begins to change. Managers learn to expect the unexpected.

Inevitably, not all of the examples of ways to modify the services and programs offered by the Anytown Public Library will work. For example, it may prove to be too difficult to develop a partnership with the recreation department to present summer programs. The new Web page for parents might not be used as heavily as anticipated. Perhaps the additional resources allocated to enhancing the easy and picture books collections were inadequate to make more than token changes. When things don't turn out the way you expected them to, what can you do?

To effectively implement your plans you need to monitor your progress and make adjustments as the implementation process progresses. Even with all of the data available, the best decision-making model is often "estimate, implement, check, adjust" and then "check and adjust" again—and again. It is important not to become so enamored with your plans that you forget that they aren't implemented in a safely controlled environment but in the real world where hundreds of unrelated issues may affect them. This is particularly true now when the real-world environment is changing daily.

Moving from Outcomes to Required Resources

When faced with having to allocate resources for a specific project or program, most of us go through pretty much the same process, whether consciously or unconsciously:

We start with a picture of the final outcome we hope to achieve.

Then we decide what resources will be required to accomplish the desired results.

Next, we look at the resources (if any) currently allocated to produce the results we want.

Finally, we determine the difference or gap between what we are allocating now and what we need and develop a plan for filling the gap or reallocating the surplus.

It may help to visualize this process if you think about it in terms of constructing, deconstructing, and then reconstructing something, perhaps a new kitchen for your home. You initially construct something in your mind when you describe the desired outcome. Let's say you want a larger kitchen with new appliances including a professional gas stove. Your architect or contractor can draw up plans that will show you exactly what the final product—your new kitchen—will look like based on your description of what is important.

Next, the contractor will separate those plans into their component parts and determine what resources are required to make each a reality. For instance, the contractor may tell you that you have to have a gas line run to your house to operate the stove you selected. Once you know what will be needed, you identify your current resources. You may discover that you live in an all-electric neighborhood and that it will be very expensive to have a gas line installed. At that point you have to make some important resource allocation decisions. Do you allocate the money to have the gas line installed, do you select a new stove that uses electricity, or do you keep your old stove? If you decide to go ahead and install the gas line, where will you get the additional financial resources required? Will you increase the overall project budget or reduce the cost of or eliminate another part of the remodeling project?

When you finish making all of these resource allocation decisions and the kitchen is finally constructed, the reality will not look exactly like the kitchen you planned. It will have been modified based on the resource decisions you made during the process of moving from a plan to a reality.

Gap Analysis

The process for determining what resources will be required to accomplish specific outcomes that was described in the kitchen remodeling story is called *gap analysis,* and it was first presented in *Planning for Results.* In fact, the emphasis on the importance of allocating the resources required to implement library priorities is among the most significant changes in *Planning for Results* from earlier Public Library Association planning models. One of the chapters in *Planning for Results* is entirely devoted to identifying resource allocation issues and helping library managers and planners make the hard decisions required to move from plans to accomplishments.[3] That chapter is organized around the gap analysis process illustrated in the previous example. That process is summarized in the *Planning for Results* Gap Analysis Workform. A miniature of the workform is shown in figure 2, and a copy of the workform can be found in appendix B.

Although the Gap Analysis Workform was designed to be used with *Planning for Results,* it can be used just as effectively with any other planning process.

The gap analysis process requires that you ask hard questions. *Managing for Results* helps you identify, collect, and analyze the information needed to answer those questions.

Let's return to the Anytown Public Library case study and see how the Anytown managers could apply the gap analysis process to their review of resources needed to reach their goal of introducing young children to the love of books and reading.

FIGURE 2
Gap Analysis Workform

Service/Response/Activity			
(Resource under review)	Have	Need	Gap
	Plan for filling the gap or reallocating the surplus		
(Resource under review)	Have	Need	Gap
	Plan for filling the gap or reallocating the surplus		

STEP 1: What is the intended outcome?

One of the desired outcomes was an increase in the circulation of easy and picture books, and one of the suggestions for increasing circulation was to add new, attractive easy and picture books to the juvenile collection.

STEP 2: What resources will be required to achieve that outcome?

$10,000 for easy and picture books for each of the next two years.

STEP 3: What resources are currently available?

$6,000 for easy and picture books in the current year budget.

STEP 4: What is the difference or gap?

There is a gap of $4,000 in the current year budget and $10,000 in the budget for next year.

STEP 5: What is the plan for filling the gap (or reallocating the surplus)?

Year 1
1. *Move $2,500 from juvenile nonfiction to easy and picture books; move $1,500 from adult nonfiction to easy and picture books.*
2. *Request a recurring increase in materials money for easy and picture books from the library's funding body.*

Year 2
1. *Use increased appropriation.*
2. *If appropriation increase is not approved, continue to use Year 1 reallocations and ask for the recurring increase again.*

Year 3
1. *Use increased appropriation.*
2. *If appropriation increase is not approved, review results of increased funding for easy and picture books and decreased funding for juvenile and adult nonfiction and decide what to do based on that data.*

What becomes clear from this example is that it isn't hard to decide what questions to ask. The difficulty comes in figuring out the answers. How did the Anytown Public Library staff decide that $10,000 was needed to reach the desired outcomes? Why not $7,500 or $15,000? Why did they decide to take the money from juvenile and adult nonfiction collections and not from fiction or media? If the Anytown Library managers who made these decisions are like most library managers, their decisions were based on minimal data combined with gut instinct and an acute awareness of which staff members would scream the loudest if the resources in the budgets they manage were reallocated.

Even if the Anytown managers had decided they wanted to try to determine their resource requirements in a more systematic way, they would have been on their own. Until recently there have been few tools to help library managers make decisions about resources. Earlier library planning models focused on helping managers and board members decide what services they wanted to provide. The unwritten assumption in these models seemed to be that the hard part of planning was deciding *what* to do and that once that was known, the *how* to make it happen could and would be addressed through the regular library budgeting process.

The reality was that this disconnect between the *what* and the *how* was reflected in the aftermath of the planning efforts in many public libraries of all sizes. These libraries selected roles; developed goals, objectives, and plans of action; and then considered their planning efforts to be complete. If there was any specific thought given to resource allocation issues in the formal planning process, it was focused on the need for new resources to implement the priorities identified in the plan. It was a rare library staff that considered *re*allocating resources to accomplish their priorities.

The processes and workforms in *Managing for Results* will help you determine *how* to achieve the outcomes defined in the library's planning process. Planning is not an end in itself. The end is improved and enhanced library services targeted to meeting critical community needs. These services require resources.

Finding the Resources You Need

Libraries have traditionally had two main sources of funding. The first, and primary, source is the governing body of the city, county, parish, etc., served by the library. The second source includes the individuals, groups, and organizations that donate funds or award grant monies to the library. The monies that come from both of these sources can be either recurring or one-time funds. Commonly, the funding received from the governing body is recurring and that received from other sources is one-time money, but that is not always the case.

In addition to appropriated and donated/grant funding, libraries may be able to obtain resources by entering into partnerships with other organizations to share responsibility for specific programs and services. Historically, this has not been a common practice for many libraries, but it is now occurring more frequently as governments look for ways to expand services without increasing expenditures. Partnerships can also be one-time or recurring.

The Challenge of Reallocating Resources

As noted earlier, library managers have tended to look for new sources of revenue to implement planning goals and objectives rather than trying to reallocate existing funding. Certainly, there is evidence that many libraries are underfunded. However, library managers cannot expect to support all new or expanded programs with new resources. Not everything the library does is equally effective, and not every program that was effective ten years ago is still effective. Changes in the resources used to support these programs may be painful—but they are also inevitable. Few libraries are still using accession books, but stopping the practice of accessioning wasn't easy even though automated cataloging services made it completely unnecessary. In fact, many libraries continued accessioning materials for years after the cataloging functions were automated because of staff resistance to what was seen as a fundamental change in "the way we have always done things in this library."

Sometimes staff and managers feel that deciding a program, service, or practice is no longer a priority implies that it was not valuable in the past. This is rarely the case. Programs, services, and practices have to evolve to meet changing community needs, just as library collections do. When a staff member evaluates the business collection and decides to discard a ten-year-old book on investing, she is not implying that the book never served a purpose. She is simply acknowledging that the book *no longer* serves the purpose it was intended to serve. It may have been absolutely the right book for the purpose ten years ago. In the same way, the programs, services, and practices you decide to change were probably right on target at one time. A decision to change the priority of those services now in no way diminishes the value of those services in the past. Change rarely means previous decisions were wrong. Normally, it simply means circumstances are different than they were when the last decisions were made.

The weeding example is interesting because it brings up another point that managers need to consider when addressing reallocation issues: Staff members have a much easier time discarding materials selected by other people than discarding materials they selected themselves. In the same way, many managers find it is easier to change programs started by other people than to change programs they started themselves. Given the average tenure of library managers in public libraries in this country, this tendency to hold onto the past is significant. Acknowledging the difficulty that people have in letting go of projects in which they have invested a lot of time and energy is an important part of effectively reallocating resources. It is equally important to recognize the contributions those projects made to the target populations they were originally designed to serve.

Other Ways to Obtain Resources

Of course, reallocation isn't the only way to obtain the resources required to implement the library's service priorities. You have a number of other choices to consider and decisions to make. As alluded to earlier, you can use appropriated funds or donated funds, or you might decide to partner with another agency or organization. In reviewing those options, you need to consider whether you can achieve the intended results with one-time funds or if it will be necessary to have recurring funds.

There are literally dozens of ways to obtain the resources needed. To get an idea of the available options, it might be helpful to return to the Anytown Public Library case study again to consider how the Anytown managers might find the increased resources they need for children's materials.

◼ CASE STUDY PART 3 ◼

In the Anytown Public Library, the library managers decided they needed to increase the budget for easy and picture books by $4,000 for at least two years. The managers chose to reallocate money from one part of the materials budget to another during the first year, and they asked their governing body for a recurring increase beginning in the second and succeeding fiscal years. The fallback plan was to continue to use reallocated funds in the second fiscal year if the increase was not granted and to again request the increase for the third fiscal year. If the increase was not granted after that second request, the managers planned to reassess the impact of reallocation and then decide what to do next. In essence, the Anytown Library managers were looking for both a one-time increase and a recurring increase in their appropriated funds.

There are a number of other ways the managers might have obtained these resources: To obtain the $4,000 for the first year (always intended to be one-time funds), they could have

- requested a grant from the state library agency if funds for such purposes are made available
- requested a grant from a private foundation that supports programs for young children
- requested that the Friends of the Library provide some or all of the funds for this project
- worked with a local organization (PTA, PTO, Boy or Girl Scouts, etc.) to raise the $4,000
- entered into a partnership with the recreation department to apply for funding for early childhood programs if such funds are available
- requested some or all of the funds from one or more of the local service organizations (Rotary, Elks, etc.)

To obtain some or all of the desired recurring funds, they might have

- requested a recurring commitment from the Friends of the Library
- requested a recurring commitment from one or more local service organizations
- entered into an ongoing fund-raising program with a local organization and earmarked all of the proceeds for easy and picture books
- continued to reallocate funds from other parts of the library budget, perhaps at a lower level

It All Comes Back to Making Decisions

There is a danger in using a book like this one: Library managers may become so involved in collecting all of the data suggested in the various chapters that they never actually use the information they gather to make decisions. It is not uncommon for managers to feel that the next piece of information they are looking for will be the one that will be the most useful—and there is always a next piece of information out there somewhere. The reality, of course, is that there is almost never one defining piece of data that makes everything clear.

It is even more important to remember that most library data, no matter how carefully collected, is at best approximate. We all know the problems with collecting data manually. In virtually every library in the country there are times when the reference staff who are supposed to note every question get busy and forget to do so. Then at the end of an hour or two they estimate the number of users they helped. Even data that is collected electronically cannot be considered to be 100 percent accurate. It is not unheard of for staff in branches with low circulation to check a few books in and out during slow times to inflate their statistics.

We rarely collect data about various aspects of library operations to analyze those discrete pieces of data. Instead, we gather data to look at in relation to other data. Therefore, many of the data collection processes included in this book recommend that data be collected through sampling.

It is also important to remember that data is not in and of itself the answer to anything. Data becomes meaningful only in the context of making specific decisions or when analyzing clearly identified processes or procedures. Collect only the data for which you have a purpose.

The workforms in this book will help you identify and collect the information you need to make decisions. The instructions suggest possible factors to consider when evaluating the information collected. However, no tool can make the ultimate resource allocation decisions for you. You, as a library manager, will finally have to stop gathering and analyzing data and have to actually decide something and move forward. Your decision will be based both on the data collected and on your understanding of the library staff, library board, and political environment in which the library operates. Remember, your library is unique. The data you collect may be similar to the data collected by a neighboring library; however, the decisions you make based on that data may be very different—and appropriately so. Ultimately, decision making is a matter of judgment. The data you collect should both support your decision and help you justify it. What the data cannot do is make the decision for you.

Finally, it is important to remember that it isn't common to make "the final" decision about any priority, program, or service. Conditions change rapidly, and you must remain flexible. The "estimate, implement, check, adjust" decision-making model described earlier provides the best guideline when plotting a course in these challenging times.

Change Is Hard

No matter what decisions you make, it is inevitable that those decisions are going to result in changing the way things are done in the library. It is important to recognize that these changes are going to be difficult for everyone involved. Most of us pay lip service to the mantra of "change is good," but in our hearts we really believe that "change *for other people* is good" and "change *for me* is hard—and unpleasant—and unnecessary."

This chapter started with the recommendation that you communicate early and often with your staff and your board, and it is appropriate that it end with the same reminder. Staff certainly need to be involved in every step of this process and to understand *why* you are making the decisions you make. In particular, staff need to be reassured that managers understand that change involves ending programs and deemphasizing services as well as creating new programs and increasing support for certain services. Many staff are skeptical about management efforts to reallocate resources, particularly in the area of staff time and duties. Staff are often afraid that rather than being asked to do *X* instead of *Y,* they will be told to do *X* and still expected to do *Y* at some level.

These staff concerns are not unreasonable. Throughout the long history of public libraries it has been easy to find stories about new programs and services initiated by libraries. It has been considerably more difficult to find examples of programs that were discontinued. When we do find such examples, they tend to focus on the unhappy reaction of the clients losing a service and not on why the resources were reallocated or the new services were provided with those resources.

Many library managers, like the managers of most other publicly supported agencies, have not been comfortable making hard choices among competing programs. They have been more inclined to reduce support for all programs equally. On the one hand, this results in the library providing mediocre services in both high priority areas and low priority areas. On the other hand, no one has been upset by the discontinuation of a little-used or overly expensive service, and so there are few if any complaints to deal with. People rarely complain about mediocrity. Of course, they don't support it much either, and that can be a problem for libraries looking for increased resources to meet new and different needs.

Little has been written about the political implications of change, but you know all too well that you work in an increasingly political environment. That, in turn, means that the decisions you make are being scrutinized more carefully than in the past. At one time, a library manager who "didn't make waves" and who changed little or nothing was making a politically safe decision. That is not always true any longer. The public expects all publicly funded agencies, including libraries, to be more accountable and more responsive. Inevitably, that requires changing the way we do business. However, changes almost always have political implications, both internally and externally. The information in *Managing for Results* will not only help you and your colleagues decide what changes need to be made; it will also help you explain and justify your decisions to staff, board members, city and county officials, and interested members of the public.

NOTES

1. Joseph Boyett and Jimmie Boyett, *The Guru Guide* (New York: John Wiley, 1998), 61.

2. Charles R. McClure and others, *Planning and Role-Setting for Public Libraries* (Chicago: American Library Assn., 1987).

3. Ethel Himmel and William James Wilson, *Planning for Results: A Public Library Transformation Process* (Chicago: American Library Assn., 1998), 40–5.

Chapter 2

Managing Your Library's Staff

MILESTONES

By the time you finish this chapter you will know how to

- deploy staff to carry out the activities associated with the selected service priorities

- determine the staff abilities needed to accomplish the service priorities and how these abilities might be acquired by the library

- determine how staff are currently spending their time and effort

- assess the difficulty and importance of activities and their staff costs in comparison with the value of those activities to the organization

- prepare a plan to reallocate staff to free up time to perform the activities related to the service priorities

Without staff, there could be no library. Who would select, organize, circulate, and reshelve materials? Who would develop and present programs? Who would answer reference questions and help students with their homework? Who would do all of the activities that are required if a library is to accomplish its goals and objectives?

However, as all library managers know, it is not a simple matter to determine how many staff members are required to carry out activities related to the library's service priorities nor is it easy to determine the abilities those staff members need. In the absence of a process for making these determinations, "not enough staff" has been, and continues to be, a common reaction to plans for initiating new activities. These days, effective organizations have to be nimble and ready to make quick responses to changing conditions, so the astute manager asks, "How can we make this work?" instead of lamenting limited staff resources. To find out "how to make it work," managers first need to gather information about current staff activities and consider how those activities contribute to library goals. Next, they need to look for ways to streamline processes, build efficiencies into the system, and eliminate tasks of lesser value to the library's goals. This chapter is intended to help managers determine the staffing required and identify the abilities needed to accomplish the library's service goals, objectives, and activities.

Considering Staff as a Resource

The term *staff,* as used here, covers both full- and part-time workers and includes all job classifications. Although some libraries have workers who volunteer their time, are assigned to work so they can collect welfare benefits, or are performing "community service" as part of a court-ordered requirement, the term *staff* as used in this chapter usually refers to only those people who are paid from the library's annual operating budget. However, if one or more of these unpaid groups or individuals makes a major contribution to library activities and your library considers them as an ongoing resource doing meaningful work, they can also be considered in the staff allotment.

Staff members are a resource, just like the collection. In fact, staff are the library's most costly resource. According to the latest figures from the Public Library Data Service, *Statistics '98,* on average, salaries account for slightly over 50 percent of total annual expenditures among all sizes of libraries—clearly the most expensive single category in any library's budget.[1] If fringe benefits were added in, the percentage of annual budget spent for staff compensation would be even higher.

Although all library staff members are employed to perform specific tasks, most organizations have established a fixed number of hours as the standard work week for full-time staff, and pay is based on the number of hours staff are expected to work. If staff members work more hours than the number included in the standard work week, additional compensation is often provided. However, in some systems library professionals are classed as exempt, meaning that they are not paid for any hours worked beyond the standard. Because staff pay is so time-based, time is an important resource emphasized in this chapter.

It is imperative that staff time and corresponding effort be used as efficiently and effectively as possible. Staff attention should be directed toward activities that are the most important to the library's mission, goals, and objectives. However, few library managers really know how much staff time is spent or should be spent on specific activities. One library manager noted, "If we had an intimate acquaintance with the cost of doing everything, we would perhaps make different decisions about how we spend our time."[2]

The overriding intent of this chapter is to stimulate your thinking about bringing the appropriate human resources to the work of the library. To do that, you and your colleagues are encouraged to use the information in this chapter in conjunction with the *Planning for Results* Gap Analysis Workform. That workform was designed to help you analyze data to answer four basic questions:

- number of professional staff required to accomplish the library service responses/priorities
- number of paraprofessional staff required to accomplish the library service responses/priorities
- number of clerical staff required to accomplish the library service responses/priorities
- training required (initial and ongoing) to accomplish the library service responses/priorities

If you did not use *Planning for Results* to determine the intended service outcomes, you can still use the Gap Analysis Workform to analyze staffing needs. A copy of the Gap Analysis Workform can be found in appendix B. In essence, the Gap Analysis Workform provides a way to consider the staff resources needed to accomplish library priorities, to identify what staff resources the library currently has, to determine the gap between the two, and then to decide how to fill that gap or reallocate the surplus. The information in this chapter will help you gather the data needed to complete the Gap Analysis Workform.

Collecting Data

The second part of this chapter includes a selection of eighteen workforms designed to help you gather the data necessary to complete a gap analysis for determining the number and classifications of staff required to accomplish the library's goals and objectives, the training those staff members will need, and the cost and value of the staff required. A complete list of the workforms in this chapter can be found in figure 3.

The workforms are divided into five categories. General instructions precede the specific directions. The first workform, S1, will help you decide which forms you need to complete. The second group of workforms, S2–S5, will help you gather data about the activities and abilities required to accomplish the library's goals and objectives. The third group of workforms, S6–S8, will facilitate gathering data about the number of staff hours available (capacity) and how these hours are used (utilization and productivity). The fourth set of workforms, S9–S14, will help you gather data about how staff members are currently spending their time. Note that these are general as well as specific directions for workforms S9–S10. The last group of workforms, S15–S18, will help you determine

---

FIGURE 3
Staffing Workforms Summary

Workform	Title	Purpose
OVERVIEW		
S1	Staff Functions Related to a Service Response/Priority	To determine the staff functions that will be affected by the library's service priorities
ACTIVITIES AND ABILITIES		
S2	Activities Involved in a Service Response/Priority	To determine the characteristics of the specific activities necessary to provide one service priority
S3	Staff Abilities Required for a Service Response/Priority Activity	To pinpoint the specific staff abilities needed for one activity related to a service priority
S4	Checklist of Abilities for Activities	To clarify when, where, and how abilities for a service priority are to be utilized
S5	Analysis of Training Needs and Costs for a Service Response/Priority	To help assess the real costs of training staff to acquire desired abilities
CAPACITY, UTILIZATION, AND PRODUCTIVITY		
S6	Estimate of Productive Work Hours Available	To calculate the hours of expected work by staff category
S7	Comparison of Public Service Indicators	To compare activity levels among public service units/teams
S8	Analysis of an Activity	To analyze the sequence of tasks involved in performing an activity

Workform	Title	Purpose
OBSERVATIONS AND TIME		
S9	Daily Direct-Observation Log	To collect data on staff activities by structured observations
S10	Unit/Team/Library Observation Summary	To show the number and variety of activities performed by various staff categories during one day
S11	Staff-Activity Analysis	To illustrate the congruence of how a staff member spends time and the tasks important to the job assignment
S12	Daily Time/Activity Log	To collect information about staff activities during one day
S13	Activity Log Summary	To categorize and summarize activities performed by one employee in one day
S14	Unit/Team/Library Activity Summary	To summarize time spent on many activities
ESTIMATING THE COSTS/VALUE OF ACTIVITIES		
S15	Conversion of Capacity to Cost	To calculate compensation costs for different time periods
S16	Estimate of the Cost/Value of Individual Staff Activities	To analyze time and money spent for individual activities
S17	Estimate of the Cost/Value of Unit/Team/Library Activities	To analyze time and money spent for unit activities
S18	Estimate of the Cost/Value of a Service Response/Priority	To calculate the anticipated or actual costs of activities related to a particular service priority

the cost and value of the activities the staff are currently performing and the cost and value of the activities required to accomplish the library's goals and objectives. General instructions precede the specific directions for this last group of workforms.

As noted earlier, it is not necessary to complete all of these workforms. Every library is different. Some libraries already have some of the information on these workforms from earlier studies; others may not need all of the information on all the workforms to make the decisions that must be made to implement the library plan. There is no point in collecting data unless you know what to do with that data. There is also little point in collecting data about a situation that you cannot change. For instance, a minimum number of staff members is required to operate even the smallest library unit. If a unit is staffed at that minimum level, it may be less helpful to study how those staff members use their time than it would be to study time usage in library units with the potential for greater flexibility in staffing.

Issues to Consider When Making Staffing Decisions

You will want to consider a number of significant issues as you decide which workforms would provide the information required to make decisions about allocating staff. These issues include

- identifying activities to be performed, and when and where they should be performed
- identifying abilities needed to accomplish the selected activities
- determining the number of staff needed in relation to patron use and staff workloads
- understanding how staff members are currently using their time
- determining how to find the staff to accomplish the library's priorities

Each of these issues is discussed in detail in the following sections. As you review them, you can decide which issues affect the choices you and your colleagues have to make to ensure that staff are being used in the most effective and the most efficient way.

Activities: What, Where, and When

The first issue to consider is quite basic: What activities should be performed to accomplish the library's goals and objectives, and when and where should those activities be performed?

If your library has gone through the planning process described in *Planning for Results,* you have already selected service responses. As noted in chapter 1, the thirteen service responses in *Planning for Results* are not intended to be add-ons to the library's present services; rather, they describe all of the services most public libraries provide. This is an important distinction for you and the staff to make. When considering the service responses as brand-new services, staff may believe that the priorities established in the planning process are beyond the library's reach in light of its current budget and staff workload. If, instead, staff are encouraged to understand that most of the service responses actually give names to activities that the library already performs, they will realize that the planning process is often a matter of increased or decreased emphasis for specific programs or services.

For example, most libraries already give information to consumers to help them make informed decisions, provide information to business and job seekers, assist with formal and lifelong learning, and acquire many current titles. Each of these services is included in the thirteen service responses in *Planning for Results.* When the library planning team members selected a number of responses from among these thirteen, they were far more likely to be making a public commitment to emphasize some services and downplay others rather than choosing to offer entirely new services. This is just as true if you have completed a library plan using some process other than *Planning for Results;* it is still very likely that areas of priority were selected from among current services.

In terms of using the information in this chapter, it doesn't matter what process was used to determine the library's priorities, nor does it matter if those priorities reflect an enhancement to an existing service or are intended to provide a new service. It is not even necessary to have recently completed a comprehensive service plan. You may be working from a project plan for a specific program or service. What is important to remember is that *Managing for Results* is intended to be used to help you and your colleagues decide how to achieve previously identified outcomes. It is not a tool to help you decide *what* outcomes to achieve.

Your desired outcomes have probably been expressed in terms of goals, objectives, and activities. In this chapter, you will be focusing most of your attention at the activity level. If *Planning for Results* was used as the model to develop the library plan, those activities are probably listed on the *Planning for Results* Activities for This Planning Cycle Workform. If you used another planning model or if you are working from a project plan, you will need to develop a list of the activities required to accomplish the intended outcomes. These activities should serve as the basis for collecting and analyzing data about staffing. A copy of the *Planning for Results* Activities for This Planning Cycle Workform has been included in appendix A if you wish to use it to record the activities, although it is not necessary.

Once you develop a comprehensive list of the activities that staff will have to perform to accomplish the library's intended outcomes, the next steps are to consider where each activity should be performed, or at least made available, and when and how the activities should be performed. For example, local history and genealogy services may be offered at only the central library, but should staff expertise be available at all times the central library is open? Should consumer information be available in all locations and at all hours the buildings are open? Should some information for consumers be available on the library's Web pages? Answering these questions about breadth and availability helps develop an understanding of the number of staff required to offer a particular activity.

You will use Workform S1 to identify which staff functions will be affected by the library's activities. Workform S2 will help you analyze in greater detail the selected activities for a given service priority.

Abilities Needed

The second staffing issue to consider focuses on the abilities required to accomplish the selected activities. The word *ability* is preferred to the word *skill. Ability* encompasses cognitive, cultural, and personality characteristics that have a broader meaning than *skill,* which connotes being able to do some particular thing. Categories of abilities that seem pertinent to a library's needs include subject knowledge, interpersonal, communication, management, technological, and physical abilities. A list showing some specific examples of these ability categories appears in figure 4. The list in the figure is intended to be generally illustrative rather than applicable to specific situations.

Some abilities seem self-evident. Certainly any activity requiring designing, mounting, creating links, and maintaining Web pages requires technological abilities. However, some abilities are more subtle and often are not considered when assigning staff. For example, the need for staff to demonstrate specific interpersonal and communication abilities is

---

FIGURE 4
Examples of General Abilities

Subject Knowledge

Business sources and business information

Reading acquisition and comprehension for basic literary programs

Genealogy sources and information

Local history sources and information

Government sources and information

Specific cultures and their histories

Grantsmanship

Child development

Interpersonal

Has welcoming manner with clients

Is responsive to clients' requests

Is patient and empathic with clients

Calms clients who seem upset or disruptive

Maintains harmonious relations with coworkers and clients

Works well with diverse clientele and coworkers

Tolerates stress and ambiguity well

Communications

Explains policies and procedures clearly and nicely

Communicates effectively verbally and in writing

Writes clearly

Understands clients' information questions

Communicates well in another language

Physical

Is able to bend and stretch

Is able to lift and carry up to __ pounds

Library Specific

Understands and is committed to goals of a particular service response

Is familiar with principles of library science

Is familiar with library policies and procedures in assigned areas

Is familiar with library's technology at least sufficiently to perform assignment

Is sufficiently familiar with library resources to assist client's request for information and materials

Management

Is able to understand problems in complex situations

Is able to think of and implement different solutions for different kinds of problems

Can assess progress toward goals and identify areas needing attention

Can motivate staff to focus on goals for the good of the library

Technological

Has familiarity with network operating systems

Has familiarity with Web page editing tools

Is able to keep the systems up and running

---

often overlooked. Staff assigned to public service activities related to Basic Literacy, Cultural Awareness, and Formal Learning Support service responses in *Planning for Results* need good communications and interpersonal abilities—but not necessarily the same abilities in each case. Those who work with literacy clients need empathy; those who are assigned to services supporting cultural awareness need the ability to communicate in the language or dialect of the culture and to understand its mores; those working with formal learning need to like children and teens and be able to communicate with them effectively.

The library's current staff has a variety of abilities, so linking current staff to needed abilities is the next step. It is also important to remember that abilities should also be linked to the appropriate classification of staff. For example, a librarian could perform all the duties involved with operating the circulation desk, but such duties underutilize the librarian's ability. If needed abilities cannot be identified among existing and available staff, then the library must consider whether present staff could or should be trained to develop the needed abilities or whether the library should recruit new staff members who already possess the abilities required.

In some cases, the abilities needed in a staff member can be learned, but they cannot really be taught—at least not in any reasonable time. For example, to accomplish activities that support the Cultural Awareness service response, it is much better to hire someone who already has the language ability and knowledge of the cultural background desired than to send staff to classes to learn these things. Such abilities require considerable time to learn—more time than is realistic to meet the library's current needs.

Personal abilities are another learnable, but often not teachable, area. Staff who are short tempered or who dislike interacting with teenagers, for instance, are not well suited for public activities related to the Formal Learning Support service response. On the other hand, some abilities, particularly those related to subject knowledge (such as business information, local history, genealogy, and current topics and titles) can be learned, although the manner in which they are learned may differ depending on the subject.

An analysis of needed abilities will also clarify the classification of staff that should be assigned to various activities connected with a particular service response or priority. Good decisions about assigning staff should be based on good information about present work patterns. Activities, tasks, and processes can be performed in various ways. The activities, tasks, and processes that are selected and the way in which they are designed are important issues in optimizing the use of staff resources. The general rule is to assign work to the lowest staff classification capable of doing that work. Not only does this practice benefit the library but it also usually makes the work more interesting and challenging for staff. Although such assignments might be difficult in libraries subject to collective bargaining agreements and in systems that favor tight job descriptions, changes can be made with patience and persistence, especially if staff want opportunities to learn new skills and to have their jobs enriched.

On the other hand, allowing senior librarians or senior library assistants to perform work that does not require their professional skills squanders staff resources in two ways. First, it drives up the costs of the processes and activities these senior staff members perform. For instance, it is obviously more expensive to have a librarian circulate materials than it is to have a circulation attendant take care of circulation functions. Second, when senior staff members spend their time on work that doesn't utilize their skills, they do not have the time to perform the activities that are more important to achieving the library's goals.

There are several reasons that staff might perform work that does not require their skills. Sometimes the library does not employ enough staff in the appropriate classification to do the work that needs to be done. In other cases, senior staff choose to do work that doesn't require their full skills because they enjoy that work. Whatever the reasons, library managers should be aware that allowing library staff to underutilize their time and abilities wastes staff resources. Workforms S3, S4, and S5 will aid in gathering and analyzing data about the abilities of the staff in relation to the activities to be completed to accomplish the library's intended outcomes.

Number of Staff Needed

The third issue to be considered when making staff decisions concerns the number of staff required to complete the selected activities. From 1933 to 1966 the American Library Association endorsed a series of published numerical standards for public libraries that recommended employment of one staff member for X thousands of residents in the service area. The ratio of staff to residents changed with each version of the standards. This recommendation was based on agreement among members of the ALA Standards Committee with no empirical tests of its validity. The standards were followed by some libraries and ignored by others.

For the past quarter century there have been no professionally recommended staffing standards at the national level. These standards were replaced by the concepts of local planning and role setting. Currently, the staff-to-population ratios that can be computed from numbers in the Public Library Data Service *Statistical Report* series show little relationship between number of staff and the population of the library's service area. For libraries serving populations of more than one million, the staff-to-population ratio ranges from a low of 1 staff member for every 6,391 persons to a high of 1 staff member per 1,831 residents. For those libraries in communities between 500,000 and 999,999, the ratios range from 1:13,536 to 1:1,383. Even in the smallest category of libraries, those serving fewer than 5,000 people, the ratio of full-time staff to population ranges from 1:4,151 to 1:215.[3]

Numerical standards have persisted at the state level, and the issue of ratio of library staff to service population is addressed in the library standards of sixteen states. As with the now-defunct national standards, these state standards are based on opinion and political reality rather than on a study of actual requirements. Most state standards call for one staff person per X population; yet, there seems to be little agreement about what that ratio should be. A few states require that a certain portion of the staff be in particular job classifications—librarians, paraprofessional, clerical—other states relate quantity and classification of staff to what are called "adequate" or "excellent" levels of library service. In essence, there is little agreement among the states having standards that address staff and silence from the thirty-four states lacking such standards.[4] Library usage or hours of service, rather than population size, seem to be more pertinent factors in estimating staff requirements than a ratio of staff to population.

The variation in library staffing patterns stems from a variety of factors. Certainly, differences exist among libraries in terms of the number or types of activities in which staff engage, although these differences are difficult to document. Data about number and types of activities do not appear in current statistical compilations at the state or national level.

Another cause of variation in staff size is the processes libraries use. Managers in each library determine for themselves how each task is to be performed. Some library managers strive to streamline processes and eliminate unnecessary steps. Some outsource tasks that others do in-house. Some have processes that might be considered baroque. Staffing patterns are also influenced by the number of facilities the library operates, the floor plans of those facilities, and the number of hours each facility is open.

In addition, both political and labor relations reasons can account for variations in staff size. Political reasons include the library administration's past and present ability to persuade local officials about budgetary matters and the financial condition of local government itself. They can also include the philosophical stance of local officials. For instance, some government administrators have a political stake in reducing the number of government employees. Contracts with labor unions affect the staffing numbers and staff assignments as well. Because of all this, in many libraries staff requirements are only tenuously related to the number of staff employed.

While political and union factors frequently define the environmental realities in which library managers work, they do not provide managers with the information they need to make optimal decisions. In fact, many of the factors given get in the way of making optimal decisions about needed staffing classifications and abilities. More quantifiable elements to consider when assessing whether the number of staff is sufficient to carry out the activities related to your service responses are capacity, utilization, and productivity.

Capacity

Capacity is concerned with the number of staff authorized and the number of hours they are actually available to perform work. Both are constrained by the library's budget.

Whatever the number of hours in the customary work week, few staff members actually work that many hours. A number of events, some predictable, some not, affect total work time. Among these are holidays, vacations, personal days, and customary or contractual break periods during the work day. A 15-minute break each morning and afternoon subtracts 120 hours—three weeks—from the work year. Paid time for sick leave, jury duty, and funerals vary among staffs, but an average for these types of unpredictable days can be calculated for each job classification in the library system. Other paid absences occur at the discretion of the library administration, including library conferences, both state and national, and staff training days. While these activities have value for both the library and the employee, they do take staff away from their regular duties. Covering public service areas can be a problem when staff are away for whatever reason.

The example in figure 5 illustrates the expected number of hours for full-time staff working 40, 37.5, and 35 hours a week. Staff members on a 40-hour-week schedule are paid to work 2,080 hours per year but actually work about 1,800 hours each year. Staff members on a 37.5-hour-week schedule are paid to work 1,950 hours per year and actually work about 1,680 hours each year. Staff members on a 35-hour-week schedule are paid to work 1,820 hours per year and actually work 1,560 hours. (These figures are illustrative. The figures for your library may be different because of policies or because of the circumstances of particular employees.)

Note that the totals in figure 5 include vacation and sick days and two 15-minute breaks each day, but they do not include time lost in common situations such as bathroom breaks, personal phone calls, interruptions, birthday cake breaks, or just chatting. In reality, productive time is lower than the actual number of hours an employee is at work. Certainly some of these social situations are necessary and others might be considered morale boosters, but supervisors need to remember that such off-task times have an impact on productive staff time.

To determine your library's total capacity, calculate the total number of hours that all staff are assigned to work over some time period—a day, week, month, or year. For instance, using the numbers from figure 5, the maximum annual capacity for a library with 10 full-time equivalent (FTE) staff members working a 40-hour week is 18,000 hours. This total does

FIGURE 5

Estimate of Productive Work Hours Available per Staff Member

	40-Hour Week	37.5-Hour Week	35-Hour Week
Predictable			
Nominal hours per year	2,080	1,950	1,820
Vacation (10 days)	−80	−75	−70
Holidays (10 days)	−80	−75	−70
Authorized breaks (30 min. per day for 48 weeks worked)	−120	−120	−120
Maximum Hours Available per Year	1,800	1,680	1,560
Unpredictable			
Sick leave	−40	−37.5	−35
Personal	−24	−22.5	−21
Other—jury duty, funerals, etc.	−8	−7.5	−7
Estimated Hours Available per Year	1,728	1,612.5	1,497

not include any time at work spent doing the necessary, common, and personal activities mentioned previously. (The International Labour Organization thinks that such time occupies about 18 percent of total working time.)[5] Nor do the 18,000 hours allow for sick days, emergencies, personal time, or jury duty. If each of the 10 staff members in the example used just 2 days a year for illness or personal time, the effective capacity of the library would be reduced by 160 hours. Workform S6 will help you determine the capacity for any unit or team or the entire library.

Utilization

The library provides a variety of services to the public. These include circulating materials, answering questions, and planning and preparing programs for groups. For the purposes here, these public services have been grouped into one category called *utilization*.

The hours of library operation provide a threshold for establishing staff needs in public service units. You must have at least one FTE available in each facility for every hour the library is open and probably need more than one FTE in most facilities. The real questions are how many staff of what qualifications should be on duty at what times? How many service points will be staffed? Will these be staffed at all times? Other factors influencing the number of staff assigned include security issues, collective bargaining agreements, and the layout of the building. For many libraries, the volume of requests for service, or utilization, is a significant factor in making these determinations.

Utilization is reflected primarily in the number of transactions provided to the public. These transactions are typically expressed as numbers of circulations, questions asked, visitors, and program attendees. Sometimes utilization figures can call attention to unused or underused capacity that might be reassigned to new or expanded activities, but such data needs to be well understood. For example, public service units frequently experience ebbs and flows in requests for service. That is, demand fluctuates by time of day and days of the week. It is important to understand these high and low flows of service demands in each library outlet or unit before you make decisions about capacity. Many libraries find that service demands are lower on weekday mornings than weekday afternoons. If that is the case, it may make sense to assign more staff in the afternoon than in the morning. Public service desks that are staffed but little used over time should raise questions about the possibility of reassigning staff to activities more important to the library's service priorities.

A justification commonly made to increase staff numbers is that some service—such as circulations or reference questions—has dramatically increased and that more staff are needed to keep up with the workload and to reduce pressure on existing staff. That reasoning was persuasive with many local government officials for a long time. However, increasing rates of utilization are no longer seen as adequate justification for authorizing more staff. These days, all organizations, including libraries, are expected to find ways to meet increasing use by doing things smarter, and most libraries are succeeding.

With assistance from technology, libraries have shifted some work formerly done by staff to the users. Libraries started self-service after World War II by opening the stacks to patrons instead of having pages retrieve items. In some libraries, patrons now check out their own books with self-circulation machines, renew materials via automated phone and OPAC machines, and place their own reserve and interlibrary loan requests. In turn, the library can send overdue notices to many borrowers via telephone with one recorded message or via one e-mail message. Not so long ago, only librarians were deemed capable of retrieving items from databases. Now even grade school students can navigate the Web and download the full text of articles for school assignments.

In essence, the nature of the work that staff members do to support utilization has fundamentally changed. Technology has eliminated many time-consuming tasks such as typing cards and filing them in the public catalog and the shelflist. It has made other things easier to do. Staff can now use the online circulation system to compile circulation statistics with the touch of a button instead of performing the laborious manual calculations once required. Borrower registration records are updated online instead of being manually typed and retyped each time there is a change. Recorded phone messages give library users information about library hours and services, freeing staff to serve the public in other ways.

On the other hand, because of technology librarians are offering new services such as Internet access.

In sum, technology has both simplified and complicated our work. The complications tend to come from the new tasks associated with this equipment—keeping the printers supplied with paper, troubleshooting the equipment, and teaching patrons how to use the new technology. Overall, face-to-face involvement between patron and staff is probably decreasing, especially over the long term, but the support of patron self-sufficiency requires staff who can deal with more-complex situations than in the past. These require higher level abilities and new positions, such as Webmaster, electronic resources librarian, and network technician. Workform S7 will help you gather data about the utilization of various public service units within the library.

Productivity

Productivity refers to the amount of work produced by staff. This can be reflected in the simple equation

$$\text{staff productivity} = \text{output} \div \text{staff input (in time or dollars)}$$

In other words, staff productivity is all the work produced by staff within a particular time divided by the number of hours of work or the compensation paid. Time and money are two sides of the same coin, so to speak.

Productivity is usually determined by the number and difficulty of the tasks or activities completed or by the number of transactions or units of work processed. Utilization, as noted earlier, reflects demand, usually by consumers of the service. Productivity can occur without demand. Many activities performed by technical services personnel are tenuously related to demand but do reflect productivity. For instance, in some libraries, technical services staff make it a priority to catalog current high-interest items as soon as they arrive (reflecting demand), but most other items are cataloged as time is available (reflecting productivity but not demand).

Examples of library staff productivity include the numbers of books cataloged, programs presented, items ordered, or new serial issues checked in. Yet, the amount of work produced is irrelevant unless the nature of the work is significant to the organization's priorities or to the service priorities selected. There is a big difference between being busy and being productive.

Often when library managers look at productivity issues in the library, they focus on efficiency and not effectiveness. In chapter 1, efficiency was defined as *doing something right* and effectiveness was defined as *doing the right thing.* It does no good to do something very well, if you shouldn't be doing it at all. (Remember the old joke about rearranging deck chairs on the *Titanic*?) On the other hand, it is critical that libraries become as efficient as possible in the areas that support the library's intended outcomes. Because materials are returned to be reused again and again, libraries have a particular problem in managing the activities and staff time that are associated with rearranging materials for circulation—sorting, moving, reshelving, and storing. These activities are necessary, and they can negatively affect service if not done in a timely and efficient manner. They can have a significant impact on resources that might be spent for collections, information service, group programs, or many other activities connected to the service responses/priorities.

PRODUCTIVITY AND PROCESS

Many activities carried out in library workrooms involve repetitive tasks—processing materials, copy cataloging, keying orders, checking in new materials, authorizing or paying invoices, sorting, and reshelving. Delays and bottlenecks in the flow of work can ripple throughout the system and disrupt public service.

Libraries are a bundle of processes. Over time, steps added to the processes become like more barnacles clinging to the hull of a ship. Just as barnacles slow the movement of the ship, each step in the process slows down completion of the task and worse, wastes time that could be spent on more-productive duties. As one librarian notes, "Yet, all too frequently, procedures take on a life of their own. Libraries become wedded to routines through time, and the rationale for the procedure becomes blurred."[6]

A good way to analyze a process is to follow the sequence of steps involved from the beginning to the end point of the activity, looking to see how many times something is handled and how long the process takes. Indicators of complexity in processes include number of steps, average time required to process a unit, the number of people handling the same item or information, the sequence of steps, and any loops in the process that go back to a previous step or a previous handler.

When you and your staff start to ask questions about why something is done a particular way, remember that "We've always done it that way" is not an answer but an indication that the procedure should be analyzed to see if the traditional way is still appropriate. Processes and procedures that were once necessary and important may no longer be either; conditions change all the time. As you prepare to implement the service priorities in the new library plan, you may find it helpful to review current processes and procedures. The following questions are a good place to start such a review of a particular process or activity:

1. Why is this being done?
2. Why is this done in this way?
3. Why is it done at this point?
4. Why is it done in this unit?
5. Does this process depend on another unit to supply work?

6. Why is it done by this person?
7. What would happen if this were not done in this way?
8. What would happen if this were not done at all?

Look at activities that take a lot of time. Consider the contribution of these activities to the library goals and objectives. The importance of the contribution should indicate whether the time involved is appropriately spent. A few examples follow.

How many times are materials stamped as library property? One stamp on any of the three edges of the pages should be sufficient. More stamping is just wasted effort.

Where are bar codes placed for circulation? Having them inside a book's cover adds two more steps to the circulation process— opening and closing the cover—for each item at checkout and check-in.

Is the same information being rekeyed as it moves from one unit to another? If so, why can't that information be captured for later use by staff who need it?

What paper files, including old shelflists, are still kept for consultation? How many times are they actually consulted? If few, why are these files being kept?

Is staff spending as much time cataloging and processing trade and genre paperbacks as hardcover titles? If so, why, since these are such ephemeral materials?

Variations in processes—from extremely streamlined to baroque— account for a large part of the differences in costs and numbers of staff among libraries of similar size. These variations in process also occur within library systems. If you work in a multiunit system, you will probably be able to find numerous examples of processes that are handled differently, unit by unit. Sometimes there are good reasons for these variations; often there are not.

There are three important things to remember as you move from analysis of an existing process to developing a new process:

• work with facts—not opinions

• work on causes—not effects

• work with reasons—not excuses

PRODUCTIVITY AND SERVICE PRIORITIES

Each service priority selected will require that a number of activities be performed in support of that priority. Those activities are based on tasks done by library staff. Traditionally, libraries have collected productivity information about tasks rather than activities. For example, a library that selected the Cultural Awareness service response from *Planning for Results* as a priority might decide on two very different activities to support that priority. The first activity might be to offer a number of programs on the African American experience. The second might be to develop suggested reading lists highlighting African American authors. The first activity requires that a variety of tasks be accomplished before a program can occur: planning, arranging, publicizing, and setting up the facility. The tasks associated with the reading list are equally varied but quite different: culling, selecting, keying, formatting, printing, and distributing. What is important to understand is that the measure of productivity should be the activity—the programs or book lists—and not the tasks.

PRODUCTIVITY AND PUBLIC SERVICES

Finally, there is a "not busy/too busy" dilemma related to productivity in public service units. Public service desks, particularly circulation and reference, depend on patron requests for service. Yet, staff needed to assist patrons must be both visible and available. Requests for service do not arrive in a steady stream as products move through an assembly line; rather, they come in spurts. Sometimes many patrons appear at approximately the same time, and other times are extremely quiet. Finding a balance between frantic and inactive times and deciding what tasks should be done during the quiet intervals is the dilemma. Staff can become so busy doing other tasks that patrons do not want to interrupt them by asking for service, even though staff presence at the desk seems to invite requests for service. Library managers and staff need to be constantly aware of this dilemma and remember one of the most important of the McDonald Corporation's Customer Ten Commandments:

> The Customer is not an interruption of our work, but the purpose of it.[7]

Workform S8 will help you gather and analyze data about the number and sequence of steps involved and, hence, give an indication of the productivity of various library processes.

Current Staff Activities

The fourth issue to be considered when making decisions about allocating staff is how staff members are currently using their time. We all know that in every library many things are done only because of custom or because no one has questioned their value, the need for them, or the methods used. Therefore, before you assign staff to activities intended to accomplish specific goals and objectives, you will probably want to identify all of the tasks and activities that staff now spend a considerable amount of time performing. Among other things, having this knowledge may allow you to reallocate staff from less cost-effective activities to more cost-effective ones.

There are several ways to collect this data. Going from easiest to most complicated, these are

existing records

observations

self-reports

You might want to start the analysis of staff productivity by using *existing records*—the statistical information the library regularly collects. Although these data reveal information at only the macro level, they can be compared among branches or units performing similar work. Some libraries have used workload figures, such as number of items circulated and number of reference questions asked, to set unit staffing patterns. However, as transactions based on patron self-service and use of resources on the World Wide Web increase, traditional statistical categories such as circulation and questions asked will provide a less-accurate reflection of staff activities.

Data about staff activities based on structured *observations* will allow you to calculate, in a general sense, the ratio of productive time to capacity in any unit or team. Staff need to be informed that such observations will occur on a particular day or within a specific week. However, information about the specific observation times should not be shared to avoid having staff modify normal behaviors during the observation period. See the generic instructions for workforms S9–S10 for other considerations when doing observations.

Other libraries may want staff to use workforms that serve as *self-reports* describing the activities they performed during a particular time period. The workforms usually ask for one of three types of information:

activities performed as percent of work time

minutes spent on major activities

activities performed during specified intervals, such as every 15 minutes during the work day

Each of these reporting methods has its own advantages and drawbacks as shown in figure 6. As you review the pros and cons of each data-collection method, consider how you might use that method to collect the information needed to make staffing decisions.

You will probably find that there is no one right method for your library. Rather you will discover that existing records work well in some instances, while self-reports are required under other circumstances. In still other cases, the only way to obtain the needed data may be through observation. For example, staff working at public service desks who per-

FIGURE 6

Collecting Data about Staff Activities

Method of Data Collection	Advantages	Disadvantages
Existing records	Data is readily available	Works best only in organizational units where staff perform a limited number of activities, such as copy cataloging, processing, etc. Data collection does not include all activities and accomplishments
Observation	Data on many activities can be collected Close in time and space to actual task performance Data tend to be objective	Time consuming Persons assigned as observers may "forget" to do observations Staff may object to being observed Who observes the observer?
Self-reports	Closest in time and space to actual task performance	Staff may resist or forget to complete workforms Administrators tend to doubt accuracy of self-reports Self-reported data may have a "halo effect"

form a variety of tasks at the desk could report the length of time scheduled for desk duty. Supplementary information about utilization might be obtained from circulation statistics for the day or from tallies of questions posed at reference/information desks. Persons performing essentially repetitive tasks in chunks of time during the day, such as checking in serials or processing invoices for payment, could record minutes spent on that activity and the number of units processed.

As a check on the accuracy of any of the methods—existing records, observations by staff, or self-reporting—a consultant or a person from outside the unit could monitor staff time in small snapshots of activity. A more complicated procedure is to employ a specialist to do time-and-motion studies of particular activities with the aim of finding the fastest and best procedure. Finally, experienced managers usually have an impression or sense of how many units of work can or should be processed in a particular time period and of the classification of staff needed to do the work. However, managers can and should exercise judgment about the amount of work accomplished.

Start with the method that best meets your needs. Collect the data and compare the results. For those situations that seem questionable—such as extremely high or low levels of activity compared with others in a similar job or similar unit—gather more data, and ask questions about the variation. Workforms S9 through S14 can be used to gather data on how staff members use their time now. The forms you use will depend on the method of data collection you have selected.

Standard Times and Outputs

Many library managers would like to know how much time it should take to do particular activities, especially repetitive high-volume tasks such as shelving. Since no library does things exactly like any other library, there are no standard times or standard costs. However, some libraries have established internal performance standards or expectations about the amount of work that people performing certain jobs should produce in a given period of time.

The number of staff needed for a particular task or process depends on the volume of work to be done, its complexity, and the manner in which the work is performed. For example, libraries that keep processes to a minimum and deal with relatively straightforward materials will need fewer cataloging staff than the library that insists on modifying cataloging records or the library that purchases materials in languages spoken in countries on the Pacific Rim.

Before determining the number of staff needed to perform a task or an activity, you need to analyze how it is performed. You do this by identifying each step in the process. This analysis isn't as straightforward as it may appear at first glance. For example, you might think it would be easy to set a standard time for a repetitive task as simple as reshelving returned items, but this task is more complex than it first appears to be. At what point does "reshelving" begin? Does it begin with the initial sorting of items after discharging them, with placing the items in order on the book trucks, with taking the book truck to the proper area of the library to begin reshelving, or with the actual placement of the item in its appropriate spot on the shelf? Unless that starting point is known, any comparisons about shelving output among library units or libraries will be misleading. It is equally important to identify the point at which "reshelving" ends.

Unfortunately, there are currently no standard descriptions of the steps in typical library tasks and activities to help libraries collect uniform data. However, it is possible to establish standards within any individual library system if the people doing the work and the administration adhere to the same definitions, procedures, and processes. The following steps show one method for collecting data about repetitive and continually processed tasks:

1. Determine the activity to be studied.
2. Identify the type of item or process to be counted.
3. Identify the starting point of this activity.
4. Identify the sequence of steps in performing the activity.
5. Identify the ending point of this activity.
6. Determine how the data about performing the activity will be collected: by the employee performing the work submitting reports of units processed or by someone else observing how work is performed and looking for ways to streamline it.

CASE STUDY

Let's say that the staff of Anytown Public Library are interested in calculating the standard times and outputs of the shelvers in the various library units. If they used the process just described, the following might be the result:

Step 1: Determine the activity to be studied.

Reshelving

Step 2: Identify the type of item or process to be counted.

The process to be counted is the number of similar items reshelved correctly. Book shelving should be compared with book shelving, videos with videos, and unbound periodicals with unbound periodicals. (Mixing materials of different types together gives misleading and inaccurate information.)

Step 3: Identify the starting point of this activity.

The starting point is the time a book truck of items is given to a staff member to be reshelved.

Step 4: Identify the sequence of steps in performing the activity.

Shelvers from each unit meet to discuss how they shelve and identify the steps involved in the activity. Based on that discussion, the staff develop a written description of the sequence of steps in shelving in the system that focuses on the similarities among the shelvers.

Step 5: Identify the ending point of this activity.

The ending point is the time when all of the items on the book truck have been shelved. (Having uniform starting and ending points are the most crucial parts of the analysis because each step in the process adds to the time needed to complete the activity and, thus, lowers the output.)

Step 6: Determine how the data about performing the activity will be collected.

The data will be collected by each supervisor, who will count the number of items on each book truck and keep track of the time taken to shelve the items on the truck.

One final thing to consider when analyzing data gathered using this process is the issue of accuracy. An employee who reshelves items inaccurately creates havoc and lowers productivity, so a balance between speed and accuracy is required. Therefore, you need to determine both numbers of items or processes completed *and* number of items or processes completed correctly.

What if one person is very fast but not very accurate and another is very accurate but not very fast? Library managers contemplating setting performance expectations for units, teams, or staff members should focus on tangible results of the task. In the shelving example, the desired result is that books are shelved accurately so that library users can find them. Rapid but inaccurate shelving isn't productive at all. Standards need to address both accuracy and speed.

Finding Staff to Accomplish the Library's Priorities

The final staffing issue to consider is how to find the staff needed to accomplish the library's priorities. Obviously, to find staff resources to perform the activities associated with the service priorities, library managers must either hire more people or reallocate and reassign present staff. You probably will not be able to hire new staff to accomplish all the priorities reflected in the new library service plan. Therefore, realistically, you are going to have to reallocate and reassign some existing staff. So now you need to decide which staff to reassign.

Before making any decisions about changing staffing patterns, you need to evaluate how staff resources are currently deployed and used. This knowledge will help you to identify those processes that seem either unnecessarily complex or are of low priority and those units or teams that seem to be underutilized. Therefore, you will need to assess the current capacity, productivity, and utilization of staff for each unit of the library using the processes and workforms described earlier, especially Workforms S10 and S11 for data from observations or Workforms S13 and S14 for data from self-reports.

Once you know what staff are doing now, you need to consider the value of each task to the library's goals. To do this, compare the list of tasks and activities from the workforms about staff (Workforms S9 through S14) with a list of tasks and activities important to the service priorities selected in Workform S2. You will find that not every service, activity, or task performed by library staff adds equal value to fulfilling the mission or meeting the library's priorities. Simply put, some things staff do are more important than others. Two tasks may take the same staff members the same length of time to complete, but if task A is vital to the library's outcomes and task B is nonessential, task A is cost-effective and task B is not. As you review each of the tasks and activities that staff are currently doing ask, "What does this contribute to the library's goals?

What does it contribute to meeting the needs identified in our services priorities?" If the contribution of any activity is not obvious, it becomes a candidate for change or even elimination.

It will also be helpful to understand something about how difficult any new activities will be so that the appropriate classification of staff can be assigned. The statements contained in figure 7 can help you decide both the classification of staff required for an activity as well as the importance of that activity to the library goals and objectives.

Those tasks and activities that occupy a lot of staff time but are of low importance to accomplishing the library's priorities are prime candidates for change. The kind of change depends on your answers to the following questions about a particular task or activity:

- Can the task be eliminated?
- Can the patrons do the task?
- Can volunteers do the task?
- Can some other organization do the task?
- Can the task be contracted out, that is, outsourced?
- Can the task be redesigned?
- If the task must be done by library staff can it be streamlined
  by automation?
  by cutting intermediate steps?
  by combining it with another task?

FIGURE 7
Criteria for Assessing Difficulty and Importance of an Activity

Rating	Difficulty Level	Importance
1	Simple to learn Simple to do No special knowledge Follows established procedure	Minor importance Errors not significant
2	Expected to meet performance standard Requires job-specific skill Small amount of discretion	Moderate importance to unit/team Errors can cause problems for unit/team
3	Special knowledge required Decision making required Knowledge needs updating	High importance Failure to perform has negative consequences for unit/team
4	High level of decision making Must balance many tasks High level of knowledge Complex to learn and do	Mission critical Failure has negative consequences for entire library system

Eliminating and Merging Tasks and Activities

Every organization and every unit performs tasks that could be discontinued, merged, or changed. For example, acquisitions staff at one library spend a lot of time rekeying bibliographic information provided by selectors in the central library and branches. Clearly, this wastes a lot of staff time and effort. Workform S8 can be used to identify tasks such as rekeying that are unnecessary.

Staff members should be given an opportunity to help identify the less important tasks that they have been assigned. Many staff are delighted to have the chance to do their jobs more efficiently or effectively. However, other staff might be reluctant to call any task unimportant because of fears about job security. You might want to point out that the purpose of identifying low importance tasks is to eliminate trivialities, not jobs. By taking part in the activity analysis, staff can have an opportunity to devote time and effort to activities that have a positive impact. All staff want their work to be an important contribution.

Outsourcing

Two key elements in managing resources of any kind are flexibility and willingness to try doing things in new ways. One way of doing things now getting considerable attention is outsourcing. Outsourcing has been defined as "hiring a contractor to manage or perform a function or to begin or complete a project."[8] Examples of outsourcing in public libraries include

> contracting for temporary staff for a limited, short-term assignment
>
> buying a one-time service such as a shelf-ready opening day collection
>
> cooperating with another organization or library to provide services (For example, many libraries offer basic literacy classes. The library supplies the meeting space and workbooks, but Literacy Volunteers or Laubach Literacy provides the tutors and the training.)
>
> buying services from commercial vendors or bibliographic utilities
>
> leasing employees from a commercial firm
>
> contracting for the provision of library services from another local government unit or from a corporation

Although some aspects of contracting for services from vendors are controversial now, libraries actually started outsourcing when they began buying catalog cards from the Library of Congress in 1913. Later many libraries joined cooperatives for cataloging and processing. The most successful of those cooperatives was the Ohio College Library Cooperative that morphed into OCLC, now providing cataloging information to some 35,000 libraries from 65 countries.[9]

Most public libraries are affiliated with local governments, and traditionally local governments did not buy many services from commercial firms. However, in the 1970s some local governments decided that competition might be a way to hold down costs and to increase productivity among their own civil service staffs. They began to put out for bids certain services, allowing their own workers to compete. Garbage pickup, custodial services, security services, and data processing were among the first services to be outsourced.

Other governmental agencies followed, and today a broad range of services from day care for children of government employees to the operation of prisons are negotiated by contracts with private firms. The reasons government organizations outsource services have remained constant since the early 1900s—the perception that the service or product can be obtained faster, cheaper, or better than doing it in-house.

Before library managers can make any decisions about outsourcing, they need data about current costs and timely productivity. These data are necessary to evaluate if outsourcing a particular service *will* result in faster, cheaper, or better ways of doing something than doing it in-house. The vendors for any service you might be interested in have already calculated the cost of providing every one of their products or services. They also have developed specifications and standards for response time and quality that usually are incorporated into their standard business contracts.

Therefore, library managers considering contracting for a service need to fully understand the specifics of the service being offered, the expected quality levels of the service, and the time frame in which the service should be delivered. Only when managers compare their in-house services in relation to outsourced services in these three areas can they accurately judge how the cost of outsourcing a service compares with using library staff to do the same work. Issues about specifications and quality are usually the most complex and the most contentious.

SPECIFICATIONS

Most vendors allow libraries to choose from among a variety of options within certain parameters. For example, when ordering preprocessed materials, library staff can usually select the classification system, the number of decimal places in the call number, the source of the subject headings, etc. However, once these options are selected, they become a controlling set of instructions that the vendor's staff will follow. If the library has not carefully determined all the features that are required or desired, staff may decide to make modifications to the service after the contract has been signed. This tinkering with the specifications after a contract has been awarded usually significantly reduces any savings in time or money that the contract was intended to provide.

QUALITY

Key staff must understand the decision to outsource certain library tasks or activities. Not only should they be involved in developing specifications but also in identifying quality standards for the service being purchased. However, even if staff are involved in these aspects, problems may still arise. In some instances library staff have raised strenuous objections about quality issues that were not anticipated and, hence, not part of the contract. Obviously, these objections take time to resolve and raise the hidden cost of outsourcing.

COMPARING COSTS

Calculating the cost of obtaining a service from an outside vendor and comparing that cost with the cost of having it done within the library can be tricky. The difficulty isn't in determining the cost of outsourcing an activity. Most vendors will quote a per-unit price based on the specifications that the library selects. The problem is trying to determine the cost of completing the activity using library staff. The library has to consider all of the following elements to determine the in-house per unit cost:

- percent of time that each staff person involved spends on the work
- salaries and fringe benefits prorated for the time involved
- prorated cost of equipment based on the percent of time that the equipment is used for the work
- cost of all supplies used in performing this work
- cost of space, including heating and lighting, custodial, and rent or lease costs

Summing the costs and dividing by the number of items processed in a particular time period, such as a month, a quarter, or a year, gives the cost of processing one item in the library. This cost can then be compared with the vendor's cost to get an initial estimate of the savings, if any, that would be gained by outsourcing.

However, before you can make a final decision about any potential savings that might be realized from outsourcing, you also need to estimate the staff time and associated personnel costs involved in overseeing the vendor and the quality of the contracted service. At least one library employee must be the contact person for the supplier and must coordinate the work. When questions or problems come up, someone in the library will have to deal with them.

You might also want to consider if the space used by staff performing the work could be used more effectively and if the staff now performing the work can be better used for something else. Only after considering all of these issues can you truly assess whether outsourcing will result in doing the activity faster, cheaper, or better.

Assessing Cost and Value

Cost is usually interpreted in terms of money, but cost can also be interpreted in terms of time or effort. In this section, staff time and effort equate with money or, more specifically, with the compensation paid to staff for their time and effort. Most libraries are not aware of the cost of each of the various activities that staff perform. Although the direct cost of operating individual library units could be fairly easily estimated by summing the dollars spent on staff, materials, supplies, and facilities, few libraries could specify the costs of circulation activities or the provision of a series of programs. If libraries were more aware of the costs of activities and the processes that underpin them, perhaps they would pay more attention to the value of those activities and processes.

As professionals we librarians like to think that everything we do is valuable. Yet, in reality, not all tasks and activities that are performed by staff add equal value. Some activities simply contribute more toward achieving the library's goals than other activities. Even in our personal or family life we start, stop, or modify activities based on some mental perception of their value.

However, if you do not know how much something costs,

how can you manage or reallocate costs?

how can you decide its value or benefit?

how can you relate its cost to outputs?

on what basis can you decide whether to contract out activities?

Workforms S15 through S18 are intended to make explicit the relationship between the cost of various activities and their value as perceived by library decision makers. Having this information will enable you to decide if an activity is worth doing in each library unit, if it should be centralized, or if it should be outsourced. For example, if essentially the same process and effort will be repeated in many libraries—such as ordering titles on the best seller lists—then the value of doing this in each library unit becomes questionable. Centralizing this activity might be more cost-effective. As another example, if you have a limited number of cataloging and processing staff, it might be more cost effective to outsource the cataloging and processing of media to a vendor.

It will be important to evaluate the new activities arising from the library's service priorities selected in terms of their cost and value to the library's overall goals. Workform S18 gives you an opportunity to calculate both cost and value before committing resources.

Interpreting and Deciding

Once you and many others have used the information in this chapter to collect all the data identified as useful, then what? How do you transform that data into information that is helpful in figuring out where and how to locate the staff resources to implement the library's priorities? Remember, this whole process is intended to help you complete the gap analysis process illustrated in Workform X of *Planning for Results* and included in appendix B. The gap analysis process suggests that you determine what resources the library currently has that support its intended outcomes, what resources are needed to achieve those outcomes, and how you plan to address the gap between the two. To make that determination, you will have to analyze the data that has been collected.

There are several ways to review and analyze the data. A list of factors to consider appears at the end of each workform in the next part of this chapter. These are intended to stimulate your thinking about allocating staff resources. There are no magic solutions because each situation is unique. However, in general, the more that the people who will be affected by staffing changes are involved in decision making, the easier it will be to implement those changes. Organizational restructuring has eliminated many middle management positions and placed responsibility for making decisions about work procedures with teams or unit staff. Since these people actually do the work, they should have ideas about how to transform or streamline processes and procedures. Decisions that are likely to affect the library as a whole will need broad discussion before consensus is reached. However, this time you will have information as a basis for the decisions.

Some teams and managers will be more comfortable with a statistical approach to resource allocation. Much of the data you will collect on these workforms is numeric. Librarians tend to report numbers about library activities as percentages or averages. Neither method may be sufficient for the decisions to be made about staffing. As you review current and projected staffing needs, it is important for you to understand if there is a meaningful difference between two or more numbers reported for the same activity or work performed. To do that you will need to know something about number distribution. If you are interested in learning more about number distribution, see appendix C, which includes both a more complete explanation of number distribution and illustrations.

However you decide to analyze the data and whatever decisions you make based on what you learn from the data, remember the recommendation that you "estimate, implement, check, and adjust" and then "check and adjust" again. The whole point is to ensure that the library is devoting time and effort to what counts—today, tomorrow, and next year.

NOTES

1. Public Library Data Service, *Statistical Report* (Chicago: American Library Assn., 1998), 41.
2. James R. Coffey, "Introduction: Costing Acquisitions: Getting More for Less," in *Operational Costs in Acquisitions,* ed. James R. Coffey (New York: Haworth, 1991), 2.

3. Public Library Data Service, *Statistical Report,* 65–66.

4. John Mooreman, "Standards for Public Libraries: A Study in Quantitative Measures of Library Performance as Found in State Public Library Documents," *Public Libraries* 36, no. 1 (Jan./Feb. 1997): 32–39.

5. Stephen A. Roberts, *Cost Management for Library and Information Services* (London: Butterworths, 1985), 60.

6. Karen Schmidt, "The Cost of Pre-Order Searching," in *Operational Costs in Acquisitions,* ed. James R. Coffey (New York: Haworth, 1991), 19.

7. McDonald Corp., "The Customer Ten Commandments" (Oak Brook, Ill.: The Corp., 1987).

8. Mary S. Konkel, "President's Program: 'The Human Side of Outsourcing,'" *ALCTS Newsletter* 9, no. 4–6 (1998): 59.

9. Internet: http://www.oclc.org (12/13/98).

General Instructions

At the Bottom of All Staffing Workforms

1. **Completed by** Enter the name of the person or people who completed this workform.
2. **Source of data** Indicate the source of the data used to complete the workform.
3. **Date** Enter the date the workform was completed.
4. **Library** Enter the library name.

Example Workforms

Examples of completed workforms accompany Workforms S6, S9–S10, and S16–S18. These are provided as a guide to assist you in completing the workforms.

Special Instructions

1. A set of general instructions is provided for those who will complete Workforms S9 and S10.
2. A page that combines instructions for Workforms S11, S12, and S13 is directed toward managers.
3. Workforms S12 and S13 are to be given to individual staff members for completion along with instructions for completing the forms.
4. Workform S11 may be completed by either the staff member who performs the activity or process or by an observer.
5. Another page of general instructions relates to Workforms S16–S18.
6. Read all these sets of general instructions carefully.

Instructions

Purpose of Workform S1

Use this workform to determine which staff functions will be affected by the selected priority or service response.

Source(s) of Data for Workform S1

1. You will complete this workform based on the service responses/priorities, goals, and objectives in the library's service plan.

2. If the library used *Planning for Results* and completed the resource allocation forms (Current Resource Allocation Chart Workform, Gap Analysis Workform, and Future Resource Allocation Chart Workform), you will find that there is a relationship between data used to complete those workforms and this workform. If those workforms have been completed, they can be helpful in completing Workform S1.

Factors to Consider When Completing Workform S1

1. Staffing requirements are different for each of the 13 service responses in *Planning for Results*. Complete a copy of this workform for each service response selected. If you used a different planning model, complete a copy of this workform for each priority identified in that plan.

2. The goals and objectives selected may also have an impact on the staff qualifications needed to perform the activities associated with the different service responses/priorities. (For example, the goals for the service response Formal Learning Support might be

   The Homework Help center will assist school children in Anytown in completing their assignments.

   Adult students enrolled in nontraditional colleges will have the support they need to pursue their degree programs or complete their courses of study.)

   Each goal will have a different impact on staff and require different abilities from staff.

3. An *activity* is what you do to attain your objectives and to make progress toward your goals. One or more tasks can constitute an activity. An activity can be a process or a transaction. (For example: "Work with school librarian(s) to develop book lists on hot topics." See other examples in *Planning for Results: The Guidebook*, pp. 43–4.)

4. You want to collect only the data that will help you decide what changes need to be made in the deployment of staff to implement the goals and objectives in the library's plan. That data will vary, depending on the plan. (For instance, in the examples for Anytown, it is probable that "programs" would be a key function. However, the programs for the homework center involving teachers and librarians in the school system will be different from those targeted toward the working adults enrolled in nontraditional colleges.)

To Complete Workform S1

1. **Line A** Write in the service response/priority under review.

2. **Column B** List the activities proposed for that service response/priority in the numbered spaces in column B.

3. **Column C–I** Next, review each activity and determine which library functions *are most important* to accomplish that activity. Place an X in the appropriate columns.

Factors to Consider When Reviewing the Data on Workform S1

1. Are these the best activities to move the library toward achieving the goals of this service response/priority? Are these activities too safe or too status quo?

2. Is the list of activities complete?

3. The staff are probably already performing activities at least somewhat related to the service responses/priorities under review. The intent here is to make explicit the relationship between the service responses/priorities and the functions needed to support them.

WORKFORM S1   **Staff Functions Related to a Service Response/Priority**

A. Service response/priority _____

B. Activity	C. Collection Management	D. Technical Services	E. Circulation Activities	F. Reference and Information Services	G. Programs/ Outreach	H. System and Technical	I. Other (Describe)
1.							
2.							
3.							
4.							
5.							
6.							
7.							
8.							
9.							
10.							
11.							
12.							
13.							
14.							
15.							
16.							

Completed by _____ Date completed _____

Source of data _____ Library _____

Purpose of Workform S2

Use this workform to stimulate your thinking about all the specific activities that will be necessary to provide one service response or meet one priority and how important the activity is to achieving the goal of the service response/priority, where and when the activity will be performed, and who or what level of staff will perform the activity.

Source(s) of Data for Workform S2

1. The goals and objectives in the library's service plan provide the information for this workform.

2. The workform also requires some thinking from staff about the scope of the activities. If the library used *Planning for Results*, review the information for each service response selected. Each service response contains a section labeled "Resource Allocation Issues to Consider" with a paragraph about pertinent staff activities.

3. If you have already completed Workform S1, use the activities on that workform to complete column C.

Factors to Consider When Completing Workform S2

1. An *activity* is what you do to attain your objectives and to make progress toward your goals. One or more tasks can constitute an activity. An activity can be a process or a transaction. (For example: "Work with school librarian[s] to develop book lists on hot topics." See other examples in *Planning for Results: The Guidebook* pp. 43–4).

2. There is a balance between being too cautious and too ambitious. Try to be realistic about where and when these activities should be carried out. It might be better to limit an activity to one location at first and then branch out based on the experience you gained.

3. Try to ensure that you have covered *all* the activities associated with the goals and objectives of the service response/priority.

4. The ratings for importance should not be clustered at the highest end—all *4s*—or at the midpoint—all 3s. They should be spread out between the lowest and highest.

5. This workform covers only one service response/priority. The process needs to be repeated for every other service response/priority selected.

To Complete Workform S2

1. **Items A–B** Provide the general information requested at the top of the workform.

   Item A Write the service response/priority under review.

   Item B Write the name of the library unit or team under consideration.

2. **Column C** List the activities you plan to accomplish for the service response/ priority being considered on the numbered lines in column C.

3. **Column D** Consider how much this activity will contribute to fulfilling your objectives and goals for this service response/priority. Rate the importance according to the scale at the bottom of the workform. Refer to figure 7, "Criteria for Assessing Difficulty and Importance of an Activity," for assistance.

4. **Column E** Place an *X* in one of the subcolumns.

   If the activity already *exists* and will continue unchanged, place an *X* in the *E* subcolumn.

   If an existing activity needs to be *redesigned* or changed in a substantial way, place an *X* in the *R* subcolumn.

   If the activity is *new* for the library or the unit to which it will be assigned, place an *X* in the *N* subcolumn.

5. **Column F** Indicate where the activity will be performed—systemwide, in multiple locations, or in a single branch or unit?

6. **Column G** Indicate when the activity will be performed. Will the activity be performed only at specific times, or will it be available during the library's hours of operation or beyond? (For example, group activities are usually location-specific at certain times. Remote access to the library's OPAC and Web pages is both systemwide and around the clock.)

7. **Column H** The responses for this column can be specifically named staff members, classification levels, or both. If the "who" is still unknown, place a ? in the column.

Factors to Consider When Reviewing the Data on Workform S2

1. Are these the best activities to move the library toward achieving the goals of this service response/priority? Are these activities too safe or too status quo?

2. Is the list of activities complete? Try to ensure that you have covered all the activities associated with the goals and objectives of the service response/priority.

3. Are the ratings for importance spread out over the list of activities and not bunched at one end or in the middle?

4. There is a balance between being too cautious and too ambitious. Try to be realistic about where and when these activities should be carried out, and then branch out based on experience gained. Are the responses for columns E–H realistic for achieving the goals?

WORKFORM S2 Activities Involved in a Service Response/Priority

A. Service response/priority _____

B. Unit/team _____

C. Activity	D. Importance*	E. Activity Status†			F. Where Performed	G. When Performed	H. Who Performs
		E	R	N			
1.							
2.							
3.							
4.							
5.							
6.							
7.							
8.							
9.							
10.							
11.							
12.							
13.							
14.							
15.							
16.							

*Importance: 1 = Minor   2 = Moderate   3 = High   4 = Critical

†Code: E= Existing activity   R= Revised or redesigned activity   N= New activity

Completed by _____   Date completed _____

Source of data _____   Library _____

Staff Abilities Required for a Service Response/Priority Activity

Instructions

Purpose of Workform S3

Use this workform to help pinpoint the specific staff abilities needed to carry out one activity listed on Workform S2 for the service response/priority selected. *There is no need to complete this workform for existing activities that are satisfactory and need no different abilities.*

This workform is primarily for new or redesigned activities.

Source(s) of Data for Workform S3

1. Each activity listed on Workforms S1 and/or S2 that is new or to be redesigned provides the information for this workform.

2. Abilities are identified by library personnel as a result of discussion and consideration of needs and levels.

Factors to Consider When Completing Workform S3

1. *Abilities* as used here can include knowledge, skill, attitude, or experience. Refer to the list in figure 4, "Examples of General Abilities," for the various categories.

2. Have all pertinent abilities been identified?

3. Are the levels specified realistic in terms of finding staff and achieving the goals related to this service response?

4. The process will have to be repeated for each new or redesigned activity listed in Workform S2.

5. Do not enter data in the shaded sections.

To Complete Workform S3

1. **Items A–B** Provide the general information requested at the top of the workform.

   Item A Write the service response/priority under review.

   Item B Write the activity under review. Note that this workform is for only one activity.

2. **Column C** On the lines provided under each of the seven numbered abilities, list the specific abilities required. There is no need to fill in every row or every category. (For example, the library might want to staff a particular branch with personnel who speak a language common in that community and who understand its ethnic culture. The abilities required might be limited to subject knowledge, communications, and interpersonal.)

3. **Column D** Further specify what is needed. (For example, if you selected the Basic Literacy service response from *Planning for Results*, the description of that service response states, "Staff providing basic literacy services should complete a literacy volunteer training program because they need to be aware of the challenges and problems faced by adult new readers" [p. 59]. Such staff also should possess patience and empathy, both of which are interpersonal abilities, and be able to communicate tactfully, but clearly, so that the adult new readers feel comfortable and motivated.)

4. **Column E** Circle the level required or desired. (For example, the basic level might call for staff with the ability to deal with easy situations, perform routine tasks, answer basic questions about library policy, and use elementary resources such as dictionaries, almanacs, etc. The medium level might call for staff with the ability to handle more-complicated situations, perform more-difficult tasks, answer questions using specialized reference resources, and deal with inquiries that require interpretation of library policy. The expert level might call for staff who are extremely knowledgeable about a particular topic, can deal well with complex situations or problems, and can perform highly specialized tasks.)

Factors to Consider When Reviewing Workform S3

1. Are the abilities specified appropriate for the service response/priority under discussion?

2. Is the need for each ability realistically described?

3. Are the levels required appropriate for the ability specified, neither too low nor too high?

WORKFORM S3 Staff Abilities Required for a Service Response/Priority Activity

A. Service response/priority _____

B. Activity _____

C. Abilities Needed	D. Description of Need	E. Required Skill Level		
1. Subject knowledge		Basic	Moderate	Expert
		Basic	Moderate	Expert
		Basic	Moderate	Expert
2. Interpersonal		Basic	Moderate	Expert
		Basic	Moderate	Expert
		Basic	Moderate	Expert
3. Communications		Basic	Moderate	Expert
		Basic	Moderate	Expert
		Basic	Moderate	Expert
4. Library specific		Basic	Moderate	Expert
		Basic	Moderate	Expert
		Basic	Moderate	Expert
5. Management		Basic	Moderate	Expert
		Basic	Moderate	Expert
		Basic	Moderate	Expert
6. Technological		Basic	Moderate	Expert
		Basic	Moderate	Expert
		Basic	Moderate	Expert
7. Physical		Basic	Moderate	Expert
		Basic	Moderate	Expert
		Basic	Moderate	Expert

Completed by _____ Date completed _____

Source of data _____ Library _____

Instructions

WORKFORM S4 **Checklist of Abilities for Activities**

Purpose of Workform S4

Use this workform to focus attention on the commitment the library has to make to obtain certain abilities that facilitate the performance of activities that, in turn, help achieve the goals associated with the selected service responses/priorities.

Another purpose of the workform is to prod you to think hard about how an ability contributes to the success of an activity. (For example, the service responses Cultural Awareness and Local History and Genealogy require specific knowledge. Formal and Lifelong Learning require persons who can relate to students whatever their age or learning ability.)

Source(s) of Data for Workform S4

1. One ability identified on Workform S3 provides the information for each copy of this workform.
2. Discussions with staff, trustees, and community leaders, as appropriate, provide information for this workform.

Factors to Consider When Completing Workform S4

1. Complete a copy of this workform for each activity under consideration.
2. Is the relationship clear between this ability and the activity it is intended to support?
3. Have the relevant stakeholders been consulted about these requirements?

To Complete Workform S4

1. **Lines A–D** Provide the general information requested at the top of the workform.

    Line A Indicate the service response/priority under review.

    Line B Indicate the activity under review.

    Line C Transfer the particular ability from Workform S3.

    Line D Tell why this ability is necessary for the success of the activity. If, in thinking this over, you decide that some ability is not needed, that decision is allowed.

2. **Items 1–7** Answer each of the numbered questions in the left-hand column by circling one of the options listed in columns E–H. Column I can be used to list other options that seem appropriate.

Factors to Consider When Reviewing Workform S4

1. Is the relationship between this ability and the activity it is to support clear?
2. Is this ability needed for only a short time? If so, can it be obtained by using temporary staff or by contracting out?
3. Is the library prepared to support the time and training this ability may require?
4. Should the library seek new staff or volunteers who already have this ability?

WORKFORM S4   Checklist of Abilities for Activities

A. Service response/priority for which this activity is needed _____

B. Activity _____

C. Ability desired _____

D. How does this ability contribute to the success of the activity listed above? _____

(Circle one option for each row below.)

	E.	**F.**	**G.**	**H.**	**I. Other (Specify)**
1. Where is this ability required?	Systemwide	Branches only	Central only	Unit/team specific	
2. When should this ability be available?	At all times	Daily	Weekly	Monthly	
3. For how long will this ability be needed?	Permanently	6–12 months	6 weeks–6 months	1–6 weeks	
4. In how much time can this ability be learned?	Years	Months	Weeks	Days	
5. In which staff can this ability be expected to be found?	All staff	Public service staff	Specific positions (specify)	Specific positions (specify)	
6. How often does this ability need to be updated?	Continually	Semiannually	Annually	Rarely/never	
7. How can this ability be learned?	Life experience	Formal classroom instruction	Continuing education	On-the-job training	

Completed by _____   Date completed _____

Source of data _____   Library _____

WORKFORM S5   Analysis of Training Needs and Costs for a Service Response/Priority

Instructions

Purpose of Workform S5

Use this workform to help you assess the real costs in both time and money of training staff to acquire abilities associated with a particular service response/priority. *If no training is needed, there is no need to proceed with this workform for that service response or priority.*

Source(s) of Data for Workform S5

1. Abilities needed as identified on Workform S3 and Workform S4 provide the information for this workform.

2. Discussions with staff, along with information about the availability of classes at local colleges or instruction provided by outside groups, such as library consortia, will provide needed information

Factors to Consider When Completing Workform S5

1. Complete a copy of this workform for each service response/priority under consideration.

2. This workform is to be used only for abilities that are teachable—such as subject knowledge or technology classes. It should *not* be used for abilities such as foreign languages or personality transformation. Are the abilities required limited to those that are teachable?

3. Are the assessments about time and place of instruction realistic?

4. Are the numbers of students to be trained realistic?

5. Is the math correct?

6. Do not enter data in the shaded sections.

To Complete Workform S5

1. **Line A**   Indicate the service response/priority under review.

2. **Row B**   Look again at all copies of Workform S4 in which you circled "formal classroom instruction" or "continuing education" in response to row 7. List those abilities on Workform S5 in row B. There is space, if needed, on this workform for four separate abilities. *All abilities, however, should relate to the same service response/priority.*

3. **Rows C–F**   Circle the appropriate response for each ability desired.

4. **Row G**   Write in the tuition or enrollment fee per student.

5. **Row H**   Write in the number of persons to be trained.

6. **Row I**   Estimate the number of hours of released time (including travel time) needed for all persons to be trained. To do this, multiply the time required for the training by the number of persons to be trained (row F × row H).

7. **Section J**   Calculate the cost for training.

    Row J1   Multiply the number of hours of released time (row I) by the average salary of the staff to be trained. Record that number in row J1.

    Row J2   Multiply the number of students by the fees for each student (row H × row G).

    Row J3   Add personnel and education costs (row J1 + J2) and write the total in row J3 for each training need.

Factors to Consider When Reviewing Workform S5

1. Is the cost of training worth the ability acquired? Consider cost in terms of staff time spent in training and dollars expended.

2. Can equally good training be obtained more cheaply?

WORKFORM S5 Analysis of Training Needs and Costs for a Service Response/Priority

A. Service response/priority _____

B. Ability Required*	Formal class		On-job training	Formal class		On-job training	Formal class		On-job training
C. Where learned	Formal class		On-job training	Formal class		On-job training	Formal class		On-job training
D. Trainer	Hired		Staff	Hired		Staff	Hired		Staff
E. Learned one time versus updated frequently	One time		Update	One time		Update	One time		Update
F. Time needed to learn	Semester	Week	Days	Semester	Week	Days	Semester	Week	Days
G. Fee per student	$			$			$		
H. Number of students									
I. Hours of released time									
J. Cost									
1. Personnel cost	$			$			$		
2. Tuition/ enrollment cost	$			$			$		$
3. Total cost	$			$			$		$

*Note: This analysis should be used only for *teachable* abilities.

Completed by _____ Date completed _____

Source of data _____ Library _____

Staff **69**

Instructions

WORKFORM S6   Estimate of Productive Work Hours Available

Purpose of Workform S6

Use this workform to calculate the total number of hours available annually for any one category of staff.

Source(s) of Data for Workform S6

Library personnel policy and library budget for staff authorized provide the information for this workform.

Factors to Consider When Completing Workform S6

1. Complete a copy of this workform for each staff category shown at the top of the workform.

2. Part of the workform focuses on predictable and unpredictable time away from work. Both kinds of time are authorized, but predictable time is routine, while the unpredictable time varies by circumstances affecting staff.

3. Be sure to account for differences in vacation days authorized for seniority among staff in the same category.

4. You might want to compile a summary sheet to calculate the total work hours available for any unit/team.

5. Do not enter data in the shaded sections.

6. For assistance in completing Workform S6, see the example.

To Complete Workform S6

1. **Lines A–D**   Complete the information at the top of the form.

   Line A   Record the number of full-time staff in a job category.

   Line B   Record the name of the unit/team in which these staff work.

   Line C   Record the total number of staff eligible for benefits. Then divide this number into two groups—those eligible for regular vacation and those eligible for seniority vacation.

   Line D   Record the number of hours in the standard work week for full-time staff in this job classification.

2. **Lines E–F**   Calculate the nominal staff hours per year by multiplying line A × line D × 52 weeks. (See the worked example of Workform S6.) Record the answer in the unshaded area of row F.

3. **Section G**   Calculate the number of predictable hours unavailable by multiplying the times authorized for vacation, holidays, and work breaks by the number of staff eligible in this job category. Record the number of hours for each in the unshaded section for each row.

   Row G5   Add all the hours in section G and record the total in the unshaded section for the row.

4. **Section H**   Record all time taken as sick or personal leave by this staff category last year. For an indication of the worst-case estimate, record all total hours for sick leave, personal days, and other (funeral time, jury duty, etc.) authorized.

   Row H4   Add the total number of hours used or authorized for sick leave, personal days, and other. Record the total in the unshaded section for the row.

5. **Row I**   Add the numbers in rows G5 and H4 and record the total.

6. **Row J**   Subtract row I from row F and enter the difference in row J.

7. **Row K**   If you know the number of hours budgeted or authorized for part-time staff for the fiscal year, record that number in row K.

8. **Row L**   Add rows J and K and record the total in row L.

Factors to Consider When Reviewing Workform S6

1. Remember that the figure for available hours is only an estimate.

2. The time worked by part-time staff needs to be included for a complete picture of a unit's available staff hours. Be sure to subtract the time these employees are on break each day.

3. If the library provides sick leave or vacation for part-time staff, use this form to determine the number of part-time staff hours available.

WORKFORM S6 Estimate of Productive Work Hours Available—*Example*

A. Indicate the number and level of staff in **one** of the categories below.

Librarians _____ Library assistants __8__ Clerical _____ Pages _____

B. Unit/team __Oakwood Branch__

C. Number of staff eligible for benefits __8__ Regular vacation __6__ Seniority vacation __2__

D. Hours in standard work week __40__

E. Nominal staff hours available per year: number of staff __8__ × hours in standard work week __40__ × 52 weeks/yr. = __16,640__

F. Nominal staff hours available/year			16,640
G. Predictable hours unavailable			
1. Vacation			
Standard hours × number eligible	480		
Seniority hours × number eligible	160		
2. Holidays (in hours)	640		
3. Daily customary breaks (2 × 15 min. × number staff)	960		
4. Other	0		
5. Total predictable hours unavailable		2,240	
H. Unpredictable hours unavailable			
1. Sick leave	192		
2. Personal days	128		
3. Other	40		
4. Total unpredictable hours unavailable		360	
I. Grand total hours unavailable			−2,600
J. Actual full-time staff hours available for year			14,040
K. Number hours of part-time staff budgeted this year			+1,000
L. Total hours available for this level per year			15,040

Completed by __Marti Manning__   Date completed __12/1/00__

Source of data __budget__   Library __Anytown Library__

WORKFORM S6 Estimate of Productive Work Hours Available

A. Indicate the number and level of staff in **one** of the categories below.

Librarians _____ Library assistants _____ Clerical _____ Pages _____

B. Unit/team _____

C. Number of staff eligible for benefits _____ Regular vacation _____ Seniority vacation _____

D. Hours in standard work week _____

E. Nominal staff hours available per year: number staff _____ × hours in standard work week _____ × 52 weeks/yr. = _____

F. Nominal staff hours available/year			
G. Predictable hours unavailable			
1. Vacation			
Standard hours × number eligible			
Seniority hours × number eligible			
2. Holidays (in hours)			
3. Daily customary breaks (2 × 15 min. × number staff)			
4. Other			
5. Total predictable hours unavailable			
H. Unpredictable hours unavailable			
1. Sick leave			
2. Personal days			
3. Other			
4. Total unpredictable hours unavailable			
I. Grand total hours unavailable			
J. Actual full-time staff hours available for year			
K. Number hours of part-time staff budgeted this year			
L. Total hours available for this level per year			

Completed by _____ Date completed _____

Source of data _____ Library _____

Purpose of Workform S7

Use this workform to compare activity levels among public service units/teams. The data obtained will give you an overview of the levels of activity in these units/teams in light of the number of staff assigned.

Source(s) of Data for Workform S7

Various library statistical reports, the personnel budget for the number of FTE authorized, and incident reports provide the information for this workform.

Factors to Consider When Completing Workform S7

1. To ensure currency, try to collect the data at the end of an annual reporting period.
2. Calculate only the indicators that are of interest.
3. Are the number of hours for each unit accurate?
4. Is the math correct?
5. If you need more space to write annual numbers, enlarge this sheet on your photocopier or create your own spreadsheet using Workform S7 as a model.

To Complete Workform S7

1. **Line A** Indicate the year during which the data was collected.
2. **Row B** List across the top of each column the public service units, either branches or departments within the central library, that engage in the activities shown under section E. If more than four units/teams are being compared, use an additional copy of Workform S7 for each.
3. **Row C** Many units operate on different schedules. Write the number of hours each unit/team provides services annually. (For example, a branch that is open 40 hours per week provides 2,080 hours of service per year [40 × 52].) Remember to adjust for holidays.
4. **Row D** Enter the number of public service FTE who work in each unit.
5. **Section E** There are eight public service indicators listed in the left column. If there are other public service indicators that you would like to consider, list them in rows 9 and 10.

6. **Yearly column, rows 1–10** For each unit/team, record the appropriate annual numbers in each row. You will use this data to calculate the "Hourly" and "By FTE" figures for each unit.
7. **Hourly column, rows 1–10** Because the magnitude of annual numbers often hinders understanding, you should look at the hourly activity. To do this, divide each number in the yearly column for each unit by the number of hours each unit provides service annually (row C). Note that some categories (such as security incidents and meeting room usage) will undoubtedly have an hourly number smaller than 1. See the following example.
8. **By FTE column, rows 1–10** You will also want to consider hourly activity per FTE staff. To do this, divide each number in the "hourly" column for each unit by the number of FTE in each unit (row D). Some categories (such as security incidents and meeting room usage) will undoubtedly have a "By FTE" number smaller than 1. See the following example.

EXAMPLE

B. Unit/Team	Branch A			Branch B			Branch C			Branch D		
C. Number of hours of service/year	2,080			2,080			2,912			3,640		
D. Number FTE public service staff	5			7			9			15		
E. Public Service Indicators	Yearly	Hourly	By FTE	Yearly	Hourly	By FTE	Yearly	Hourly	By FTE	Yearly	Hourly	By FTE
1. Circulation	275,000	132	26	450,000	216	31	475,000	163	18	650,000	178	12
2. Meeting Room Usage	200	.096	.019	240	.115	.016	300	.103	.011	375	.103	.007

Factors to Consider When Reviewing Workform S7

1. The data indicates activity at the macro level, so it is quite likely that some of this data will raise questions that can be answered only by more-detailed analysis.
2. Look closely at the hourly and FTE numbers. These will give an indication of how busy the units are in relation to the number of FTE staff.
3. If there are wide discrepancies in activity levels among the units/teams, could local conditions be one cause? (For example, units/teams whose security incidents seem high may need more staff.)

WORKFORM S7 Comparison of Public Service Indicators

A. Year _____

B. Unit/team

C. Number of hours of service/year

D. Number FTE public service staff

E. Public Service Indicators	Yearly	Hourly	By FTE	Yearly	Hourly	By FTE	Yearly	Hourly	By FTE
1. Circulation									
2. Door count									
3. Number of programs held*									
4. Program attendance									
5. Number of reference questions									
6. Number of special classes									
7. Meeting rooms booked									
8. Security incidents									
9. Other (specify)									
10. Other (specify)									

Programs refers to those prepared by library staff, not those created by other groups or individuals.

Completed by _____ Date completed _____

Source of data _____ Library _____

Manager's/Observer's Instructions

WORKFORM S8 **Analysis of an Activity**

Purpose of Workform S8

Use this workform to analyze all the steps or tasks involved in performing an activity or process. This workform can also be used to help standardize an activity or process among all library units/teams to establish standard times or performance expectations.

Who Should Complete Workform S8

The workform should be completed either by an observer or by the persons involved in the activity or process. The work of every person who performs tasks associated with the activity or process under consideration should be noted either by the observer or by the staff involved to show in sequence the steps in performing each person's part.

Source of Data for Workform S8

1. Either self-reports from persons performing tasks for this activity (or process) or the observations of persons performing the activity provide the basis for this information. Observations are more accurate than self-descriptions because some steps might not be recorded. Furthermore, although the procedure manual might list steps for performing the activity or process, the instructions may or may not be followed by individual staff.

2. *Note* that self-reports have separate instructions that follow these for observers.

Factors to Consider in Completing Workform S8

1. Staff being observed may be nervous. Their apprehensions need to be allayed by informing them that the library is looking at processes, not at their performance.

2. If the same task is performed by many persons in the library system (such as shelving items), it is important to know how the task is performed by each person.

3. Data about work passed along from person to person should be compiled to produce a summary of the steps involved in the activity or process. Use a separate form for each person involved.

4. If you are providing self-reports, provide the separate instructions and make sure respondents understand what they are to do to complete Workform S8.

To Complete Workform S8 (Observer)

1. **Line A** Write the name of the person performing the activity or process.

2. **Line B** Briefly describe the activity under consideration.

3. **Line C** Identify what gets counted. (The reshelving example noted in the chapter's narrative recommends that books, videos, and periodicals be counted as separate types of materials.) In other words, how would the accomplishment of this activity be noted in the library's annual statistics?

4. **Line D** Record the number of staff in each classification who work on this activity or process.

5. **Line E** The starting point for each individual is extremely important for establishing standards. Where or what is the first point of contact for this person?

6. **Section F** List on the numbered lines—in sequence—all the steps done by the person named in line A. Use additional numbers if necessary.

7. **Line G** Identify the endpoint performed *by the person named.* (For the reshelving example, it could be placing the last item in its correct spot on the shelf.) The end point for one person could be passing some item to another. If that is the case, indicate who is the receiver.

8. **Section H** Note the abilities required for this work. See figure 4, "Examples of General Abilities," for assistance in identifying abilities. (For reshelving, these might include the ability to alphabetize and the ability to bend down to place items on the lowest shelf, etc.)

Factors to Consider in Reviewing Workform S8

1. Are any steps redundant, unnecessary, or cumbersome?

2. Could wasted movement by the staff member going from one point to another be streamlined by reconfiguration?

3. Are the abilities required realistic in light of the steps involved?

4. Is the level of staff required appropriate?

Self-Report Instructions

Purpose of Workform S8

This workform is intended to identify all the steps or tasks involved in performing an activity.

Who Should Complete the Workform

Every person who performs tasks associated with the activity under consideration should complete this workform. Each person is to show in sequence the steps he or she takes when performing the task.

Factors to Consider in Completing Workform S8

1. Write down each step as you go along. This way you are unlikely to forget any part of the process.

2. If the same task is performed by many persons in the library system, such as shelving items, then it is important to know how the task is performed by each individual.

WORKFORM S8 Analysis of an Activity

To Complete Workform S8

1. **Line A** Write your name.

2. **Line B** Describe, in general terms, your part in performing the activity.

3. **Line C** Identify what gets counted. (For example, you may be counting orders processed, books reshelved, items charged out, etc.) In other words, how would you calculate the accomplishment of this activity?

4. **Line D** Identify the classifications of those who work with you on this activity.

5. **Line E** What is the first thing that you do to start this activity?

6. **Section F** List—in sequence—all the steps you perform for this activity. Use another sheet of paper if necessary, but number the additional steps in sequence.

7. **Line G** Identify the end point of the activity. (The end point for you could be passing some item to another person. If so, name the person.)

8. **Section H** Note the abilities required. What do you have to know how to do to perform this activity well? (For reshelving, these might include the ability to alphabetize and the ability to bend down to place items on the lowest shelf, etc.)

Staff

WORKFORM S8 Analysis of an Activity

A. Name of person completing activity _____

B. Activity performed _____

C. What gets counted _____

D. Number of other staff involved   Librarians _____   Library assistants _____   Clericals _____   Pages _____

E. Starting point of activity _____

F. List in sequence the steps involved

1. _____
2. _____
3. _____
4. _____
5. _____
6. _____
7. _____
8. _____
9. _____
10. _____
11. _____
12. _____

G. End point of activity _____

H. Abilities required _____

1. _____
2. _____
3. _____

Completed by _____   Date completed _____

Source of data _____   Library _____

General Instructions

Staff are observed by the public, by their coworkers, and by their supervisors every day. The difference in using structured observations is that the observations are recorded with the intent to use the data for planning. Staff may be apprehensive; therefore, they need to be informed about the administration's intentions and be assured that the data concerns units and teams, not individuals.

A number of the questions that arise about collecting data by observations are addressed in the following sections. Before using Workforms S9–S10, persons designated as observers should have at least one group-training session and one practice session to facilitate understanding and to ensure that the instructions are understood by all designated observers.

Who will be observed?

All staff in public and technical services and in support units should be observed. Singling out one unit or one type of service will seem "unfair."

Who will observe?

Supervisors are candidates to do the observations when they are on duty in the unit. At other times, the senior person on duty could be the observer.

Where will the observations be done?

Observations should be done in the designated work areas for the unit or team. The areas include both public and nonpublic space.

When should the observations be done?

Ideally observations should cover all the times that the unit is providing service. For public service units that means nights and weekends. Observers should be instructed not to disclose the observation times and not to record the information in a way that draws attention to the observation.

How long should the observation period be?

The observation period should cover at least three days. The period can be done in a single week or over three weeks. If other observation periods are planned, the days of the week and times of day selected should be different from previous periods.

The observation period should allow for all employees working those days to be included.

How many observations should be done?

There are three types of observations: observation periods, observation days, and single observations. The observation days should cover the employees' entire shift. To ensure that the data concerns the administration's intentions and be as-

The number of single observations depends on the size of the staff. To ensure reliability, a minimum of 30 single observations should be made in each unit per day. The greater the number of staff, the larger the number of single observations. Follow this guide:

Number of Staff	Number of Single Observations
3–10	30
11–20	33–40
21–30	42–60
31+	62

The number of observations per person depends on staff size to a large extent. For example, a staff of 3 would each be observed 10 times during a day. A staff of 10 would each be observed 3 times over the same period. All employees working the same number of hours should be observed the same number of times to ensure equal treatment.

Observations of part-time employees should be prorated according to the number of hours of their shift.

At what time should the observations be done?

The observation times depend on the number of observation periods and on the number of observations to be made. Spread them out over each shift the employees work.

In the unlikely event that there are more than 20 employees in a unit, do not try to observe all 20 at the same time. Instead, plan to observe a small number at each observation period, but make sure that each employee is observed the same number of times as the others.

Make the observations some time during the hour, rather than on the hour or half hour when staff are likely to expect them. Subsequent observations should occur at different minutes in the hours following. The point is to randomize the times at which observations are made.

Instructions

WORKFORM S9 Daily Direct-Observation Log

Purpose of Workform S9

Use Workform S9 to collect data through structured observations of staff activities in both public and nonpublic services.

Source(s) of Data for Workform S9

Direct observations as recorded by designated observers provide the information for this workform.

Factors to Consider When Completing Workform S9

1. Choose the observers for each unit to be observed. These people may be supervisors, staff members, or from outside the unit. However, it is necessary that the observers be able to recognize individual staff members and have access to nonpublic areas.

2. At least two or perhaps more persons will need to be designated as observers to cover all the time periods. The identity of the observers should not be disclosed to avoid skewing the results. (See appendix C for more information on analyzing numeric data.)

3. Provide the observers with the General Instructions for Workforms S9–S10, the examples of completed Workforms S9–S10, and these instructions.

4. Refer to the General Instructions for Workforms S9–S10 for details on how many observations to make. The observation times should cover the entire range of service hours for the unit/team being observed, including evenings and weekends.

5. Use a new workform for each day of observations. Begin a new workform when the observers change. Begin a new workform when staff shifts change.

6. Staff should be informed that the observations will occur during a certain period, but the exact times should not be announced.

To Complete Workform S9

1. **Items A–C** Complete the information on the workform.

   Item A Write the day of the week (for example, Wednesday).

   Item B Record the date the observations are being made.

   Item C Write the name of the unit/team being observed.

2. **Section D** Record the name and job classification of the staff members working on the day of the observations. As noted in "Factors to Consider When Completing Workform S9," if the number changes during the day, use a new form.

3. **Column E** Either record the exact time (10:10) or the hour (10). Using only the hour figure is easier for the observer. Whichever you choose, be consistent.

4. **Column F** Each staff member on duty is to be observed. Write the name and job classification of the staff member being observed on the Observation Log and refer to it when recording in column F.

5. **Column G** Indicate the location of the staff member being observed. For staff who cannot be located, write "not located" in this column. Use the letters *OBLB* for staff who are out of the building on library business.

6. **Column H** If you are not sure what the person is doing, leave the line blank. If the staff member is assigned to a public service desk and there is no activity, write "no activity."

Factor to Consider When Reviewing Workform S9

Do not base judgments on a small number of observations. Observations should be repeated several times over the year to allow data to accumulate to see the larger picture of activities.

WORKFORM S9 **Daily Direct-Observation Log—*Example***

A. Day of the week ___Wednesday___

B. Date of observation ___12/15/99___

C. Unit/team observed ___Oakwood Branch___

D. Staff on duty on this date:

1. Name ___Mary Smith___   Classification ___Librarian___

2. Name ___Joe Jones___   Classification ___Library Assistant___

3. Name ___Nancy North___   Classification ___Library Assistant___

4. Name ___Bill Blue___   Classification ___Clerk___

5. Name ___Betty Johnson___   Classification ___Clerk___

6. Name _____   Classification _____

7. Name _____   Classification _____

8. Name _____   Classification _____

9. Name _____   Classification _____

10. Name _____   Classification _____

11. Name _____   Classification _____

12. Name _____   Classification _____

13. Name _____   Classification _____

14. Name _____   Classification _____

15. Name _____   Classification _____

16. Name _____   Classification _____

17. Name _____   Classification _____

18. Name _____   Classification _____

19. Name _____   Classification _____

20. Name _____   Classification _____

(Continued)

WORKFORM S9 **Daily Direct-Observation Log — *Example (Cont.)***

E. Time	F. Name/Classification	G. Location	H. Activity
10:15	Smith/Librarian	Children's area	Conducting story hour program
10:18	Jones/LA	Reference desk	Helping patron
10:20	North/LA	OPAC	Helping patron
10:21	Blue/Clerk	Circulation desk	Checking out items
10:23	Johnson/Clerk	Stacks	Shelving items
12:34	Smith/Librarian	Staff room	Lunch
12:36	North/LA	Reference desk	No activity
12:36	Jones/LA	Circulation desk	Issuing new card
12:36	Johnson/Clerk	Circulation desk	Checking out items
12:36	Blue/Clerk	Circulation desk	Loading a book truck
2:20	Smith/Librarian	OBLB	
2:20	Jones/LA	Reference desk	Reading Library Journal
2:23	North/LA	Stacks	
2:25	Blue/Clerk	Circulation desk	On phone
2:26	Johnson/Clerk	Workroom	Sorting returned items

Completed by ___Marti Manning___

Source of data ___Direct Observation___

Date completed ___12/15/00___

Library ___Anytown Library___

WORKFORM S9 **Daily Direct-Observation Log**

A. Day of the week _____

B. Date of observation _____

C. Unit/team observed _____

D. Staff on duty on this date:

1. Name _____ Classification _____

2. Name _____ Classification _____

3. Name _____ Classification _____

4. Name _____ Classification _____

5. Name _____ Classification _____

6. Name _____ Classification _____

7. Name _____ Classification _____

8. Name _____ Classification _____

9. Name _____ Classification _____

10. Name _____ Classification _____

11. Name _____ Classification _____

12. Name _____ Classification _____

13. Name _____ Classification _____

14. Name _____ Classification _____

15. Name _____ Classification _____

16. Name _____ Classification _____

17. Name _____ Classification _____

18. Name _____ Classification _____

19. Name _____ Classification _____

20. Name _____ Classification _____

(Continued)

82 Staff

WORKFORM S9 **Daily Direct-Observation Log (Cont.)**

E. Time	F. Name/Classification	G. Location	H. Activity

Completed by _____ Date completed _____

Source of data _____ Library _____

Instructions WORKFORM S10 **Unit/Team/Library Observation Summary**

Purpose of Workform S10

Use this workform to summarize the data obtained from observations taken over one day or several days within one unit, team, or library.

Source(s) of Data for Workform S10

All copies of completed Workform S9 from the same unit/team/library on the same date provide the information for this workform.

Factors to Consider When Completing Workform S10

1. Are the numbers for each day correctly totaled?

2. Is the math correct?

3. For assistance, study the example for Workform S10.

To Complete Workform S10

1. **Item A**   Record the day or days of the week the observations were made.

2. **Item B**   Record the date(s) of the observation period.

3. **Item C**   Record the name of the unit/team/library observed.

4. **Item D**   Total by job classifications the number of FTE staff working during the observation period.

5. **Columns E and F**   List all of the locations and activities reported in columns G and H of the copies of Workform S9 completed on this date. Do not record breaks, lunch, or any activity that is not clearly identified.

6. **Section G**   Total the instances of each type of activity observed and the associated job classifications of the persons performing those activities. Record the totals in the appropriate places. (See the worked example of Workform S10.)

Factors to Consider When Reviewing Workform S10

1. Are activities being performed by the appropriate level of staff?

2. Does the level of activity seem appropriate for the number of staff?

3. Do not base judgments on a small number of observations. Allow time for data to accumulate to see the larger picture of activities.

WORKFORM S10 Unit/Team/Library Observation Summary—*Example*

A. Day of week __Tuesday__

B. Date of observation __12/15/00__

C. Unit/team/library observed __Oakwood Branch__

D. Number of staff on duty this date

Librarians __1__   Library Assistants __2__   Clerks __2__   Pages __1__

E. Location	F. Activity	G. Staff Observed				Total
		Librarians	Library Assistants	Clerks	Pages	
Children's area	Story hour	1				1
Reference desk	Helping patron		1			1
OPAC	Helping patron		1			1
Circulation desk	Checking out items			2		2
Stacks	Shelving items			1	1	2
Circulation desk	Issuing card		1			1
Circulation desk	Loading book truck			1		1
Workroom	Sorting returned items			1		1

Completed by __Marti Manning__   Date completed __12/15/00__

Source of data __Direct observation__   Library __Anytown Library__

WORKFORM S10 Unit/Team/Library Observation Summary

A. Day of week __Tuesday__

B. Date of observation _____

C. Unit/team/library observed _____

D. Number of staff on duty this date

Librarians _____ Library Assistants _____ Clerks _____ Pages _____

E. Location	F. Activity	G. Staff Observed				
		Librarians	Library Assistants	Clerks	Pages	Total

Completed by _____ Date completed _____

Source of data _____ Library _____

Manager's Instructions

Purpose of Workforms S11–S13

Use these workforms to elicit information about the activities that occupy staff members' time.

Workform S11 asks about time-consuming and important activities.

Workform S12 is a record of time spent and activities performed in one work day.

Workform S13 categorizes and totals the times and activities reported in Workform S12.

Sources of Data for Workforms S11–S13

Perceptions of the employees completing the workforms provide the information for Workform S11.

Each person who completes Workform S12 will use it to provide the information for Workform S13.

Factors to Consider When Distributing Workforms S11–S13

1. Workform S11 is separate and should not be distributed with S12 or S13.
2. Workforms S12 and S13 are paired, in that S13 summarizes information on S12. Therefore, Workform S13 and its instructions should be distributed with Workform S12 and its instructions.
3. Be sure that staff understand the purpose of each workform.
4. Be sure that staff understand the instructions for each workform.

Factors to Consider When Reviewing Workforms S11–S13

1. **Workform S11**

   Are time-consuming activities and important activities listed by the staff members congruent or divergent?

   The information is based on perceptions that may or may not be accurate.

2. **Workform S12**

   Not all staff members may have understood the instructions or interpreted them in the same say.

   In considering reliability and accuracy, remember the information is self-reported. Staff may report data that makes them "look good."

   If a running record of time and activities was not kept, the data may be faulty.

   Realize that information about one day of activities is not sufficient for making informed decisions.

3. **Workform S13**

   Does the list of activities seem complete?

   Is all work time accounted for?

   Is the math correct?

Staff Instructions

WORKFORM S11 **Staff-Activity Analysis**

Purpose of Workform S11

Use this workform to identify the activities that occupy most of your time and those activities that are most important to your job duties. Also use this workform to provide suggestions about better use of your time.

To Complete Workform S11

1. **Items A–C** Provide the information requested at the top of the workform:

   Item A Write your name.

   Item B Provide your job title or job classification.

   Item C Provide the name of your library unit or team.

2. **Sections D–F** Answer the questions related to each of the three sections (D, E, and F) about time-consuming activities, important activities, and suggestions for better use of your time.

3. Give the completed workform back to your manager.

WORKFORM S11 Staff-Activity Analysis

A. Name _____

B. Job title _____

C. Unit/team _____

D. List from most to least time-consuming, the five activities on which you spent the **most time** during the past year.

1. _____

2. _____

3. _____

4. _____

5. _____

E. Based on your job description and work assignments, list the **three most important** activities you perform.

1. _____

2. _____

3. _____

F. How could the library make better use of your time?

_____

_____

Completed by _____   Date completed _____

Library _____

Staff Instructions

Purpose of Workform S12

Use this workform to provide information about your activities during one work day.

Factors to Consider When Completing Workform S12

Keep a running record of your time and activities. Trying to remember what you did some hours earlier will result in an inaccurate record.

To Complete Workform S12

1. **Items A–D**   Provide the general information requested at the top of the workform.

    Item A   Write your name.

    Item B   Provide your job classification.

    Item C   Provide the name of your team/unit.

    Item D   Give the date, including the day, month, and year.

2. **Column E**   Record the activities at the time you perform them during one work day. Fill in the hours of your shift. You will be recording your activities at 15-minute intervals during the work day.

3. **Column F**   Write what you did during each time period indicated. Be as specific as possible. If the activity covered more than one 15-minute block, draw an arrow down column F to the time block the activity concluded. (For example, if you shelved books from 10:15 until 11, write "shelved books" in column F at 10:15 and draw an arrow to the line above the row for 11:00.)

    If you perform more than one activity in a 15-minute interval, record only the task that occupied the most time except as instructed below.

    When assigned to a public service desk, it is possible to perform activities other than direct assistance during slow periods. If you do something else, record that.

    Be sure to record lunch periods and breaks.

4. Use the information on this workform to complete Workform S13.

WORKFORM S12 Daily Time/Activity Log

A. Name _____ **B.** Job classification _____ **C.** Team/unit _____ **D.** Date _____

E. Time	F. Activity	E. Time	F. Activity
:00		:00	
:15		:15	
:30		:30	
:45		:45	
:00		:00	
:15		:15	
:30		:30	
:45		:45	
:00		:00	
:15		:15	
:30		:30	
:45		:45	
:00		:00	
:15		:15	
:30		:30	
:45		:45	

Staff Instructions

Purpose of Workform S13

Use this workform to categorize and summarize the activities you listed on Workform S12.

Who Should Complete the Workform?

If you completed Workform S12, you should summarize your time and activities on this workform.

Source(s) of Data for Workform S13

Workform S12 Daily Time/Activity Log provides the data for this workform.

Factor to Consider When Completing Workform S13

Is the math correct?

To Complete Workform S13

1. **Items A–D**   Provide the general information requested at the top of the workform.

    Item A   Write your name.

    Item B   Provide your job classification.

    Item C   Provide the name of your team/unit.

    Item D   Give the date the data being recorded was collected.

WORKFORM S13   Activity Log Summary

2. **Column E**   In the numbered rows in column E, list the major activities on which you spent time. If other tasks were completed while you were staffing a public service desk, note all tasks, the amount of time spent, and add the words "on desk." If you need more numbered rows, make another copy of the workform.

3. **Section F**   Compute the amount of time spent on each major activity for each 15 minutes of the work day. Time should be stated in decimal equivalents, not fractions (1.5 hours, not 1-1/2 hours).

4. **Column G**   Add all the numbers across each row and record the totals in column G for each row.

5. **Row H**   Add the minutes in each column 1–8 for section F, and record the sum in row H for the appropriate column.

    Add the numbers in column G and write the total in row H for column G. The total can exceed 8 hours because of double recording of activities while at the public service desk. The column G final total and the sum of row H should be the same or nearly so. (You should have the same total adding down or across.)

6. Give both the daily log (Workform S12) and the summary workform (S13) to your manager.

Factors to Consider When Reviewing Workform S13

1. Does the list of activities seem complete?

2. Is all work time accounted for?

WORKFORM S13 Activity Log Summary

A. Name _____ **B.** Job classification _____ **C.** Team/unit _____ **D.** Date _____

E. Activity	F. Hours and Minutes Spent								G. Total
	Hour 1	Hour 2	Hour 3	Hour 4	Hour 5	Hour 6	Hour 7	Hour 8	
1.									
2.									
3.									
4.									
5.									
6.									
7.									
8.									
9.									
10.									
11.									
12.									
13.									
14.									
15.									
16.									
17.									
18.									
19.									
20.									
H. Totals									

Completed by _____ Date completed _____

Source of data _____ Library _____

Instructions

WORKFORM S14 Unit/Team/Library Activity Summary

Purpose of Workform S14

Use this workform to summarize time spent on major activities by units, teams, or the entire library.

Source(s) of Data for Workform S14

Data from Workform S13 completed by employees in the unit, team, or collected and summarized for the library provide the information for this workform.

Factor to Consider When Completing Workform S14

Is the math correct?

To Complete Workform S14

1. **Items A–D**   Provide the general information requested at the top of the workform.

   Item A   Write the name(s) of the unit or units being analyzed.

   Item B   Enter the number of hours worked by the unit or units being analyzed. If you are recording for more than one unit, total all the times. (For example, time for three units should be the combined total.)

   Item C   Record the total full-time equivalent staff for all units providing data.

   Item D   Indicate the dates that the data was collected from Workform S13.

2. **Column E**   List the major activities on which time was spent.

3. **Section F**   Using data from Workform S13, add all the time spent on each activity by each of the four levels of staff and record that information in the row corresponding to that activity.

4. **Column G**   For each activity, total the times for all four levels of staff (section F) and enter the combined total in the appropriate box in column G.

5. **Row H**   Add the time spent for each column in section F and record it in row H. Also total column G.

Factors to Consider When Reviewing Workform S14

1. Is the time period reported sufficient to make a reasonable judgment?

2. Is time spent on activities by each level of staff appropriate?

3. Does the information from Workform S13 seem reasonable? Should any of it be double checked?

WORKFORM S14 Unit/Team/Library Activity Summary

A. Unit/team/library _____ **B.** Total of work hours _____ **C.** FTE _____ **D.** Period covered _____ to _____

E. Activity	F. Time Spent by Level of Staff				G. Total Hours
	Librarian	Library Assistant	Clerical	Page	
1.					
2.					
3.					
4.					
5.					
6.					
7.					
8.					
9.					
10.					
11.					
12.					
13.					
14.					
15.					
16.					
17.					
18.					
19.					
20.					
H. Totals					

Completed by _____ Date completed _____

Source of data _____ Library _____

Instructions

Purpose of Workform S15

The purpose of this workform is to simplify computations about compensation costs that you will need to complete Workforms S16–S18.

Source(s) of Data for Workform S15

The library personnel budget or unit personnel budget for the fiscal year under consideration provides the information for this workform.

Factors to Consider When Completing Workform S15

1. Completing this workform simply allows you to "plug in" the average compensation paid over different time periods to different levels of staff. This information should also raise consciousness about staff costs.

2. Have you remembered to include all paid employees?

3. Is the math correct?

To Complete Workform S15

1. **Items A–B** Provide the general information requested at the top of the workform.

   Item A Enter the name of the unit/team/library being analyzed.

   Item B Indicate the fiscal year and personnel budget on which compensation is based.

2. **Columns C–G** Provide the compensation information for each block. Based on your circumstance, fringe benefit costs can be included or excluded in compensation costs.

Column C Write in the name of each person within the appropriate job and time category *above the row* for the average for that group. (For example, the names of full-time librarians Ginger and Elaine would be written in above "Average, full-time librarians.") Note that the column on the left is divided by job classification and by full-time and part-time staff.

Note: If it is not possible to fit all the names on Workform S15, expand the form on your own spreadsheet.

Column D Write in the annual compensation for each name in the column. For part-time help who are paid from one budget line, write in the amount budgeted this year for each job category.

Column E Divide the amount for each annual compensation by 12 and write in the amount associated with each person or group in the appropriate block.

Column F Divide the amount for each annual compensation (column D) by 52 and write in the amount associated with each person or group in the appropriate block.

Column G Divide each weekly compensation (column F) by the number of hours in the standard work week. Write in the amount associated with each person or group in the appropriate block.

Average Rows Compute the average compensation for each time period for each group of employees. For full-time staff, total all compensation costs paid to that job category and divide by the number of employees in the group. For part-time staff who are paid from one budget line—such as pages—simply divide the wages for each time period by the number of persons in the group.

WORKFORM S15 Conversion of Capacity to Cost

A. Unit/team/library _____

B. Fiscal year _____

C. Name/Classification	D. Annual Compensation	E. Monthly Compensation	F. Weekly Compensation	G. Hourly Compensation
Average, full-time librarians				
Average, part-time librarians				
Average, full-time library assistants				
Average, part-time library assistants				
Average, full-time clericals				
Average, part-time clericals				
Average, full-time other				
Average, part-time other				

Completed by _____ Date completed _____

Source of data _____ Library _____

General Instructions

Purpose of Workforms S16–S18

These workforms can be used to assess the cost/value of activities:

performed by one staff member or proposed new position (Workform S16)

performed by staff within one unit or team (Workform S17)

associated with a particular service response (Workform S18)

Source(s) of Data for Workforms S16–S18

The source of information depends on the purpose for which the workform is being completed. See the specific instructions.

Factors to Consider When Completing Forms S16–S18

1. Do not confuse the purposes outlined above.
2. Time periods and costs for the various purposes will differ.
3. Do not enter data in the shaded sections.

To Complete Workforms S16–S18

1. Specific instructions are provided for each of the three purposes.
2. An example of a completed workform for each purpose appears after the instructions for that workform.
3. These workforms are intended to give information about the cost and monetary value of activities. *If you want only cost data, there is no need to complete the value portion of the workform.*

Factors to Consider When Reviewing Workforms S16–S18

1. To be valid, comparisons can be made only with workforms reflecting the same elements:

   Branch libraries may be compared with other branch libraries.

   Service response activities should be compared only with activities for other service responses.

   Workforms reflecting activities of individuals should be compared only with those of individuals performing similar work and having equivalent job classifications.

2. Data that seems to fall outside normal boundaries should be questioned and perhaps recalculated. (See appendix C for more information on distribution.)

WORKFORM S16 Estimate of the Cost/Value of Individual Staff Activities

Instructions

Purpose of Workform S16

Use this workform to calculate the actual costs and associated values of activities or tasks performed by one staff member. The workform can also be used to estimate the cost/value of creating a new position.

Source(s) of Data for Workform S16

1. Use actual or average salary for the job classification as computed on Workform S15. If desired, fringe benefit expenses can be included in the compensation.

2. Time estimates may be obtained from observations or estimations or from Workform S13 activity logs completed by the employees.

3. Guidance about difficulty and importance can be obtained from figure 7 and from staff recommendations.

Factors to Consider When Completing Workform S16

1. Is the time that is covered matched to the compensation paid for that time period: week to week or hour to hour?

2. Are the ratings for difficulty and importance reasonable?

3. Is the math correct?

4. Hours spent can be used in place of percent of time, if desired.

5. For assistance, study example S16 as a guide.

6. Data collection can and should be repeated from time to time for a more accurate picture. Estimates can be made on an annual basis.

7. Do not enter data in the shaded areas.

To Complete Workform S16

1. **Items A–B**   Provide the general information requested at the top of the workform.

   Item A   Write the job classification and/or name of the staff member.

   Item B   Write the time period covered. Data should cover only a short time—days or a week. It is simply too cumbersome to have a staff member's time analyzed over a longer period.

2. **Column C**   List each of the activities or major tasks that the staff member has performed or will perform for the time period under consideration.

3. **Column D**   Rate the level of difficulty of each activity on a scale of 1 to 4, with 1 being the easiest. For guidance in determining the level of difficulty, refer to the ratings in figure 7, "Criteria for Assessing Difficulty and Importance of an Activity." (Ratings shown in the example are for illustrative purposes only.)

4. **Column E**   Rate the level of importance of each activity on a scale of 1 to 4, with 1 being the least important. Refer to the ratings in figure 7 for determining the level of importance. (Ratings shown in the example are for illustrative purposes only.)

5. **Column F**   Enter the percent of time or hours spent on each activity. For new positions, estimate the time requirements. Total column F on row 11.

   Note: Some time may remain unaccounted for. This is not unusual. To show the cost of unaccounted time, enter it as an activity and rate both its difficulty and importance as 1. Then compute costs as instructed in the following directions.

6. **Column G**   Compute the index for each row by multiplying the difficulty rating (column D) by the importance rating (column E) by the percent of time spent (column F). (In the example for preparing and telling stories: 4 × 2 × 25 = 200.)

   Row 11   Enter the total for the column in row 11.

7. **Column H**   Divide the index number (column G) for each activity by the total index number (column G, row 11). Record the quotient in the corresponding row of column H. (For example, the weighting for reference desk is 270/815 = .331.)

   Row 11   Total column H on row 11. The total may be slightly more or less than 100% because of rounding up or rounding down.

8. **Column I**   To complete this column, refer to the amount paid this person for the time period covered from Workform S15. Record the salary for the time period covered in the row immediately below the heading "Compensation." (In the example, the time covered is a week. The weekly salary used for illustration in this example is $893. In doing your own calculation, you will, of course, use the person's salary computed for the appropriate time period on Workform S15.) For new positions relate average costs for the job classification (Workform S15) to time estimates.

   Rows 1–10   For each activity, multiply the compensation paid by the percent of time spent as shown in column F. (In the example, that amount for collection development would be $893 × .10 = $89.30.)

   Row 11 Enter the total for column I on row 11.

(Continued)

Instructions

9. **Column J** For each activity multiply the *total* compensation paid (column I, row 11) by the weighting (column H). (In the example, that amount for collection development would be $893 × .147 = $131.71.) This reflects the value of staff activities based on the time expended, the level of difficulty, and the importance of the activity to the service response. You will note that some activities have a greater value than cost and vice-versa. (Note: In the example, the value of reference desk activities [$295.58] is more than the actual cost [$267.90], whereas the cost of attending meetings [$89.30] is more than the value perceived [$43.76]. Also note that the cost of miscellaneous [unaccounted time] is $44.65, but its value is $5.36.)

   Row 11 Enter the total for column J on row 11.

Factors to Consider When Reviewing Workform S16

1. Are cost/value outcomes reasonable in terms of benefit to the library?

2. How do the costs and values of the activities reflected here compare with those of individuals doing similar jobs or at similar levels?

3. If the purpose is to estimate the cost/value of activities for a new position, do these results seem reasonable?

4. Do you want to extrapolate the time and costs data to an annual estimate? If so, it would be best to repeat gathering information on times expended for several more periods throughout the fiscal year.

100   Staff

WORKFORM S16 Estimate of the Cost/Value of Individual Staff Activities—*Example*

A. Classification/name   Librarian/Ginger Wax

B. Time period covered   9/10/00   to   9/16/00

C. Activity	D. Level of Difficulty	E. Importance to Library	F. % Time Spent	G. Index	H. Weighting	I. Compensation	J. Task Value
						$893.00	
1. Preparing and telling stories	4	2	25%	200	.245	223.25	$218.79
2. Reference desk	3	3	30%	270	.331	267.90	295.58
3. School visits	3	3	20%	180	.221	178.60	197.35
4. Collection development	3	4	10%	120	.147	89.30	131.71
5. Meetings and travel	2	2	10%	40	.049	89.30	43.76
6. Miscellaneous	1	1	5%	5	.006	44.65	5.36
7.			%				
8.			%				
9.			%				
10.			%				
11. Total			100%	815	.999	$893.00	$892.55

Completed by   Marti Manning   Date completed   12/15/00

Source of data   Personal reporting   Library   Anytown Library

Staff   **101**

Estimate of the Cost/Value of Individual Staff Activities

A. Classification/name _____

B. Time period covered _____ to _____

C. Activity	D. Level of Difficulty	E. Importance to Library	F. % Time Spent	G. Index	H. Weighting	I. Compensation	J. Task Value
						$	$
1.			%				$
2.			%				
3.			%				
4.			%				
5.			%				
6.			%				
7.			%				
8.			%				
9.			%				
10.			%				
11. Total			%			$	$

Completed by _____ Date completed _____

Source of data _____ Library _____

WORKFORM S17   Estimate of the Cost/Value of Unit/Team/Library Activities

Instructions

Purpose of Workform S17

Use this workform to calculate the costs and associated value of activities performed within one library unit, by one team, or for the entire library.

Source(s) of Data for Workform S17

1. Average salaries for each job classification involved as computed on Workform S15, and, if desired, fringe benefit costs can be included as a part of the compensation.

2. Time estimates spent on activities may be obtained from observations or estimations or by forms such as activity logs (Workforms S12 and S13) completed by the employee.

3. Guidance about difficulty and importance can be obtained from figure 7 and from staff recommendations.

Factors to Consider When Completing Workform S17

1. Is the time that is covered matched to the compensation for that time period: week to week or day to day?

2. Are the ratings for difficulty and importance reasonable?

3. Is the math correct?

4. For assistance study example S17 as a guide.

5. Data collection should be repeated throughout the year for a more accurate picture.

6. Do not enter data in the shaded areas.

To Complete Workform S17

1. **Items A–D**   Provide the general information requested at the top of the workform.

   Item A   Write the name of the unit/team/library to be analyzed.

   Item B   Write the time period covered. Data will cover only a short time—days or a week. It is simply too cumbersome to have staff time analyzed over a much longer period.

   Item C   Write the number of hours this unit is staffed for the time period covered (noted in item B).

   Item D   Add together the time scheduled to be worked for all full- and part-time staff during the time period covered and record the total here.

2. **Column E**   List each major activity that staff members in this unit/team/library have performed during the time period under consideration.

3. **Column F**   Rate the level of difficulty of each activity on a scale of 1 to 4, with 1 being the easiest. For guidance in determining the level of difficulty, refer to figure 7, "Criteria for Assessing Difficulty and Importance of an Activity." (Ratings shown in the example are for illustrative purposes only.)

4. **Column G**   Rate the level of importance of each activity on a scale of 1 to 4, with 1 being the least important. Refer to figure 7 for determining the level of importance. (Ratings shown in the example are for illustrative purposes only.)

5. **Column H**

   Rows 1–9   Include in this column the hours worked by one or more staff members on each activity. Volunteer time can be included as appropriate here. The hours spent can be estimated, or they can be calculated from data collected through observations. These hours can also be obtained from activity logs or other forms completed by staff reporting time spent on various activities.

   Row 11   Total all hours spent on activities (rows 1 to 9) and write that number in row 11 of the column.

   Row 10   Subtract the total for column H, row 11 from item D. The difference equals the amount of unaccounted time. Write "unaccounted for" in the activity section and the number of hours represented in column H, row 10. Note: Some hours may remain unaccounted for. This is not unusual. Rate both difficulty and importance for "unaccounted for" as 1 and compute costs as instructed in the following sections.

6. **Column I** Compute the index number for each row by multiplying the difficulty rating (column F) by the importance rating (column G) by time spent in hours (column H). (In the example, circulation activity is $1 \times 4 \times 90 = 360$.)

   Add the numbers in column I and enter the total in row 11.

7. **Column J**

   Rows 1–10   Divide the index number (column I) for each activity by the total (column I, row 11). Record the quotient in the corresponding row of column J. (In the example, the weighting for collection development is $120/1,572 = .076$.)

   Row 11   Add the weights for column J and enter the total in row 11. The total may be slightly more or less than 100% because of rounding.

(Continued)

8. **Column K**   Using Workform S15, total the staff compensation for the time period covered, and write that total in the row immediately below the heading.

For each activity, multiply the compensation paid (from Workform S15) by the hours spent (column H) by that level of staff. (In the example, that amount for collection development would be the average hourly amount of the librarian's compensation [$16 × 10 hours = $160].)

For activities involving several levels of staff, prorate the cost. (If a librarian worked at the circulation desk for 4 of those 90 hours, the computation would be 86 hours × average clerical costs + 4 hours × the average librarian cost.)

Be sure to include part-time staff wages for the activities they perform.

Row 11   Write the total for column K in row 11.

9. **Column L**   For each activity, multiply the *total* compensation paid (column K, row 11) by the weighting in column J. This reflects the value of activities based on the time expended, the level of difficulty, and the importance of the activity. You will note that some activities have a greater value than cost and vice-versa.

(In the example, the value of collection development activities [$273] is more than the actual cost ($160], whereas the cost of circulation [$918] is more than the value perceived [$822]. The total value of all activities is computed at $3,583, but the cost is $3,590. This means that cost and value are in harmony.) These two sets of numbers *do not have to balance*. Value can be either higher or lower than actual cost.

Factors to Consider When Reviewing Workform S17

1. Is time in this unit being appropriately used? If not, how could it be directed to more important activities?

2. How do the cost and value of the activities on this workform compare with those of similar units or teams doing similar jobs?

3. Do you want to extrapolate the time and costs data to an annual estimate? If so, it would be best to repeat gathering information on times expended for several more periods throughout the fiscal year.

WORKFORM S17 Estimate of the Cost/Value of Unit/Team/Library Activities—*Example*

A. Unit/team/library Oakwood Branch   **B.** Time period covered 9/10/00 to 9/16/00

C. Hours of service per time period 62   **D.** Total staff hours scheduled 263

E. Activity	F. Level of Difficulty	G. Importance to Library	H. Hours Spent	I. Index	J. Weighting	K. Compensation	L. Task Value
1. Circulation	1	4	90	360	.229	918	$ 822
2. Reference	3	3	75	675	.429	1,200	1,540
3. Collection development	3	4	10	120	.076	160	273
4. Sorting and reshelving	1	4	40	160	.102	241	366
5. Group services	3	1	5	15	.009	240	32
6. Meetings	2	2	5	20	.013	262	47
7. Supervision	4	3	5	60	.038	94	136
8. Story hours	4	2	15	120	.076	240	273
9. Communications	2	2	8	32	.020	105	72
10. Unaccounted for	1	1	10	10	.006	130	22
11. Total			253	1,572	.998	$3,590	$3,583
						$3,590	

Completed by Marti Manning   Date completed 12/15/00

Source of data Workform S16 and time logs   Library Anytown Library

WORKFORM S17 Estimate of the Cost/Value of Unit/Team/Library Activities

A. Unit/team/library _____ B. Time period covered _____ to _____

C. Hours of service per time period _____ D. Total staff hours scheduled _____

E. Activity	F. Level of Difficulty	G. Importance to Library	H. Hours Spent	I. Index	J. Weighting	K. Compensation	L. Task Value
1.	$					$	$
2.							
3.							
4.							
5.							
6.							
7.							
8.							
9.							
10.							
11. Total						$	$

Completed by _____ Date completed _____

Source of data _____ Library _____

WORKFORM S18 Estimate of the Cost/Value of a Service Response/Priority

Instructions

Purpose of Workform S18

Use this workform to judge the value of various activities that are involved in fulfilling a service response/priority in relation to their costs. *This analysis may be done before any of the activities are begun as well as at any time during or after their completion.* This analysis will help you assess whether the activities need to be redesigned, increased, decreased, or eliminated.

Source(s) of Data for Workform S17

1. Workform S2 provides the list of activities chosen for this service response.

2. Guidance about difficulty and importance can be obtained from figure 7 and from staff recommendations.

3. Hours allocated are based on estimates from staff and supervisors about the time needed to fulfill this service response/priority, or they can be calculated from data collected through observations or self-reports from staff for the time period covered.

4. For compensation data, use the average compensation costs that you calculated for the various classifications and time periods from Workform S15.

Factors to Consider When Completing Workform S18

1. Are the time allocations or hours spent reasonably accurate? If you are considering planning activities, are estimates realistic?

2. Did you use the same unit of measure for the compensation and the time costs? (For example, do not calculate a day of time data with a week of compensation costs.)

3. Have you checked the math?

4. For assistance study example S18 as a guide.

5. Do not enter data in the shaded areas.

To Complete Workform S18

1. **Items A–C** Provide the general information requested at the top of the workform.

   Item A Write the name of the unit concerned.

   Item B Indicate the months/year or years covered *(or to be covered)* by the data being recorded on the form.

   Item C Write the service response or priority being analyzed.

2. **Column D** List each activity that appears on Workform S2 for the same service response. (The activities on example S18 are from the *PFR Guidebook*, p. 88.)

3. **Column E** Rate the level of difficulty of each activity on a scale of 1 to 4, with 1 being the easiest. For guidance in determining the level of difficulty, refer to the ratings in figure 7, "Criteria for Assessing Difficulty and Importance of an Activity." (Ratings shown in the example are for illustrative purposes only.)

4. **Column F** Rate the level of importance of each activity on a scale of 1 to 4, with 1 being the least important. For guidance in determining the level of importance, refer to the ratings in figure 7. (Ratings shown in the example are for illustrative purposes only.)

5. **Column G** Record the time estimated or spent.

   Row 11 Add the time, and record the total for the column in row 11. (Row 11 in the worked example is illustrative.)

6. **Column H** Compute this number for each row by multiplying difficulty ratings (column E) by importance ratings (column F) by hours to be allocated for each activity. (In the example, row 1, column H, is computed as $4 \times 4 \times 160 = 2,560$.)

   Row 11 Add the numbers in the column, and enter the total in row 11.

7. **Column I** Divide the index number for each activity (column H) by the total index number (column H, row 11). Record the quotient in the corresponding row of column I. (In the example, the weighting for reading lists is $360/6,756 = .053$.)

   Row 11 Add the numbers in row I, and record the total in row 11.

(Continued)

Instructions

8. **Column J**   Indicate the job classification and estimated hours associated with each activity in this column. Abbreviate classifications as indicated in the key at the bottom of the page.

9. **Column K**   Refer to the average hourly compensation of the staff performing that activity as computed on Workform S15 for the time period covered or to be covered.

   For each activity, multiply the hourly cost by the number of hours allocated for each level of staff assigned to that activity. (In the example, that amount for Programs on African Americans might be L$ × 120 hours + C$ × 40 hours = $3,000.) Be sure to add the compensation costs for all levels of staff involved in an activity.

   Row 11   Total column K and record it in row 11.

10. **Column L**   For each activity, multiply the *total* compensation paid (column K, row 11) by the associated weighting (column I). (In the example, the value of the program on African Americans would be computed as $8,576 × .378 = $3,242. Note that the actual cost is only $3,000.)

The numbers in column L reflect the value of staff activities based on the time expended, the level of difficulty, and the importance of the activity to the service response. You will note that some activities have a greater value than cost and vice-versa.

   Row 11   Add the numbers in column L, and record the total in row 11.

Factors to Consider When Reviewing Workform S18

1. Relate the task value to the activity. Are the costs of less-important activities disproportionate to their perceived worth?

2. If costs are disproportionate to perceived value, consider what activities can be eliminated, combined, or redesigned.

3. Do you want to extrapolate the time and costs data to an annual estimate? If so, it would be best to repeat gathering information on times expended for several more periods throughout the fiscal year.

WORKFORM S18 Estimate of the Cost/Value of a Service Response/Priority—Example

A. Unit/team Oakwood Branch

B. Time period covered 6/30/99 to 12/30/99

C. Service response/priority Cultural Awareness

D. Activity	E. Level of Difficulty	F. Importance to Library	G. Hours Allocated	H. Index	I. Weighting	J. Level of Staff and Hours*	K. Compensation	L. Task Value
1. Program on African Americans	4	4	160	2,560	.378	L–120, C–40	$3,000	$3,242
2. Community forums	4	4	200	3,200	.474	L–180, C–10	3,750	4,065
3. Information booth	2	2	35	140	.021	LA–35	473	180
4. Reading lists	3	3	40	360	.053	L–40	640	455
5. Budgeting	4	4	10	160	.024	L–10	188	206
6. Recruiting	3	4	28	336	.050	L–25, C–3	525	429
7. Parade float	1	3				Outsourced	2,500†	
8.								
9.								
10.								
11. Total			473	6,756	1.00		$8,576	$8,577

*Code: L = Librarian LA = Library Assistant C = Clerical P = Page
†Note: Float cost not included in total.

Completed by Marti Manning

Source of data Workforms S2, S15, and estimates

Date completed 1/15/00

Library Anytown Library

WORKFORM S18 Estimate of the Cost/Value of a Service Response/Priority

A. Unit/team _____

B. Time period covered _____ to _____

C. Service response/priority _____

D. Activity	E. Level of Difficulty	F. Importance to Library	G. Hours Allocated	H. Index	I. Weighting	J. Level of Staff and Hours*	K. Compensation	L. Task Value
1.							$	$
2.								
3.								
4.								
5.								
6.								
7.								
8.								
9.								
10.								
11. Total							$	$

*Code: L = Librarian   LA = Library Assistant   C = Clerical   P = Page

Completed by _____   Date completed _____

Source of data _____   Library _____

Chapter 3

Managing Your Library's Collections

MILESTONES

By the time you finish this chapter you will know how to

- evaluate the library's existing collections—print, media, and electronic

- determine how the existing collections are being used

- identify the collections needed to meet the library's service goals and objectives

- determine the format or formats that are most appropriate for those collections

- prepare a materials budget that reflects the library's new priorities

Public libraries of all sizes offer hundreds of different programs and services. However, no matter how unique those services are, they all have one thing in common—they are supported by the library's collections. At one time a library's collections were primarily in print format, but over the past fifteen years that has changed. Now, even the smallest public libraries offer materials in a wide variety of formats. With the emergence of the Internet as an affordable mechanism for accessing online electronic resources, libraries are expanding their definitions of collections to include resources that can be accessed electronically as well as physical information that can be purchased, processed, and housed on library shelves.

If your library is a typical public library, you lack the funding to purchase all of the print, media, and electronic resources that are published each year, and you do not have the space to house all of those items even if you could afford to purchase them. As a result, you and your colleagues must select from among the available resources those items you want to include in the collections. This is not an easy task. Effective collection development can occur only within the context of meeting identified service priorities, and those, in turn, must be based on clearly understood community needs. This chapter will help you determine the specific collection and information resources you need to accomplish your service goals and objectives.

Considering Collections as a Resource

The term *collections,* as used here, includes all of the library's print, media, and electronic resources, both circulating and noncirculating. The issues surrounding the selection and use of electronic databases and CD-ROM information products are addressed in this chapter and not in the technology chapter. That may seem strange to some library staff members and managers. Because widespread use of electronic resources is relatively new, those resources are managed quite differently by libraries around the country. A number of libraries treat the decisions concerning electronic databases and access to information on the Internet as technology issues and not as collection development issues at all. In many of these libraries, one group of staff members selects print and media titles and a completely different group selects electronic resources. The result is a great deal of duplication of resources and little meaningful conversation about formats appropriate for specific kinds of information. In this chapter all types of information resources are addressed together, and the emphasis is on meeting the library users' needs by providing the right information in the most effective format.

Every library's collections are constantly changing. New print and media titles are purchased, new databases are leased, new links to existing Web-based resources are created, and new Web-based resources are developed. Just as print and media items are regularly lost through accident, theft, or damage, access to Web-based resources is lost because of changing URLs, and access to some online databases is lost because of changes in licensing agreements. As noted previously, this ever-changing environment is made even more complex because in most libraries the responsibility for collection development is divided among staff members, based on location, subject, format, or various combinations of these factors.

Before you can begin to make effective resource allocation decisions about any new materials you intend to purchase, it is very helpful to have an overview of the current collections and the changes that have occurred in the past five years. It is always a good idea to know where you have been and where are you are *now* before deciding where you want to be in the future and how you want to get there. That would seem to be self-evident, but in the hectic and demanding world of librarianship, acquisition decisions are often based on assumptions about the collection that have not been validated by an actual collection assessment in years—or even decades (time flies . . .).

One convenient way to get an overview is to complete the materials section of the Library Scan Workform from *Planning for Results.* If you have not used *Planning for Results* to develop the library plan, you can find a copy of that section of the workform in appendix D. Use this workform to record general data about the library's collections as they were five years ago and as they are now. You will probably want to leave the "in 5 years" column blank until after you have completed the evaluation of the collections and you have the information needed to make informed projections.

Gap Analysis

The intent of this chapter is to help you and your colleagues develop library collections that support the outcomes identified as important to your community. To do that you are encouraged to use the information in this chapter in conjunction with the *Planning for Results* Gap Analysis Workform. (See appendix B.) That workform is designed to help you analyze data to answer three basic questions about collection resources:

- money needed for library materials (print and media) to accomplish intended service responses/priorities
- money needed for information resources (electronic, CD, etc.) to accomplish intended service responses/priorities
- adequacy of current collections/resources (quantity, type, recency, location) in relation to intended service responses/priorities

If you did not use *Planning for Results* to determine your library's intended outcomes, you can still use the Gap Analysis Workform to analyze your collection needs. The gap analysis process encourages you first to identify the collection resources appropriate to the accomplishment of library priorities and then to assess the current collections. Based on that data, you determine the gap between what the library has and what is needed and finally decide how to fill that gap.

Collecting Data

The second part of this chapter includes a selection of seventeen workforms designed to assist you to gather the data required to complete a gap analysis. This, in turn, will help you determine the collections necessary to accomplish the library's service goals, objectives, and activities. Figure 8 provides a complete list of the workforms for this chapter. The workforms are divided into six groups.

The first workform, C1, will help you decide which of the remaining workforms will provide the information needed to determine if the collections adequately support the library's selected service priorities. Once you have decided what you need to know, use the appropriate workforms to gather the data required. General instructions precede the specific instructions for each workform. The workforms are intended to be used independently of one another. Don't be put off by the number of workforms or the seeming complexity of any given one. Most libraries

FIGURE 8

Collections Workforms Summary

Workform	Title	Purpose
	OVERVIEW	
C1	What's Important	To determine the data needed to complete the gap analysis process
	SIZE	
C2	Volumes—Print and Media	To record information about the number of volumes in the collections that support a specific activity
C3	Titles—Print and Media	To record information about the number of titles in the collections that support a specific activity
C4	Titles—Electronic	To record information about the number of electronic titles in the collections that support a specific activity

Workform	Title	Purpose
	UTILIZATION	
C5	Circulation—Print and Media	To record information about the circulation of print and media items that support a specific activity
C6	In-Library Use—Print and Media	To record information about the in-library use of print and media materials that support a specific activity
C7	In-Library Use—Electronic	To record information about in-library use of electronic resources that support a specific activity
C8	Off-Site Use—Electronic	To record information about the off-site use of electronic resources that support a specific activity
	ACCESS	
C9	Document Delivery	To record information about the number of days it takes users to get materials that support specific activities when those materials are not available at the time the user visits the library
C10	Materials Availability	To record information about the success users have in obtaining materials that support a specific activity when they come to the library
C11	Electronic Text Availability	To record information about the level of access provided to electronic resources that support a specific activity
	AGE	
C12	Copyright—Print	To record information about the age of the print titles in the collections that support a specific activity
C13	Copyright—Media	To record information about the age of the media titles in the collections that support a specific activity
C14	Periodicals—Print and Microform	To record information about the coverage of the print and microform periodical titles that support a specific activity
C15	Periodicals—Electronic	To record information about the coverage and the timeliness of the electronic periodical titles that support a specific activity
	CONDITION	
C16	Worn or Damaged—Print	To record information about the condition of print items in the collections that support a specific activity
C17	Worn or Damaged—Media	To record information about the condition of media titles in the collections that support a specific activity

will complete only a few of the workforms for each activity and will gather data only about the specific portions of the collection that support that activity. More information on selecting workforms appears later in this chapter.

The remaining five groups of workforms will help you collect, organize, and analyze the data you have decided you need about the library's collections. The first group of workforms, C2–C4, is concerned with the number of titles and volumes in the collections that support the library's goals and objectives. The second group of workforms, C5–C8, focuses on how the library collections are being used. Workforms C9–C11 address the level of access users have to your collections. The fourth group of workforms, C12–C15, will help you determine the age of part or all of the collections. The last two workforms, C16 and C17, will help you evaluate the condition of selected portions of your collections.

Issues to Consider When Making Collections Decisions

Library managers should consider a number of significant issues as they make decisions about allocating materials resources. These issues include

- how to define collection needs based on service priorities
- how to evaluate the library's current collections
- how to address the question of format
- what resources are required to develop collections that support the library service priorities

Defining Collection Needs Based on Service Priorities

The first issue to address when making collection development decisions concerns how the collections under review are intended to be used and by whom. It is important to reiterate that the process described in this book will not help you identify the library's service priorities. The underlying assumption is that some combination of library managers, staff, board members, and other stakeholders have gone through a planning process that resulted in the identification of service goals, objectives, and activities. This chapter will help staff develop collections that support the library's intended outcomes.

Every library collection has been tailored in some fashion to the community it serves. Even if the only criterion for selecting titles has been that a staff member thinks someone will want to use them, the collection is still being tailored—to what, in a staff member's judgment, will be of interest to one or more library users. The assumption in this book, however, is that library staff will allocate collection development resources in a more focused way to meet the service priorities that the library's planning committee selected to meet the unique needs of community residents. Even if you are working from a specifically focused project plan rather than a full library service plan, that plan should identify the services to be provided.

First you have to determine if the library's collections support those services. To determine this, you start by identifying the specific portions of the collection to review. For example, if you used *Planning for Results* as your planning model and selected Business and Career as one of the library's service responses, you might start with a review of the Dewey decimal classifications 330 (economics) and 650 (management) or the Library of Congress classifications HF 5001-6182 (business). If the goals written to support the service response have narrowed the focus, you might identify even more specific portions of the collection. If the library's goal or objectives target small-business owners, you might focus on a review of Dewey number 338.6542 (small business). However, as any business librarian can testify, the information needs of businesspeople aren't limited to these narrow classification ranges. It will be important to involve the staff members who serve the audience targeted in the goal, objective, or activity under review in the identification of the materials that will be affected. It is equally important to look at all library materials—print, media, and electronic—in the identified subject areas.

Each library will have to decide which portions of its collections support a given service priority. This is not a "one-size-fits-all" process. Each library will interpret its service priorities a little differently, just as each library will create unique goals and objectives based on the special needs of the community. Furthermore, every library collection is unique, and every library has made local classification decisions that do not conform to current national practice.

Evaluating the Library's Collections

The second issue to address concerns the adequacy of the existing collections. Once you have identified the portions of the collection that support each of the selected service responses or priorities, you will want to review those portions to determine if they are sufficient to meet the goals and objectives. To do that you will look at one or more of five specific elements: size, use, access, age, or condition.

You and your colleagues will have to decide which of these elements are most relevant to your decision-making process based on the library's service goals and objectives. For example, if one of the objectives is to increase the circulation of a portion of the collection, then you will obviously want to look at one or more of the use indicators. You might also want to consider both the size and the access elements because they have a significant impact on use. On the other hand, if the objective is to increase the number of business owners who report that the library provides current information that is conveniently accessed, you might want to analyze the access and age elements of the collection.

Providing a Context for Evaluation

As stated previously, there is no need to collect data about all the library's collections. In fact, trying to use the workforms in this chapter to assess every part of every collection would be counterproductive. Assuming you could actually amass all of that data, you would still face the nightmare task of trying to analyze it in a way that provides meaningful information. It is far more useful to collect limited data that relate directly to the library's services and objectives.

However, there is one exception. You may want to collect some data not specifically related to the library's service priorities to help place the data about those priorities into a context. This will allow you to compare information about the part of the collection under review with data about the collection support provided for other service priorities, and it will allow comparisons with the collection support given to areas that are not a priority. The question, of course, is what part of the collections you want to use to provide that context.

The areas of collection emphasis are different for each of the service priorities selected, and these will be further affected by the nature of the goals and objectives. Returning to one of the previous examples, the library planners had selected the Business and Career service response with a focus on the business aspect. As noted, library managers would first identify areas of the collection—print, media, and electronic—that support business services. They then need to decide which data elements would provide useful information. Let's say they decide it will be useful to know the number of titles available in the business areas of the collection. When gathering data about the number of titles that support business services, they might find that the library has a total of 625 print titles (monograph and serial), 75 media titles, and access to 5 databases. But what do those numbers mean? There is no way to answer that question without having a context to measure the number of business-related titles against and without knowing what other service priorities relating to adults are included in the library plan.

Many managers would probably decide to compare the number of business-related titles available against the entire adult nonfiction collection to get a context. Let's say they find that 7 percent of their print titles, 2 percent of media titles, and 20 percent of electronic titles are business-related. They could then look at the other priorities for services to adults and count the titles in the areas of the collections that support those services. That data becomes a starting point for comparing the number of titles currently available to support business services with the number of titles available to support other priorities—and perhaps other areas in the adult nonfiction collection that are not a priority, as well.

If, on the other hand, the library staff had just collected the information about the total number of business-related titles in the collection and no other data, they would be hard-pressed to decide what that data meant in terms of the library's overall collections and the resources available to change those collections.

Selecting the Most Appropriate Workforms

The workforms for collections are much less interrelated than the workforms in the other chapters of this book. The five categories of collections workforms are organized around five different evaluation elements—each of which can stand alone. In almost every case, each of the workforms within those categories can also stand alone. That makes the task of selecting the most appropriate collections workforms for your environment both more important and more challenging than it is for the other areas covered in this book. It may be helpful to explore how one library staff might go through the process of identifying the workforms that would provide the collection information needed to achieve the library's goals and objectives.

CASE STUDY

In the case study in chapter 1, the Anytown Public Library staff decided that one intended outcome should be an increase in the circulation of easy and picture books. They had agreed that reaching that outcome depended on purchasing a number of new, attractive easy and picture books. They had then decided to increase the budget for easy books and picture books from $6,000 to $10,000 for two years. The increase was to come from reductions in the juvenile and adult nonfiction allocations in the first year and from an increased appropriation in the second year. These resource decisions were based on minimal data, gut instinct, and an awareness of probable staff reaction to reallocation decisions.

What kinds of information would have been useful to the managers of the Anytown Public Library in making these decisions? What data would help them explain their decisions to the staff involved? What data would provide persuasive justification to the members of their funding body when they ask for additional funds for the next fiscal year?

To answer these questions, the library managers in Anytown would need to start with the intended outcome—the increase in circulation of easy and picture books. They have already decided that the purchase of a number of new attractive easy and picture books would help accomplish this outcome. The issues remaining to be resolved are how many new books to purchase, at what cost, and where they will find the source of the additional monies to purchase the new materials. These are clearly materials allocation issues, so the managers would begin by reviewing the workforms that are available in this chapter to see which of them might provide useful information.

Because Anytown Public Library's particular decision is about resources for easy and picture books, the managers could eliminate immediately all of the workforms that exclusively relate to electronic resources, periodicals, and media (C4, C7, C8, C11, C13–C15, and C17). Of the two remaining size workforms, C2: Volumes—Print and Media and C3: Titles—Print and Media, C2 is far more useful in this instance because there is often a significant duplication of titles in easy and picture book collections. In addition, two workforms could be considered in the utilization category: C5: Circulation—Print and Media and C6: In-Library Use—Print and Media. Because easy books and picture books are far more likely to be checked out and used at home, C5 is probably the better choice. Neither of the two remaining access workforms are likely to provide useful information. C9: Document Delivery includes information about interlibrary loans and reserves, which don't typically apply to children's materials. C10: Materials Availability might provide data useful in some libraries, but most will decide that the information gathered using this workform will not be worth the effort of collecting it in this instance. Age is not a particularly significant issue with easy books and picture books (in fact, older is often good) so the entire age category also can be eliminated.

That leaves the Anytown managers with three workforms (C2: Size: Volumes—Print and Media, C5: Utilization: Circulation—Print and Media, and C16: Condition: Worn or Damaged—Print); each of those would probably provide pertinent information.

The Anytown staff would probably start with C2: Size: Volumes—Print and Media to determine how many volumes of easy and picture books are currently in the collection. The actual number of items in the easy and picture book collection could then be compared with the total number of items in the juvenile collection to give staff some idea of the percent of the juvenile collection represented by easy and picture books. Because the activity under review specifically concerns print items, they would not need to complete the media portion of the form.

The staff will then move to C5: Utilization: Circulation—Print and Media to collect data about the current circulation of easy and picture books. Again, they would not need to collect data about media circulation for this activity. They might compare the circulation of easy and picture books against circulation for the entire juvenile collection. This data might also be used to calculate the turnover rates for easy and picture books and for the juvenile collection as a whole. Turnover rate is the average number of times each item in a collection circulates and is calculated by dividing the total circulation by the number of items in that collection.

The third important factor to consider is condition, and for this the staff would use C16: Condition: Worn and Damaged—Print. Easy and picture books get a lot of hard wear and tear, and in many libraries the bulk of the collection is in poor condition. Certainly the general condition of the collection will affect circulation. Clean, attractive books circulate more than dirty, damaged ones. The condition of the collection may also be used to determine the percent of the budget increase that will be used for replacement items as opposed to new titles or additional copies.

When the managers have completed these workforms and analyzed the data gathered, they will know the number of easy and picture books they own now, the current circulation of those books, and the physical condition of the books. Based on this information they can extrapolate how many additional easy and picture books will be required to increase the circulation by the amount projected.

The managers then need to decide where to get the money to purchase these materials. In this case study, they decided to reallocate funds from other parts of the collection budget. The data they collected on the first two workforms—number of volumes and use of collection: circulation—included information about the entire juvenile collection that might be helpful in deciding where to get the required funds. For example, they may have found that although less than 25 percent of the juvenile collection is classified as easy and picture books, those books account for 40 percent of the juvenile circulation. If that is the case, it might be useful to go back and look at the juvenile circulation in greater detail. What percent of the circulation is fiction? What percent is nonfiction? Have circulation patterns changed significantly over the past five years?

If the managers decide to reallocate part but not all of the money needed from the juvenile nonfiction collection based on the number of volumes and use statistics, they will have to expand their data gathering to other parts of the collection to determine where to get the rest of the money required. Collecting data on the number of volumes in the adult fiction and nonfiction collections and on the circulation of those items will probably provide the information needed to reallocate the remainder of the money required.

A Closer Look at the Five Collection Evaluation Elements

The following sections discuss each of the five elements pertinent to evaluating library collections. Reading these sections should help you and your colleagues decide which of the elements will provide the information you need.

Size

The two indicators to consider when looking at the size of one or more of the library's collections are the number of individual items and the number of titles in the collection. Workforms C2 through C4 will help you gather and organize data about the size of selected portions of the collection.

As you know, every library has more items than titles. Most libraries buy multiple copies of popular titles in response to demand for those titles. Even if staff in a particular library never purchase multiple copies, the library would still have more items than titles because multiple-volume publications such as encyclopedias are considered to be one title while each volume in the encyclopedia set is counted as a separate item.

The ratio of titles to items varies among libraries. These differences are caused by a variety of factors, including the library's service priorities, the resources available for collection development, the library's reserve policies, and even the attitudes of the selectors toward popular materials. Of these, the service priorities should be the most important factor. Libraries that place an emphasis on providing high-demand, high-interest materials (the Current Topics and Titles service response in *Planning for Results*) will probably have a lot of multiple copies. On the other hand, libraries that emphasize services that require in-depth collections—reference services or local history and genealogy, for example—will have far fewer multiple copies.

Actually, rather than describing levels of collection development as *either* popular materials *or* in-depth, most libraries consider a *range of levels* when deciding the appropriate scope of specific collections. Figure 9

FIGURE 9

Levels of Collection Development

Popular/recreational	Current titles, best sellers, hot topics in a variety of formats
	Multiple copies of many items
	Items replaced regularly as new titles become available
Basic or general	Carefully selected materials in appropriate formats based on quality and popularity and intended to meet the reading needs of a diverse reading public
	Emphasis on recent publications but recognized standard works from the past included
	Standard reference titles purchased
	Access to some electronic resources provided
	Items replaced as new titles become available
Instructional	Broad collection that includes virtually everything in all formats recommended by an established authority
	Includes a considerable number of retrospective titles and all of the works of significant writers in the field
	Circulating collection supported by most-recommended reference materials and a selection of representative journal titles
	Titles may be specialized or technical
	Access to some specialized electronic resources provided
	Materials discarded when they have outlived their usefulness, but collection expected to grow in size
Research	Comprehensive collection of materials in all formats that are likely to be of interest to anyone working in the field—layperson or expert
	Includes all the subject's bibliographies and reference tools, all important journals, selected research reports, virtually all current titles published in the field, standard or classic titles, and appropriate media materials
	Access to all available electronic databases provided
	Few materials discarded, and the collection will grow each year
Exhaustive	Everything published on a subject in all formats, editions, and translations throughout history
	Includes ephemeral materials, manuscripts, archival materials, etc.
	Intended for the researcher
	No items discarded

describes five levels of collection development and is based on a combination of models used by various organizations and libraries. Obviously, the level of development in the section of the collection to be evaluated will have a significant impact on the ratio of titles to volumes.

As noted earlier, in an ideal world, decisions about the levels of collection development would be determined by the library's service priorities. In the real world, decisions about the collection are often affected by the availability of other resources. For instance, even if the money is available to build new or enhanced collections to meet the library's service priorities, the capacity to shelve and display a large number of new materials or new formats of material may be limited. Therefore, when assessing the size of the collection, you also need to develop estimates of the linear feet of shelving used for various subsets of the collection. Some materials, such as children's picture books or CDs, take very little space for each item. Other materials, such as art books or art prints, require considerably more space on a per-item basis. Items that circulate heavily need less shelf space than slower-moving items. Electronic materials require space for PCs to make them accessible, although the materials themselves don't need shelving. Most nonprint materials require specialized shelving to make them available for browsing. As you assess various subsets of the collection, you will want to estimate both the linear feet of shelving used to house that section and the proportion of the available space devoted to that material. Knowledge of these proportions will also be valuable in developing collection enhancement plans and resource reallocation strategies. See chapter 4 for more information on space and collections.

Utilization

Utilization is a count of how frequently the public uses the materials in the collections. This count can be reflected in a variety of ways including circulation figures; in-house use of print, media, and electronic resources; and dial-in or Internet access to the library databases.

Staff members who are responsible for building specific collections to support the library's service priorities need the most detailed data available about the use of those collections. That data provides the staff with the only real tool they have to determine if the collections are doing what they are intended to do. It is all very well to buy materials that are highly recommended from one source or another and to work to shape a "perfect" collection based on some theoretical model. However, if that collection isn't used, it isn't meeting the needs of residents in your community—and that, after all, is what the library is all about.

There are no magic numbers for utilization that validate a collection. It isn't possible to say that four or more circulations per capita clearly indicate that a specific part of the collection is meeting user needs better than another part of the collection that generates two circulations per capita. In the first place, circulation is just one measure of collection use. Collection use is also measured by in-library use and by use of electronic resources. Secondly, not every part of the collection is used by the public in the same way. The per capita circulation figures for picture books are expected to be considerably higher than the per capita circulation of items in the business collection. By the same token, there is no point in comparing the per capita circulations with the in-house use of local history and genealogy materials.

Finally, per capita numbers are normally derived by dividing the circulation of the collection by the *whole* population of the community. A per capita number is not helpful for measuring the use of specific portions of the collections that have been targeted to meet the needs of *certain groups* of residents. In those instances, the circulation of the part of the collections under review should be divided by the approximate number of people in the target population. For example, you might divide the circulation of items in the preschool collection (picture books, I-Can-Read books, concept books, preschool videos, book kits, etc.) by the number of children under the age of five in your community. The resulting figure is far more meaningful than one obtained by dividing the circulation of that portion of the collection by the entire population of the community.

CIRCULATION STATISTICS

Circulation figures were among the earliest statistics that public libraries collected. Once, library staff members had to physically count each circulation card to determine how many items had been checked out. Needless to say, this labor-intensive task did not encourage libraries to collect circulation data about specific portions of the collections. Many libraries just collected a single aggregate figure representing total circulation. In other libraries circulation counts were separated by adult and juvenile materials. Still others went one step farther and counted the total adult and juvenile fiction and nonfiction circulation. Very few attempted anything more complex.

With the advent of automated circulation systems, library staff members discovered they could have access to a vast array of data about how the collections were being used. However, being *able* to collect the data and *choosing* to collect the data are two very different things. Many libraries have chosen to continue to collect exactly the same circulation data that was collected when staff hand-counted circulation cards.

Unfortunately, it is not always easy to adjust automated circulation systems to collect statistics that were not requested when the library established the original statistical profile. If the library's current circulation system provides only limited circulation data, you may want to see if the data collected can be easily expanded. If it is not cost-effective to adjust the current system, begin now to develop a list of the kinds of information about use that you would like to have so that you will be ready when the vendor upgrades your system or when you select a new system.

IN-LIBRARY USE OF MATERIALS

Not all library use results in an item being checked out for use off-site. Many library patrons use materials in the library rather than checking them out. In-Library Materials Use was one of the twelve output measures included in the second edition of *Output Measures for Public Libraries, second edition*.[1] (See appendix F.) It continues to be an important measure of use, particularly for service priorities that rely heavily on noncirculating materials such as local history and genealogy or reference. If you decide to collect data about in-library material use, you may want to consider limiting data collection to the specific areas of the collection that support the service priority under review. Obviously, library patrons can choose to wander all over the building with selected items, but generally they sit as close as possible to the source of the materials they are using. Signs can be put up asking that materials in the classifications under review be put on a book truck rather than reshelved no matter where they are found.

ELECTRONIC USE STATISTICS

It is important to collect and analyze use figures for materials in all formats that support the specific service priorities under review. Libraries across the country are finding that the increased use of electronic resources is negatively affecting circulation figures for printed materials, particularly for nonfiction.

Most libraries have been offering public access to electronic databases for less than a decade. Library managers are still trying to determine the best way to count the use of those databases along with the use of the library's print and media collections and to report that use in ways that will be meaningful.

Electronic use can be measured by sessions or log-ons, searches, and items retrieved.

session Occurs when a library user connects to a specific database either in the library or from a remote site using dial-in or Internet access

search Occurs when a library user types an inquiry into a database's search engine during a session

items retrieved Occurs when a library user receives an electronic document, abstract, or full-text article that was identified during a search

To see how these terms are used in a real situation, consider the following example. A library user might connect to the library's network from the Internet or through a dial-in connection. The user could then use that connection to log on to a business periodical collection, which would be counted as one session. During that session, the user might search for information on investing, which would count as one search. Let's assume that the search produced twenty-five responses, three of which were articles by John Q. Expert. The user might choose to open and read all three articles, which would be counted as three items retrieved.

As you can see, a single user can initiate multiple searches and retrieve multiple items in each session and might very well initiate more than one session while connected to the library's network from an external site. This is not unlike what happens in other areas of service. A library user might spend the morning doing research at the library. If he takes a break every hour and goes outside to smoke a cigarette, the library people-counter will consider him to be a new user every time he comes back into the building. That same user may ask several reference questions during his time at the library and may check out multiple items as he leaves. He may think of another reference question on his way home and call the library to ask that question when he gets home. The library will count each of these transactions separately. We can look at electronic resources in much the same way.

In this book, dial-in or Internet sessions are considered to be a measure of number of users, searches are considered to be reference transactions, and items retrieved are considered to be a measure of actual use.

> *Number of sessions initiated off-site* Another measure of "number of users." Most libraries currently count the number of people who walk in the door and report that number as "total users." A comparable statistic would be the number of people who access the library from off-site, either through dial-in access or using the Internet.

> *Searches* Another form of "reference transactions." Virtually every library currently counts the number of reference questions asked by users. In essence, an online search is the equivalent of a self-service reference question. Logically, searches could be reported as one type of reference transaction.

> *Items retrieved* Another use of library resources comparable to "circulation" and "in-library use." Libraries currently count the number of items checked out as circulation. Some libraries also count in-library use of materials as a measure of the use of the collection. A third measure of the use of the collection is the number of abstract or full-text items that users request during a session. In this instance, it doesn't matter if the session was initiated off-site or on a library computer. An item retrieved is a use of resources in either case.

When comparing electronic use to the use of print and media resources in a specific part of the collection, you will be comparing items retrieved to circulations and in-library use of materials.

Every vendor who provides access to electronic resources provides some sort of statistics, although each statistical package is a little different. Libraries can begin to collect meaningful data if they consider the use statistics provided by the vendors in the context of the three general terms of sessions, searches, and items retrieved. In most cases, this is easy for sessions and searches; those are the most commonly used terms for those activities by most vendors. Unfortunately, vendors report items retrieved in a number of different ways. For example, at the time of this writing, OCLC provided reports detailing the number of sessions, searches, and documents ordered, which would be considered to be items retrieved. EBSCO reported the numbers of sessions and searches for all databases and the number of searches for each database in the network. EBSCO also reported the number of "abstracts browsed," the number of "abstracts downloaded," and the number of "full-text articles browsed." Both "abstracts browsed" and "full-text articles browsed" would be considered to be items retrieved. In many cases, the abstract provides the library patron with the information needed; in other cases the full article is required. In EBSCO's case, "abstracts downloaded" would not be considered as items retrieved because they were already counted in the "abstracts browsed" category.

Clearly, it is important to understand what your vendors are actually counting in the reports you receive if you are planning to use those reports in meaningful ways. It is also important to remember that the types of information provided by each vendor change regularly. Don't assume that because you couldn't get certain data last year, it is not available this year. Always request the data you need to make good decisions. If it is not available, ask the vendor to consider ways to provide the data you need.

Workforms C5 through C8 will help you gather and analyze data about the utilization of specific parts of the library's collections.

Access

Access refers to the availability of print, media, and electronic items. Availability can be determined by using statistics relating to materials availability and document delivery and by evaluating the type of access to electronic resources the library provides.

document delivery Measured by the length of time it takes for a library user to obtain an item that was not available at the time it was requested; waiting-time measures can be applied to reserves, interlibrary loans, intralibrary loans, and items purchased specifically because a user requested them

electronic access Measured according to which of three types of databases are provided: indexes, abstracts, or full-text

materials availability   Measure of the library users' success in obtaining the materials they want when they come to the library

Prior to online catalog systems, most library facilities, including the branches of large systems, had catalogs only of their own holdings; if a union catalog of the entire collection existed, it was usually housed only at the main library. If a union catalog in printed form (book or microform) was distributed to all facilities, it was typically months out of date due to the time and expense of updating it. This meant that materials not owned by the local branch were all but invisible to library users. Although staff would happily identify and request materials from other branches, it was incumbent on the library user to initiate that action. Needless to say, it was difficult for users to request specific materials that they didn't even know existed.

With the introduction of online catalogs, the public had immediate access to the library's entire collection, regardless of where the materials were physically housed. Users could not only identify materials housed in other library units but they could see whether those materials were available for checkout. Online catalogs made it possible for library users to place holds on materials throughout the collection rather than on only those materials listed in the local catalog. Self-service reserves, in which library users place their own requests directly into the online catalog, make it even easier for them to obtain the titles they are interested in. With self-service the library user no longer has to "bother" a staff member to request material. Any library that has implemented self-service reserves can attest to the dramatic increase in reserves that results. Dial-in and Internet access to online catalogs have similar effects on the use of library materials.

Online reserves give a library user the opportunity to request the transfer of any item in the circulating collection to his or her local branch. With this "transfer on demand" option, the issues surrounding access are altered. If any item in the entire collection is available for request by any library user and can be delivered to any branch, the decisions surrounding what items should be included in branch collections change.

Collection developers need to consider the specific collections under review to determine if the types of materials in those collections are selected primarily by physical browsing or are most likely borrowed on impulse, as is typical in collections supporting the Current Topics and Titles service response in *Planning for Results*. These are the types of materials that need to be equitably distributed among all outlets. On the other hand, subject-specific materials, typically identified through searches of the library catalog or from other reference sources and requested as known items, can be housed anywhere throughout the system and still be equitably available.

As a result of this improvement in accessibility, many multibranch libraries are able to build deeper collections with more titles and fewer copies per title in many subject areas. The composition of physical collections may be based on usage patterns, shelving availability, and delivery system positioning rather than relying solely on the traditional funding equity formulas. "My branch needs a copy" is no longer necessarily true. The collection needs a copy, and the patron needs access to it, but that copy may not need to be shelved in "my" branch.

DOCUMENT DELIVERY

Document delivery measures how long it takes users to obtain the titles they request when those titles are not immediately available. Document delivery was one of the twelve measures included in *Output Measures for Public Libraries,* second edition.[2] (See appendix G.)

The issue of the time taken to deliver a title to a user is important and becoming more important in our fast-paced society. Library users want instant gratification as much as everyone else does. If an item on the shelf in one location can be delivered to another location in 24 hours, most users will find that delivery time acceptable. On the other hand, few people are going to be happy to wait for a week. Remember, more and more people are measuring time not in weeks or even days, but in hours and minutes.

Providing access to titles not currently available anywhere in the library system is a somewhat different challenge. Library users normally have three choices for obtaining such titles. If the library owns the title and all copies are in circulation, many libraries allow the user to put a reserve or hold on the title. If the library does not own the title, the user may be encouraged to request it through interlibrary loan. Libraries also occasionally decide to purchase some titles that users request. No matter which option the user selects, the real question is how long it takes for the user to obtain the requested item.

The waiting time for each of these three options—reserve, interlibrary loan, or purchase—can vary widely. Libraries have some control over the maximum length of time it takes to get a title that has been reserved. They can implement a policy to purchase a new copy of a title for every X number of reserves placed on the title. However, such a policy does not guarantee that the user will get the title in any time frame that comes close to being defined as instant gratification. If the normal loan period is two weeks and the library owns five copies of a title that has been reserved by fifteen patrons, the wait for the fifteenth person on the reserve list could be six weeks. In the real world, the wait is often considerably longer for very popular titles.

As most librarians know, it can also take a long time to get titles requested through interlibrary loan, and in this instance the library has no control over the arrival time. Sometimes libraries decide to buy items that users request that are not currently available in the system. At first glance, it appears that this purchase option would get the requested title to the user relatively quickly. Of course, that depends on the library's acquisition policies and time lines, the backlog in cataloging, and the procedures established to notify the user that the book is now available. Again, the length of time involved is unlikely to be considered "quick" by the user who requested the title.

There is no one right answer to the question of "how long is too long" to wait for materials. Those decisions need to be made by the staff and managers in each library based on their service priorities, current collections, and the available resources. It is important to remember, however, that access is a significant concern to library users, and for most users faster is always better. Use Workform C9 to determine the time it takes for users to get the materials they want that are not available to them at the time they visit the library.

MATERIALS AVAILABILITY

Library users who come to the library for specific materials do not always find the materials they want. Materials Availability Measures were among the twelve output measures included in the second edition of *Output Measures for Public Libraries*.[3] (See appendix H.) They continue to be important measures of the access the library provides to the collections, particularly for service priorities that emphasize meeting client demand, such as the Current Topics and Titles service response in *Planning for Results*. The three basic materials availability measures are title fill rate, author/subject fill rate, and browser's fill rate. The first two measure the proportion of searches that were successful. For example, a user might come to the library looking for the newest best seller by a popular author and for a low-fat cookbook. That would be considered two searches, one for a title and one for a subject. The browser's fill rate, on the other hand, measures the number of users who were satisfied when they left the library.

There has been a considerable amount of discussion about materials availability measures since they were first introduced. Many libraries have collected the data for these measures at least once. Some found the data useful, but others thought that the data collection was more trouble than it was worth. Most of the libraries that used these measures collected data about the entire collection. That, in turn, often resulted in a glut of data that didn't seem to be helpful in any particular instance. Very few libraries have used these measures to determine the availability of items in one or more particular portions of the collection that support a specific activity. This focused data collection should provide information that is useful in making decisions. Use Workform C10 to collect data about the availability of materials that support the specific activity under review.

ACCESS TO ELECTRONIC RESOURCES

The issues to be addressed when considering access to electronic resources are somewhat different from those surrounding materials availability and document delivery. In these latter cases, access was defined as getting the item to the user. Access to electronic resources, on the other hand, is a little more complex. Certainly, it is important that the user be able to get to the database that contains the desired information. That means that the library needs to provide sufficient terminals onsite, adequate bandwidth to access online databases, and perhaps dial-in or Internet access. These infrastructure issues and other related issues are discussed in detail in chapter 5.

However, electronic access is defined by more than just being able to get to a database. It is also defined by the kinds of databases available. There are three basic kinds of databases commonly used in libraries: those that provide only index citations; those that provide index citations and abstracts; and those that provide the full text of documents. Index databases provide citations to items in printed sources such as journals. Databases that include abstracts provide citations along with a summary of the important points of a print document. Databases that provide full-text access always include indexes, sometimes include abstracts, and allow the user to choose to read the entire document.

In the not too distant past when libraries first began to offer access to electronic resources, the most common databases available were indexes to printed documents. As the equipment used to connect to databases became more sophisticated and the bandwidth available to transmit data enlarged, more and more libraries began offering full-text access. There is little question that library users want and expect full-text access, and demand for full-image access is increasing as well.

If the library's databases provide only indexes or abstracts, you may need to consider both materials availability and document delivery in this context as well. For instance, it might be helpful to know what percent of the users did not find all of the information they needed using the electronic resources available (materials availability) and how long it took them to get the resources they identified as being of probable value (document delivery). Workform C11 can be used to gather data about the levels electronic access provided in specific parts of the library's collections.

Age

Age refers to the average publication date of all the items in the part of the collection under review. Age can also refer to the years or depth of coverage and frequency of updates for print, microform, and electronic periodicals.

PUBLICATION DATE

While most librarians would agree that currency is an important consideration in collection assessment, very few library managers actually know much about the age of their collections. Data on age has been tedious to obtain, and most librarians haven't been sure what to do with the data once they got it. The first problem—difficulty in data collection—can be addressed by using automated circulation systems or by using sampling techniques that are explained in the directions for Workforms C12 and C13.

The second problem—what to do with the data when you get it—is more complex. There is no "right" age for the average title in your library. A fifteen-year-old average age may be fine for standard fiction or a history collection. On the other hand, if the average title in your 500 section (sciences) is fifteen years old, the information in many of those titles is probably obsolete. The average useful life of titles is influenced by format, target audience, and subject area. For example, most children's titles are in demand longer than most best sellers are; as a result, we often replace worn copies of children's titles but discard worn copies of old best sellers. *The CREW Method,* a manual intended to help staff from small and medium-sized public libraries evaluate and weed their collections, provides some useful guidelines on the appropriate age for items in various Dewey classifications.[4] Workforms C12 and C13 will help you collect data about the publication dates of print and media items in the sections of the collections that support the library's service priorities as reflected in the activities.

COVERAGE AND TIMELINESS OF PERIODICALS

Coverage is defined as the number of years that are available for a particular periodical title. It is a measure of collection depth and applies to both print and electronic periodicals. A collection of *Time Magazine* from 1976 to 1981 will probably not be used as much as a collection of the same journal from the past five years. On the other hand, providing electronic access to *Time Magazine* for just the past year will not be as useful as providing access for a longer period of time in either print or electronic format. The challenge, of course, is that many vendors provide electronic access to a wide range of periodicals for a specified period of coverage, often five years. Not every library can afford to purchase print copies and electronic copies of every periodical; therefore, the library coverage is limited to five years. This may be fine for some subject areas, but other subject areas require broader coverage. You will want to assess how important coverage is in the areas of the collections that support the service priorities under review.

Timeliness is normally only an issue with electronic access to periodicals. It measures the frequency with which an electronic database is updated. If the library provides access to a database that includes daily or weekly publications, it is important that the database be updated daily or weekly. It is not particularly helpful to get twelve issues of *Time Magazine* every three months, but that is what happens if the database providing access to that magazine is only updated quarterly. Timeliness can be a real problem when providing CD-ROM access to periodicals. Online databases accessible over the Internet can be updated at a central site, and those updates are transparent to the host libraries. In other words, they appear to happen magically, and no staff member has to worry about them. CD-ROM updates, on the other hand, have to be created, purchased, shipped, and installed—very different from being transparent! Workforms C14 and C15 can be used to gather data about the coverage and timeliness of specified portions of a library's periodicals collection.

Condition

Condition refers to the physical state of the print or media items in the collection. It is important to look at the physical condition of the items during your assessment because physical condition has a significant impact on use. For better or worse, most library borrowers *do* judge a book by its cover. If you have every standard title in a given field but the pages are yellowed with age or stained with use and the binding is shabby or broken, the collection will not attract the usage it would if the items were more attractive.

The CREW Method includes a list of reasons to consider discarding an item from the library collection. The list is arranged to form the mnemonic MUSTIE, each letter of which corresponds to a reason for discarding an item:

M = Misleading

U = Ugly

S = Superseded

T = Trivial

I = Irrelevant to the needs and interests of your community

E = Elsewhere (the material may be easily borrowed from another source)[5]

"Ugly" is a succinct and accurate description of far too many items in our collections. See figure 10 for more information on judging the condition of items in the collection.

Many librarians find it difficult to consider discarding an item from the collection solely because of its condition. They say, often with justification, that there isn't any money to replace the item. They go on to say, with less justification, that something is better than nothing, which may be true for some parts of the collection. Scholarly items in the areas of history, literature, etc. are far less likely to be judged by their appearance than are items in the fiction collection; but even in the former areas, library users are more likely to select an attractive book than one that is heavily worn or damaged.

If the library's service priorities include goals, objectives, and activities intended to encourage children or young adults to use the library,

FIGURE 10
Condition of Items in the Collection

	Wear	**Print Examples**	**Media Examples**
Excellent	Mint condition	Like new	Like new
Good	Shows light wear	Has plastic jacket, clean pages, no marks	All parts available and in good working order Software loads and runs under the intended operating system All supporting documentation, booklets, etc. complete Cases and display bags may be showing slight wear but remain usable
Fair	Shows considerable wear	Has plastic jacket, unbroken spine, yellowed or lightly marked pages, minor damage to cover, etc.	May be showing wear but still is operational All parts available Audio and visual tapes may need cleaning Cases and display bags need replacing or repair Supporting documentation may have torn or missing pages
Very poor/damaged	Shows extensive wear or is damaged	Has no plastic jacket; has broken spine, pages torn or heavily marked, etc.	Sound or visual quality is diminished or distorted

you may want to pay special attention to the condition of the children's and YA collections. It is particularly important that these items are attractive and appealing. Books must compete with toys, TV, videos, computer games, and a myriad of other activities in a child's or young adult's life. A shabby or torn book doesn't compete very effectively. Yet, in many libraries, it is the items in the youth collections that are in the worst repair. Youth materials circulate heavily, and young people are not always as careful in handling library materials as adults are. In addition, items in the youth collections often have longer shelf lives than items in the adult collection. Parents read the same picture books to their children that were read to them a generation ago. Sadly, in some cases, they also are reading from the same physical book.

Use is also seriously affected by the condition of items in the recreational reading/viewing sections of the collections. Books in fair or poor condition are passed over for those that look newer and cleaner. Videotapes with tracking problems are returned by irate borrowers. These same borrowers are likely to assume that any tape in an old case will have similar problems. If your library used *Planning for Results* and selected the Current Topics and Titles service response, you will want to pay special attention to the condition of the items in the collection supporting that service response. Workforms C16 and C17 will help you tabulate information about the condition of selected portions of the library's collections.

The Question of Format

Once upon a time it was simple to decide the format of materials to be included in the library's collections. The choices for most titles were print, print, and print. Libraries could choose bindings (library, mass-market, or paperback) and size of print (regular or large print), but that was about all. Interestingly, even when the differences were this minimal, libraries made distinctions based on the differences. Hardbacks were treated one way, and paperbacks were treated another way. These distinctions were usually intended to make it clear that the only "real" books were hardbacks.

Of course, libraries have been circulating phonograph records, filmstrips, 16mm films, 8mm films, etc. for many years. However, these items have always been considered to be supplementary to the print collection. The advent of the VCR and the incredible popularity of videotapes caught many library staff members by surprise. Suddenly, this new format was in as much or greater demand than books were. Libraries adapted to the video world slowly—indeed many are still coming to terms with the implications of circulating videos. Large numbers of libraries have different circulation rules for print and video items. For instance, video items often circulate for shorter loan periods than print items, and overdue fines for videos are usually considerably higher.

One of the big problems that many library staff members, managers, and board members had with the video revolution was their deeply held belief that print resources were intrinsically superior to media resources. This certainly seems to have been reflected in the relative amount of money allocated for print and media resources over the years.

For most of us, the print versus video conflict is old news. Today's significant format issues concern access to electronic resources. However, the attitudes that made many librarians prefer hardback to paperback books and any print item to any media item have carried over to electronic resources. Yes, we pay lip service to the importance of being able to access vast quantities of information via the Internet, and yes, we provide access to some electronic resources, but many of us still believe that "real" books are better.

The only effective way to address format issues is to understand that all formats are valid. The question that librarians responsible for developing collections should be asking is "Which format or formats are the most appropriate to deliver specific information to specific client groups?" That, in turn, suggests that collection development decisions should be made in a holistic environment rather than by committees charged with selecting items based on format. In keeping with that philosophy, a number of the workforms in this chapter include data about both print and media items. When data collection about print and media items has been separated into two workforms, it is because of layout issues with the workforms and not because the data should be considered separately.

Remember, too, that electronic and print collections are not mutually exclusive. It is probable that some titles will be purchased in both print and electronic formats. However, the expense of purchasing duplicate resources as well as the cost of housing physical collections and providing sufficient PCs to deliver electronic materials will mean that in most instances staff will have to choose to purchase items in either print or electronic formats. So what criteria can you use in determining which format meets your users' needs best? The three main criteria to consider when making decisions about format are

Who will be using this resource?

How will the resource be used?

Where will the users of the resource be located?

Who Will Use the Resource?

"Who" refers both to the target audience and the number of people expected to use the resource simultaneously. If the materials under consideration are targeted for a specific audience, it will be important to consider the probable level of technical expertise in the target audience. For instance, when you are trying to decide the appropriate format for basic literacy materials, one important factor to consider is that adult new readers are unlikely to have strong technology skills. It is also important to remember that although the Web is a graphic environment, it is a graphic environment surrounding primarily text-based materials and using text-based command structures. As such, it is not a terribly user-friendly environment for people who don't read well. If, on the other hand, your target audience is high school students and you are selecting materials to provide homework help for them, you can probably safely assume that the target audience has reasonably good technical skills.

How Will the Resource Be Used?

The choice of format also depends on how the resource is most likely to be used. When building a collection of materials to reinforce reading instruction in adult new readers, for example, the target audience will probably want print materials that are easily transportable so they can carry them and use them whenever they have the time. Each new reader will want materials at the appropriate reading level on subjects of interest to him or her. These will be very individualistic choices, and the materials will be selected to offer as many different choices as possible. Therefore, the format of choice for most basic literacy materials will probably be print.

On the other hand, the significant factor about the use of homework help materials targeted for high school students is that they are likely to be in very high demand for the relatively short duration of each assignment. What reference librarian doesn't have a story of spending hours looking for materials for the student who comes in at the last minute, long after everything on the assigned topic has been checked out? One of the real advantages of providing homework support to students using electronic resources is that electronic resources are never checked out. They are also accessible to as many simultaneous users as the technology and licensing agreements support. Unlike a book, which is generally best used by one person at a time, an electronic database can be used from many PCs by many people at the same time. Therefore, materials in electronic formats would be good choices for homework help centers.

There are other considerations about how the resource will be used. Some materials are best collected in print because that is the format in which most users want to use them. As Crawford and Gorman point out in *Future Libraries: Dreams, Madness, and Reality,* "print-on-paper (the 'book') is the best vehicle for sustained reading and is likely to remain so for the foreseeable future."[6] For the materials people want to curl up with or use at their leisure, physical formats (print, video, and audio) remain the formats of choice. However, for information resources, those materials people use to find facts or compile sets of data, timeliness and greater functionality make electronic resources the format of choice.

Michael Buckland defines five circumstances in which electronic formats can be the best choice:

> Electronic documents are preferable in the following circumstances:
> 1. When documents are highly *volatile* . . .
> 2. When *manipulation* of the document is desired . . .
> 3. When *scanning* for names or particular words or phrases in a lengthy document . . .
> 4. When light use of *remote material* is needed . . .
> 5. When rapid *communication* is desired . . .[7]

Remember, too, that the work habits and working environments of library users are changing as well. Increasingly, library users are functioning in automated environments themselves. Businesspeople may be looking for data to include in a spreadsheet for a presentation. Students might want information to incorporate into their own electronic word processing program to produce a school report. Even family cooks download recipes into electronic cookbooks that can be used to create shopping lists to take to the grocery store. These people don't want to key in the information they found at the library; they want to download it. They intend to use the information in electronic format, and they want to retrieve it that way.

Where Will the Resource Be Used?

Finally, think about where people are likely to be when they need to use the resources. As Buckland points out, ". . . paper is a localized medium. Paper can be used only if the reader and the paper are in the same place at the same time."[8] Electronic materials, on the other hand, can be available anywhere and at any time. Distribution of electronic resources is limited only by licensing agreements and the availability of the technology needed to access them.

Users no longer have to physically go where the print materials are housed. They can use electronic information from any computer anywhere. All kinds of information can be accessed from home or office, even during hours when the library itself is not open. This means that libraries that have licensed electronic resources to provide off-site access don't even need to supply the PC for each of the users. Library users can access the information from their own home, school, or office PCs. Think of it: serving more users without having to buy more PCs!

Making Format Choices

What seems clear is that library staff members responsible for making collection decisions that will lead to accomplishing the library's service priorities are going to have to be familiar with materials in all available formats. Libraries can no longer afford to divide selection responsibilities by the format of the items being selected. Instead, selection teams should be composed of print experts, media experts, and electronic resources experts. These team members can pool their knowledge of the intended audience and the resources available to make the appropriate format choices.

Budget and Funding Issues

A library can build and maintain collections that adequately support the selected service responses in a number of ways. These include purchasing new materials, licensing new databases, providing access to information through Web pages and links, and creating new information resources. Each of these has specific resource allocation implications.

Buying new materials or licensing new databases requires additional collection money. This, in turn, will have an impact on other library resources. In *Collection Development and Finance: A Guide to Strategic Library-Materials Budgeting,* Murray Martin notes that "a long-standing problem has been the virtual separation of the library materials budget from other parts of the library budget. This custom has always been shortsighted, since the acquisition of a certain flow or mix of materials has always carried with it other costs—acquisition, processing, and shelving to name only a few."[9] These may be particularly important issues to consider if the library is planning to make major changes in the proportion of print versus media materials purchased or in the proportion of mass-market titles versus the number of small-press and locally produced titles.

Changes in the collections will not just affect technical services. As noted previously, one of the major issues facing public library managers today is the impact of electronic resources on collection development. Information that is simply too expensive to provide in print format may be made available in electronic format in a cost-effective manner. Even the smallest library can have a 1,200-title periodical collection with a full five-year back-run in electronic format. However, when you decide to license new databases, you will not only need money for the license fees but you might also need more terminals, staff training, etc. If you are going to create library Web pages to link to Web-based resources or create new information resources, you may need additional staff. If you find that developing the collections needed to support the library service priorities will have an impact on staffing or technology budgets, you may want to refer to chapters 2 and 5 for more information. This chapter focuses specifically on allocating the resources needed to improve the library collections and not on the broader implications of those collection decisions.

Materials Allocation Formulas

No two libraries allocate their materials funds in the same way. In *Developing Library and Information Center Collections,* G. Edward Evans noted that "one can think of allocation methods as being a continuum with impulse at one end and formulas at the opposite end. Between the two extremes are several more-or-less structured methods."[10] Figure 11 lists four common materials allocation methods and the advantages and disadvantages of each.

Regardless of the allocation strategy or formula currently in use, if you intend to "put your money where your mouth is" and develop collections that support the library's service priorities, you may well need to revise or adjust the existing process for allocating funds for materials. Implementing a service priority means providing library users with access to the information resources associated with that service. It means making a commitment to building a current, high-quality collection of resources beyond the minimal level. (See figure 9: Levels of Collection Development for more information about this.)

FIGURE 11
Materials Allocation Methods

	Description	Advantages	Disadvantages
Historical	"We have always done it this way"	Easy to understand and no one gets too angry because there are never any real surprises	Difficult to adjust to changing demands and new formats; the only flexibility comes from new funds
Zero-based budgeting	Starts from zero each year to build a materials budget that reflects current needs and conditions	Very flexible, and allows quick responses to changing circumstances	Difficult and time-consuming
Formulas, ranking, and percentages	Uses mathematical models to determine allocations for specific subsets of the collection	Can recalculate the materials allocation annually, making it easier to adapt to changing circumstances	Not easy to select a mathematical model that satisfies everyone; often political considerations become more important than the actual elements of the model in making decisions
Local modeling techniques	Develops an individual methodology to allocate materials	Lets staff address special, unique circumstances	Time-consuming to develop a unique model, and few library staff members have the skills required

Your assessment of the library collections may indicate that the current collection fully supports the chosen service responses at the levels appropriate for the library's intended outcomes. If so, the current budget allocations for collection development are fine. However, it is far more likely that your assessment of current collections will indicate a need to invest more heavily in specific parts of the collection to bring them up to the required levels; therefore, you will need to look carefully at the library's allocation process.

Obviously, libraries using the historical approach will have to make the greatest changes in the way they determine their allocations. However, libraries using mathematical models will also have to examine the elements in those models carefully. As noted in figure 11, the selection of the elements to include in the allocation model can become political.

In that case, it may be difficult to change the model to reflect more accurately the library's current service priorities.

Monitoring Collection Expenditures

Developing allocation plans or formulas is only the first step. Accountability is equally important. Accountability implies not only setting up a budget that reflects goals and priorities but also monitoring that budget to ensure that those goals and priorities are met.[11] This, in turn, means tracking collections expenditures to ensure that formulas are adhered to. It may even mean reviewing actual purchases to ensure that materials selected support the library's priorities. Not too long ago library managers who wanted to track acquisitions expenditures had to develop cumbersome and time-consuming manual systems. Fortunately, automated acquisitions software has made monitoring collections expenditures both easier and more cost-effective. This is one area in which you may have access to far more data than you know about. The departmentalization common in most public libraries has tended to mean that technical services staff have some information, acquisitions staff have other information, subject selectors have yet another set of information, and library managers have bits and pieces of each. The first step in developing a monitoring plan is to bring all of the interested parties together to share what they know and describe the kinds of data each has available. Based on that information, managers can assign responsibilities for monitoring and develop procedures to ensure continuing communication and cooperation.

Interpreting and Deciding

The collection development issues presented in this chapter are intended to provide you and your colleagues with a common understanding of the forces that affect collection development in our rapidly changing environment. Based on that understanding you can select from among the collections workforms those that will help you gather data you think will be useful. When you have finished discussing the issues and gathering data, you should be in an excellent position to make informed decisions about the allocation and reallocation of your collection resources.

However, that is just the beginning of using your resources effectively. Don't forget that there is often a big difference between what we plan and what we actually end up with. You have been encouraged throughout to "estimate, implement, check, and adjust" and then "check and adjust" again. This continual monitoring is the critical final step required to ensure that the library's collections support its service priorities.

NOTES

1. Nancy Van House and others, *Output Measures for Public Libraries: A Manual of Standardized Procedures,* 2d ed. (Chicago: American Library Assn., 1987), 44–7.

2. Van House, 62–5.

3. Van House, 44–7.

4. Belinda Boon, *The CREW Method: Expanded Guidelines for Collection Evaluation and Weeding in Small and Medium-Sized Public Libraries* (Austin, Tex.: Texas State Library, 1995).

5. Boon, *The CREW Method,* 31.

6. Walt Crawford and Michael Gorman, *Future Libraries: Dreams, Madness, and Reality* (Chicago: American Library Assn., 1995).

7. Michael Buckland, *Redesigning Library Services: A Manifesto* (Chicago: American Library Assn., 1992), 45.

8. Buckland, 45.

9. Murray S. Martin, *Collection Development and Finance: A Guide to Strategic Library-Materials Budgeting;* Frontiers of Access to Library Materials, no. 2 (Chicago: American Library Assn., 1995), 3.

10. G. Edward Evans, *Developing Library and Information Center Collections,* 3d ed. (Englewood, Colo.: Libraries Unlimited, 1995), 370.

11. Martin, *Collection Development and Finance,* 4.

Instructions

WORKFORM C1   What's Important?

Purpose of Workform C1

Use this workform as the basis for deciding what changes need to be made in the materials budget to implement the goals and objectives in the library's plan.

Source(s) of Data for Workform C1

The goals, objectives, and activities in the library plan are the sources of the data for this workform.

Factors to Consider When Completing Workform C1

1. The areas of collection emphasis are different for each of the 13 service responses in *Planning for Results*. The goals, objectives, and activities selected may also have an impact on the areas of emphasis in the library's collections. (For example, if the library planners identified "Lifelong Learning" as a service response, the plan might include these two goals:

   The preschool children in Anytown will be introduced to books and a love of reading.

   Seniors in Anytown will have the support they need to pursue their avocations.)

   Each goal will result in different objectives and activities, and they in turn will have different impacts on the library's collections.

2. You have access to a wide variety of data about your collections. These data have been divided into five major categories shown across the top of Workform C1.

To Complete Workform C1

1. **Activity column**   List the activities that will have an impact on the library's collection resources in the left column headed Activity. Use additional copies of the workform, if needed.

2. Review the activities to determine which data elements are most important for each activity and place an *X* in the appropriate columns.

3. Complete the information requested at the bottom of the workform.

   Completed by   Enter the name of the person or persons who completed the workform.

   Source of data   Indicate the source of the data used to complete the workform.

   Date completed   Enter the date the workform was completed.

   Library   Enter the library name.

Factors to Consider When Reviewing the Data on Workform C1

1. Have you reviewed the goals and objectives in the library plan to be sure that you understand the results expected from the activities?

2. Have you identified all of the activities that will have an impact on the library's collection resources?

Workform Number	Size			Utilization				Access			Age					Condition	
	C2	C3	C4	C5	C6	C7	C8	C9	C10	C11	C12	C13	C14	C15	C16	C17
Activity	Volumes—Print and Media	Titles—Print and Media	Titles—Electronic	Circulation—Print and Media	In-Library Use—Print and Media	In-Library Use—Electronic	Off-Site Use—Electronic	Document Delivery	Materials Availability	Electronic Text Availability	Copyright—Print	Copyright—Media	Periodicals—Print and Microform	Periodicals—Electronic	Worn or Damaged—Print	Worn or Damaged—Media

Completed by _____ Date completed _____

Source of data _____ Library _____

General Instructions

At the Top of Workforms C2–C17

1. **Activity**   Indicate the activity being reviewed.

2. **Collection**   These workforms can be used to record information about the entire collection, or they can be used to record information about a portion of the collection. That decision will be based on the activities, goals, and objectives you are reviewing. (For example, if you are evaluating your collection support for the service response "Lifelong Learning" and the goal is "The preschool children in Anytown will be introduced to books and the love of reading," you might be interested in reviewing only the juvenile collection.) Place an *X* on the line for the portion(s) of the collection under review. On several workforms you will be asked to list subject areas rather than parts of the collection.

3. **Month/year data collected**   Indicate the month and/or year the data being recorded on the workform was collected.

4. **Library unit**   If the data on a workform is from an individual library unit, indicate the name of the unit. If the data is from the whole library, write the library's name.

At the Bottom of All Collections Workforms

1. **Completed by**   Enter the name of the person or persons who completed the workform.

2. **Source of data**   Indicate the source of the data used to complete the workform.

3. **Date completed**   Enter the date the workform was completed.

4. **Library**   Enter the library name.

Tally Sheets

Tally sheets are included following Workforms C6, C9, C12, C13, C16, and C17. You may want to use them to collect data prior to completing those workforms.

Instructions

Purpose of Workform C2

Use this workform to record information about the number of volumes in the collection that support the activity under review.

Source(s) of Data for Workform C2

1. Count each physical item as one volume. You may be able to get information from your automated circulation system. If you do not have an automated system or can't get the data you need from your system, you can determine this information by sampling. (See item 2, following.)

2. To determine the total number of print or media volumes in a specific portion of the collection by sampling:

   Measure a one-foot area of shelving in the portion of the collection being counted.

   Count the number of books shelved in that one-foot space.

   Measure two more one-foot areas in the same section of the collection, and again count the number of books shelved in each.

   Total the three numbers and divide by three to get an average number of volumes per foot in that portion of the collection. (Obviously, this is going to be a very different number in picture books than in business books.)

   Measure the total number of feet of books on the shelf in the portion of the collection being evaluated.

   Multiply the total number of feet of books by the average number of books per foot. Add the approximate number of books checked out. This will give you an approximate number of volumes in a specific section of the collection.

3. For software, count each diskette or CD-ROM as a single volume. If the diskettes or CD-ROMs have more than one program, each program would be considered as an individual title.

Factors to Consider When Completing Workform C2

1. *Volumes* are defined as "the number of physical items in both the print and media collections." (For example, a single encyclopedia set normally includes 24–26 volumes.)

2. Complete a copy of the workform for each activity for which you checked the "Size: Volumes—Print and Media" column on Workform C1.

3. If the library has multiple units, complete a copy of this workform for each unit. Then create a summary copy of the workform that shows the entire library's resources.

4. Be sure you are counting the same things in all parts of the workform.

To Complete Workform C2

1. **Column A** In the numbered rows above the double line, indicate the specific sections of the collection that support the activity under review.

2. **Columns B and C** Enter the numbers in the appropriate boxes in the print and media columns. See "Source(s) of Data for Workform C2" if you need more information on where to find the data required.

3. **Rows D–F** The data in these rows will help you determine how the number of volumes that support the activity under review compares with the number of volumes in other parts of the collection.

   Row D Total all of the numbers in the columns and enter that data in row D.

   Row E Determine what portion of the collection you want to use as the basis of comparison. In most cases, this will be the part of the collection you indicated in the "Collection" section at the top of the workform. Enter the total number of volumes in that portion of the collection in row E.

   Row F To determine the percent of volumes or the portion being used as the basis of your comparison supporting this activity, divide the number in row D by the number in row E. (For example, if you have a total of 1,250 volumes in your picture books, E books, and I-Can-Read books, and a total 5,000 volumes in your whole juvenile collection, 25% of your juvenile volumes are supporting your preschool activity [1,250 ÷ 5,000 = .25 = 25%].)

Factors to Consider When Reviewing the Data on Workform C2

1. How does the number of volumes in the parts of the collection that support the activity under review compare with other parts of the collection?

2. What is the title/volume ratio? To determine the ratio, divide the number of volumes by the number of titles. See Workform C3 for the number of titles. (If you have no duplicate titles, the ratio would be 1:1. If you have 350 titles and 500 volumes, the ratio would be 1:1.4.)

(Continued)

Instructions

3. What is the turnover rate for the volumes in the portion of the collection that support the activity under review? The *turnover rate* is "the average number of times each volume circulates." To determine the turnover rate, you will need to complete Workform C5: Circulation—Print and Media. Then you will divide circulation of the items in the portion of the collections under review by the number of volumes in that part of the collections. (For example, if there are 400 volumes in the section under review and they circulated 1,200 times, the turnover rate would be 3 [1,200 ÷ 400 = 3].)

4. What level of collection development is appropriate for the portion of the collection under review? See figure 9 in the text for more information.

WORKFORM C2 Size: Volumes—Print and Media

Activity _____

Month/year data collected _____

Collection   All _____   Adult _____   Juvenile _____   YA _____

Library unit _____

A. Call Number/Subject Area	B. Print (including microforms)			C. Media			
	Books	Periodicals	Other	Video	Audio	Software	Other
1.							
2.							
3.							
4.							
5.							
6.							
7.							
8.							
9.							
10.							
D. Total number of print and media volumes supporting this activity							
E. Total number of print and media volumes in the portion of the collection used for comparison							
F. Percent of print and media volumes supporting this activity	%	%	%	%	%	%	%

Completed by _____   Date completed _____

Source of data _____   Library _____

WORKFORM C3   Size: Titles—Print and Media

Instructions

Purpose of Workform C3

Use this workform to record information about the number of titles in the collection that support the activity under review.

Source(s) of Data for Workform C3

1. For books and media count the unique bibliographic records. You may be able to get this number from your automated circulation system. If you do not have an automated system or can't get the data you need from your system, you can gather the data by sampling. (See item 2, following.) Be sure to include microforms in your count of print books and periodicals.

2. To determine the number of unique bibliographic records of books and media in a specific portion of the collection by sampling:

   Mark the beginning and ending of the sections in your shelf list that represent the call numbers/subject areas that support the activity under review.

   Estimate the number of titles in the sections of the shelf list you marked using the following method:

   measure one inch of cards

   count the number of cards in that inch

   multiply the number of cards in one inch of cards by the total number of inches of cards (100 cards per inch × 2.75 inches = 275 cards = 275 titles)

3. For periodicals, count individual periodical titles, whether they are in print or microtext format.

4. For software, count individual titles, whether in diskette or CD-ROM format.

Factors to Consider When Completing Workform C3

1. *Titles* are defined as "unique bibliographic records." This information includes the number of titles in both print and media collections.

2. Complete a copy of the workform for each activity for which you checked the "Size: Titles—Print and Media" column on Workform C1.

3. If the library has multiple units, complete a copy of this workform for each unit. Then create a summary copy of the workform that shows the entire library's resources.

To Complete Workform C3

1. **Column A**   In the numbered rows above the double line, indicate the specific sections of the collection that support the activity under review.

2. **Columns B–D**   Enter the numbers in the appropriate places in the books, periodicals, and media columns. See "Source(s) of Data for Workform C3" if you need more information on where to find the data required.

3. **Rows E–G**   The data in these rows will help you determine how the number of titles that support the activity under review compares with the number of titles in other parts of the collection.

   Row E   Total all of the numbers in the columns and enter that data in row E.

   Row F   Determine what portion of the collection you want to use as the basis of comparison. In most cases, this will be the part of the collection you indicated in the "Collection" section at the top of the workform. Enter the total number of volumes in that portion of the collection in row F.

   Row G   To determine the percent of titles (or the portion being used as the basis of the comparison) that support this activity, divide the number in row E by the number in row F. (For example, if you have a total of 800 titles in your picture books, E books, and I-Can-Read books, and a total 4,000 titles in your whole juvenile collection, 20% of your juvenile titles are supporting your preschool activity [800 ÷ 4,000 = .20 = 20%].).

Factors to Consider When Reviewing the Data on Workform C3

1. How does the number of titles in the parts of the collection that support the activity under review compare with other parts of the collection?

2. What is the title/volume ratio? To determine the ratio, divide the number of volumes by the number of titles. (If you have no duplicate titles, the ratio would be 1:1. If you have 350 titles and 500 volumes, the ratio would be 1:1.4.)

3. What level of collection development is appropriate for the portion of the collection under review? See Figure 9 in the text for more information.

4. Are there enough copies of popular titles to meet demand? Refer to data collected on Workforms C9: Document Delivery and C10: Materials Availability for more information on access.

WORKFORM C3   Size: Titles—Print and Media

Activity _____

Collection   All _____   Adult _____   YA _____   Juvenile _____

Month/year data collected _____

Library unit _____

A. Call Number/Subject Area	B. Books (including microforms)		C. Periodicals (including microforms)	D. Media		
	Circulating	Reference		Video	Audio	Software
1.						
2.						
3.						
4.						
5.						
6.						
7.						
8.						
9.						
10.						
E. Total number of print and media titles supporting this activity						
F. Total number of print and media titles in the portion of the collection used for comparison						
G. Percent of print and media titles supporting this activity	%	%	%	%	%	%

Completed by _____

Date completed _____

Source of data _____

Library _____

Instructions

WORKFORM C4 Size: Titles—Electronic

Purpose of Workform C4

Use this workform to record information about the number of electronic reference materials in your collection that support the activity under review.

Source(s) of Data for Workform C4

This information should be available from the vendor(s) from whom you leased or purchased the databases.

Factors to Consider When Completing Workform C4

1. In databases that include a number of titles, such as periodical indexes with full text, you will be evaluating individual periodical titles rather than the database as a whole, since many collections cover a broad range of topics.

2. Complete a copy of the workform for each activity for which you checked the "Size: Titles—Electronic" column on Workform C1.

3. If the library has multiple units, complete a copy of this workform for each unit. Then create a summary copy of the workform that shows the entire library's resources.

To Complete Workform C4

1. **Column A** In the numbered rows above the double line, record the databases that include titles that support the activity under review.

2. **Column B** Enter the number of titles in the database that are relevant to the activity.

3. **Rows C–E** The data in these rows will help you determine how the number of titles that support the activity under review compares with the number of titles in other parts of the collection.

   Row C Total column B and enter that data in row C.

   Row D Determine what portion of the electronic collection you want to use as the basis of your comparison. In most cases, this will be the part of the collection you indicated in the "Collection" section at the top of the workform. Enter the total number of titles in that portion of the collection in row D.

   Row E To determine the percent of the collection that you designated at the top of the workform (or the portion being used as the basis of your comparison) supporting this activity, divide the number in row C by the number in row D.

Factors to Consider When Reviewing the Data on Workform C4

1. How does the number of electronic titles in the parts of the collection that support the activity under review compare with the total number of electronic titles?

2. What level of collection development is appropriate for the portion of the collection under review? See figure 9 in the text for more information.

3. What kind of access is provided to the electronic titles? Refer to data collected on Workform C11: Electronic Text Availability for more information on this.

Size: Titles—Electronic

Activity _____

Month/year data collected _____

Collection   All _____   Adult _____   Juvenile _____   YA _____

Library unit _____

A. Database	B. Number of Titles
1.	
2.	
3.	
4.	
5.	
6.	
7.	
8.	
9.	
10.	
11.	
12.	
13.	
14.	
15.	
C. Total number of electronic titles supporting this activity	
D. Total number of electronic titles in the portion of the collection used for comparison	
E. Percent of electronic titles supporting this activity	%

Completed by _____   Date completed _____

Source of data _____   Library _____

Purpose of Workform C5

Use this workform to record information about the circulation of print and media items in the collection that support the activity under review.

Source(s) of Data for Workform C5

1. If you have an automated circulation system, information about the circulation of the entire collection is readily available through the system statistics program. However, your ability to get circulation information about specific sections of the collections is based on the choices made when the statistical profile for the circulation system was established.

2. If the library does not have an automated circulation system, you probably maintain accurate records of the circulation by counting the number of checkout cards at the end of each day. Many libraries divide this manual count into four groups: adult fiction, adult nonfiction, juvenile fiction, and juvenile nonfiction. If the data currently collected is not specific enough to determine the use of materials that support the activity under review, you may obtain the data you need by sampling. (See item 3, following.)

3. To obtain sampling data about the circulation of a specific portion of your collection through a manual count of checkout cards during a period:

   Determine the sample period; this is when you will measure the circulation. You should collect the sample for at least two one-week periods, ideally at two different times of separate months and during two different times of the year.

   At the end of each day during the sample period, divide the checkout cards for that day into groups based on the sections of the collection you have identified as supporting the activity under review as listed in column A.

   Count the cards representing materials in the portions of the collection that support the activity and record that number on a tally sheet.

   Re-sort the cards to separate all of the cards from the portion of the collection you will be using as a comparison. (In the business example, this might be the entire adult nonfiction collection.) If you are using a portion of the collection for which you normally record circulation statistics for this comparison, such as adult nonfiction, you can skip this step. See the directions for row D for more information on the comparison process.

   Count the cards that are from the materials in the portion of the collection you are using as a comparison and record that number on a tally sheet.

   Re-sort the cards into whatever groups you normally tabulate and recount your circulation for your ongoing statistics.

4. At the end of the sample period, total the circulation for each portion of the collection from which you collected data. That should give you the circulation for two weeklong periods. Then multiply the total for the two weeks by 26 to determine the approximate annual circulation of the portions of the collection under review. This data may not be as accurate as the information from an automated circulation system, but it will provide you with a clear indication of the relative use of various parts of the collection.

Factors to Consider When Completing Workform C5

1. *Circulation* is defined as "the number of times these items were checked out for use outside the library."

2. Complete a copy of the workform for each activity for which you checked the "Utilization: Circulation—Print and Media" column on Workform C1.

3. If your library has multiple units, complete a copy of this workform for each unit. Then create a summary copy of the workform that shows the entire library's resources.

4. Be sure that you are counting circulation from the same time period in all parts of the form. Select a period of time for gathering data (weekly, monthly, or yearly), and use it consistently throughout workforms C5–C11.

To Complete Workform C5

1. **Column A** In the numbered rows above the double line, indicate the specific sections of the collection that support the activity under review.

2. **Columns B–C** Enter the numbers in the appropriate places in these columns. See "Source(s) of Data for Workform C5" if you need more information on where to find the data required.

3. **Rows D–F** The data in these rows will help you determine how the circulation of the collection that supports the activity under review compares with the circulation of other parts of the collection.

   Row D Total all of the numbers in the columns and enter that data in row D.

   Row E Determine what portion of the collection you want to use as the basis of comparison. In most cases, this will be the circulation of the part of the collection you indicated in the "Collection" section at the top of the workform. Enter the total circulation of that portion of the collection in row E.

(Continued)

Instructions

Row F To determine the percent of circulation supporting this activity, divide the number in row D by the number in row E. (For example, if your picture books, E books, and I-Can-Read books circulated 9,000 times and the materials in your entire juvenile collection circulated 25,000 times, 36% of your juvenile circulation comes from materials that are supporting your preschool activity [9,000 ÷ 25,000 = .36 = 36%].)

Factors to Consider When Reviewing the Data on Workform C5

1. What is the library loan period? Circulation will be higher in a library with a two-week loan period than in a library with a three-week loan period.

2. What is the library renewal policy? If the library allows renewals and counts them as a separate circulation transaction, circulation will be higher than if renewals are not counted as separate transactions.

3. Are there restrictions on loans of new materials? If a library restricts users to a minimum number of new materials, circulation may be lower than in libraries with unrestricted circulation.

4. If you collected data though sampling, when did you collect the sample? Data collected from December 15 to January 1 is not typical. Neither is data collected during the first week of the summer reading program.

WORKFORM C5   **Utilization: Circulation—Print and Media**

Activity _____

Month/year data collected _____

Collection   All _____   Adult _____   YA _____   Juvenile _____

Library unit _____

A. Call Number/Subject Area	B. Print (including microforms)			C. Media			
	Books	Periodicals	Other	Video	Audio	Software	Other
1.							
2.							
3.							
4.							
5.							
6.							
7.							
8.							
9.							
10.							
D. Total circulation of print and media supporting this activity							
E. Total circulation of print and media in the portion of the collection used for comparison							
F. Percent of circulation of print and media supporting this activity	%	%	%	%	%	%	%

Completed by _____   Date completed _____

Source of data _____   Library _____

Instructions WORKFORM C6 Utilization: In-Library Use—Print and Media

Purpose of Workform C6

Use this workform to record information about the in-library use of the print and media items in the collection that support the activity under review.

Source(s) of Data for Workform C6

The only way to collect data about in-library use of materials is to physically count the items taken from the library shelves during a specified period. Libraries with automated systems may be able to use the system to record in-library use on an on-going basis, using portable terminals or scanning devices. Libraries that record in-library usage through sampling typically record data for at least a week.

1. To determine the in-house use of the materials that support the activity under review, use the following procedures:

   In-library use of materials (print and media) is one of the output measures included in ALA's *Output Measures for Public Libraries: A Manual of Standardized Procedures*, second edition. The section of *Output Measures for Public Libraries* that includes instructions for collecting this data has been reprinted in appendix F. Please note that for this workform you will not need to determine the in-library use per capita. Instead, you will use the annual in-library material use figures.

   If the activity under review relates to children, follow the instructions for collecting data about in-library use of materials found in *Output Measures for Public Library Services to Children: A Manual of Standardized Procedures,* also in appendix F.

   If the activity under review is focused on young adults, follow the instructions for collecting data about in-library use of materials found in *Output Measures and More: Planning and Evaluating Public Library Services for Young Adults,* in appendix F.

   Use separate tally sheets to count the materials in the call numbers/subject areas you have identified as supporting the activity under review and listed in the numbered section of column A of Workform C6.

   At the end of the data collection period, tabulate the tally sheets for the in-house use of materials that support the activity under review and record that data in row D of Workform C6.

2. To determine the in-house use of the materials you are using as a basis for your comparison, use the following procedures:

First, determine what portion of the in-library use you want to use as the basis of your comparison. In most cases, this will be the in-library use for that portion of the collection you marked in the "Collection" section at the top of the workform.

Tabulate all of the tally sheets completed during the data collection period for the call numbers/subject areas you used as a comparison.

Enter that data in row E of Workform C6.

Factors to Consider When Completing Workform C6

1. *In-library use* is defined as "any item that is removed from the shelf by the public or by a staff member but not circulated."

2. Complete a copy of the workform for each activity for which you checked the "Utilization: In-Library Use—Print and Media" column on Workform C1.

3. If the library has multiple units, complete a copy of this workform for each unit. Then create a summary copy of the workform that shows the entire library's in-library use.

4. Be sure to gather all of the data about in-library use during the same time period.

5. If you wish to use the tally sheet provided, see appendix F for instructions.

To Complete Workform C6

1. **Column A**   In the numbered rows above the double line, indicate the specific sections of the collection that support the activity under review.

2. **Columns B–C**   Enter the numbers in the appropriate places in these columns. See "Source(s) of Data for Workform C6" if you need more information on where to find the data required.

3. **Rows D–F**   The data in these rows will help you compare the in-house use of materials that support the activity under review with the in-house use of other materials.

   Row D   Total all of the numbers in the columns and enter that data in row D.

   Row E   Determine what portion of the collection you want to use as the basis of your comparison. In most cases, this will be the in-library use of the part of the collection you indicated in the "Collection" section at the top of the workform. Enter the total in-library use of that portion of the collection in row E.

(Continued)

Instructions

Row F To determine the percent of in-library use supporting this activity, divide the number in row D by the number in row E. (For example, if 100 items from subject areas that support activities to serve the business community were used in-house and a total of 1,000 items were used during the same time period, then 10% of your in-house use would be in support of your business activity [1,000 ÷ 10 = .10 = 10%].)

Factors to Consider When Reviewing the Data on Workform C6

1. When did you collect the data? Data collected from December 15 to January 1 is not typical. Neither is data collected during the first week of the summer reading program.

2. Is there sufficient space for people to use materials comfortably in the library? See chapter 4 for more information on space.

3. Are the materials in question appropriate for use in the library? (If you are considering current fiction, for instance, in-library use is irrelevant.)

WORKFORM C6 Utilization: In-Library Use—Print and Media

Activity _____

Collection All _____ Adult _____ Juvenile _____ YA _____

Month/year data collected _____

Library unit _____

| A. Call Number/Subject Area | B. Print (including microforms) | | | C. Media | | | |
	Books	Periodicals	Other	Video	Audio	Software	Other
1.							
2.							
3.							
4.							
5.							
6.							
7.							
8.							
9.							
10.							
D. Total in-library use of print and media supporting this activity							
E. Total in-library use of print and media in the portion of the collection used for comparison							
F. Percent of in-library use of print and media supporting this activity	%	%	%	%	%	%	%

Completed by _____ Date completed _____

Source of data _____ Library _____

Utilization: In-Library Use—Print and Media Tally Sheet

Subject area/call number _____

Type of Material	Hour													Total
Totals														

Completed by _____ Date completed _____

Source of data _____ Library _____

Instructions

WORKFORM C7 **Utilization: In-Library Use—Electronic**

Purpose of Workform C7

Use this workform to record information about the in-library use of the electronic reference resources in the collection that support the activity under review.

Source(s) of Data for Workform C7

1. Many vendors can provide the following information about the databases accessed through the library's PCs to complete this portion of Workform C7:

   number of sessions (when a library user logs on to a specific database)

   number of searches (when a library user types an inquiry into the databases search engine during a session)

   number of items retrieved (when a library user requests an electronic document that was identified during a search)

   (For example, a user in the library might use a computer to log on to a business database, which would be counted as one *session.* During that session, the user might search for information on investing, which would count as one *search.* Let's assume that the search produced 25 responses, one of which is an article by John Q. Expert. The user might choose to open that article to read, which would be counted as one *item retrieved.* As you can see, a single user can initiate multiple *searches* and *items retrieved* in each *session* and might very well initiate more than one *session* while at the computer terminal.)

2. Most stand-alone CD products do not include an electronic way to measure the use of the product. You will probably have to count the number of people who use them, just as you do with the in-library use of print and media materials.

   Some libraries ask users to register to use CD-ROM products. If your library does this, you have the data you need to determine the number of people who used the product.

   If you do not normally register users, you can do so for one or two sample weeks to collect the usage data.

   If you choose not to register users by name, ask a staff member to keep a tally of users during the sample period.

   See Technology Workforms T9 and T10 for more information on collecting data on the use of electronic resources.

3. Metering software is available that will indicate how many users accessed each of the CD products on your network. Check with your vendor for more information.

Factors to Consider When Completing Workform C7

1. Electronic reference sources include the use of online licensed databases, CD-ROM products, and the information on the library's Web server when these resources are accessed from the PCs in the library.

2. Complete a copy of the workform for each activity for which you checked the "Utilization: In-Library Use—Electronic" column on Workform C1.

3. If the library has multiple units, complete a copy of this workform for each unit. Then create a summary copy of the workform that shows the entire library's electronic resources.

4. Be sure to gather all of the data used on the workform during the same time period.

5. Record the same type of data in the rows above and below the double line. If you recorded information on "Sessions" in the boxes above the double line, you need to count "Sessions" below the line, as well.

To Complete Workform C7

1. **Column A** In the numbered rows above the double line, indicate the specific subject areas of your electronic resources that support the activity under review. Smaller libraries may be able to list the actual titles of the resources in this column.

2. **Columns B–C** Enter the numbers in the appropriate places in these columns. See "Source(s) of Data for Workform C7" if you need more information on where to find the data required.

3. **Rows D–F** The data in these rows will help you compare the in-house use of electronic resources that support the activity under review with the in-house use of other electronic resources.

   Row D Total all of the numbers in the columns and enter that data in row D.

   Row E Determine which electronic resources to use as the basis of comparison. Many libraries will use all of their electronic resources. Enter the total use numbers for those electronic resources in row E.

   Row F To determine the percent of the use of electronic resources (or the portion being used as the basis of your comparison) that supports this activity, divide the number in row D by the number in row E for each column. (For example, if you have a total of 1,000 sessions on the online databases that support this activity and a total of 10,000 sessions on all of the online licensed databases, 10% of the use of online licensed databases supports this activity [1,000 ÷ 10,000 = .10 = 10%].)

(Continued)

Instructions

Factors to Consider When Reviewing the Data on Workform C7

1. How many opportunities does the public have to use the resources being evaluated? If some resources are available only at a limited number of devices, their percentage of use may seem comparatively low, even if they are in use 100% of the time.

2. What is the ratio of searches to sessions for each resource? Can you account for the differences based on the resources? (For example, is one resource more focused in its content?)

3. What percentage of the searches done result in items retrieved from each resource? Can you speculate on reasons for the differences? (For example, does one resource have a higher percentage of full text? Or more complete abstracts?)

Utilization: In-Library Use—Electronic

Activity _____

Month/year data collected _____

Collection   All _____   Adult _____   YA _____   Juvenile _____

Library unit _____

A. Subject Area	B. Online Licensed Databases			C. CD Products		
				Stand-alone		Networked
	Sessions	Searches	Views	People/Time		Number Accessed
1.						
2.						
3.						
4.						
5.						
6.						
7.						
8.						
D. Total in-library use of electronic resources supporting this activity						
E. Total in-library use of electronic resources in the portion of the collection used for comparison						
F. Percent of in-library use of electronic resources supporting this activity	%	%	%	%		%

Completed by _____   Date completed _____

Source of data _____   Library _____

Instructions

Purpose of Workform C8

Use this workform to record information about the off-site use of the library's electronic reference resources that support the activity under review.

Source(s) of Data for Workform C8

1. The information to complete the online licensed databases portion of the workform will come from the vendor of the database(s) being measured. Most vendors can provide the following information:

   number of sessions (when a library user logs on to a specific database)

   number of searches (when a library user types an inquiry into the databases search engine during a session)

   number of items retrieved (when a library user requests an electronic document that was identified during a search)

   (For example, a library user might use a computer in the library to log on to a business database, which would be counted as one *session*. During that session, the user might search for information on investing, which would count as one *search*. Let's assume that the search produced 25 responses, one of which is an article by John Q. Expert. The user might choose to open that article to read, which would be counted as one *item retrieved*. As you can see, a single user can initiate multiple *searches* and retrieve multiple items in each *session*, and might very well initiate more than one *session* while at the computer terminal.)

2. Metering software is available that will indicate how many users accessed each of the CD-ROM products on your network. Check with your vendor for more information.

Factors to Consider When Completing Workform C8

1. Off-site use includes the use of online licensed databases, CD products, and the information on the library's Web server when those resources are accessed from PCs outside the library.

2. Complete a copy of the workform for each activity for which you checked the "Utilization: Off-Site Access" column on Workform C1.

3. It is likely that all of the off-site access to electronic resources goes through a single network. If this is the case, you can complete one copy of this workform for the entire network. However, if the library has more than one network, complete a copy of this workform for each network.

4. Be sure to gather all of the data used on this form during the same time period in which you gather the data for Workform C7.

To Complete Workform C8

1. **Column A**   In the numbered rows above the double line, indicate the specific subject areas of the electronic resources that you have determined support the activity under review.

2. **Columns B–C**   Enter the numbers in the appropriate places in these columns. See "Source(s) of Data for Workform C8" if you need more information on where to find the data.

3. **Rows D–F**   The data in these rows will help you compare off-site electronic use with data about the collection support provided to other activities—and about the collection support provided to areas that are not priorities.

   Row D   Total all of the numbers in the columns and enter that data in row D.

   Row E   Determine which electronic resources to use as the basis of comparison. In most cases, libraries will use all of their electronic resources. Enter the total use numbers for those electronic resources in row E.

   Row F   To determine the percent of the use of electronic resources (or the portion being used as the basis of your comparison) that support this activity, divide the number in row D by the number in row E. (For example, if a total of 400 sessions on the online databases supports this activity out of a total of 2,500 sessions on all of the online licensed databases, 16% of the use of your online licensed databases supports this activity [400 ÷ 2,500 = .16 = 16%].)

Factors to Consider When Reviewing the Data on Workform C8

1. Are there any licensing restrictions that limit the use of electronic resources by off-site users? How might these restrictions be affecting the counts of use?

2. What is the ratio of searches to sessions for each resource? Can you account for the differences based on the resources? (For example, is one resource more focused in its content?)

3. What percentage of the searches done result in items retrieved from each resource? Can you speculate on reasons for the differences? (For example, does one resource have a higher percentage of full text? Or more complete abstracts?)

WORKFORM C8 Utilization: Off-Site Use—Electronic

Activity _____

Month/year data collected _____

Collection All _____ Adult _____ Juvenile _____ YA _____

Library unit _____

| A. Subject Area | B. Online Licensed Databases | | | C. Networked CD Products |
	Sessions	Searches	Views	Number Accessed
1.				
2.				
3.				
4.				
5.				
6.				
7.				
8.				
D. Total off-site use of electronic resources supporting this activity				
E. Total off-site use of electronic resources in the portion of the collection used for comparison				
F. Percent of off-site use of electronic resources supporting this activity	%	%	%	%

Completed by _____ Date completed _____

Source of data _____ Library _____

Instructions

Purpose of Workform C9

Use this workform to record information about the number of days it takes for users to get materials in the subject areas that support the activity under review when those materials are not available at the time the user visits the library.

Source(s) of Data for Workform C9

Document delivery is one of the output measures included in *Output Measures for Public Libraries: A Manual of Standardized Procedures*, second edition. Instructions for gathering the data to determine how long it takes to provide a library user with material not available during the user's visit have been reprinted in appendix G. The instructions in appendix G are intended to be used to measure the time needed to fill all reserves, interlibrary loan requests, intrasystem loans, requests for purchase, etc. If the activity under review relates to children, follow the instructions for collecting data about document delivery found in *Output Measures for Public Library Services to Children: A Manual of Standardized Procedures*, also in appendix G. If the activity under review is focused on young adults, follow the instructions for collecting data about document delivery found in *Output Measures and More: Planning and Evaluating Public Library Services for Young Adults*, in appendix G.

To determine how long it takes to fill requests in the subject areas that support the activity:

1. Follow the instructions for collecting document delivery data in appendix G.

2. At the end of the data-collection period, review all of the requests and mark those that are in the subject areas/call numbers of the collection that supports the activity noted at the top of Workform C9.

3. Following the instructions in appendix G, tabulate the data for the requests on Workform C9.

Factors to Consider When Completing Workform C9

1. Materials might not have been available because they were in use or because the library does not own the materials. It is useful to know which is the case.

2. Complete a copy of the workform for each activity for which you checked the "Access: Document Delivery" column on Workform C1.

3. If the library has multiple units, complete a copy of the workform for each unit. Then create a summary copy of the workform that shows the entire library's resources.

4. If you want to use the tally sheet provided, see appendix G for instructions.

To Complete the Workform

1. Gather the data to complete the workform. Enter the numbers in the appropriate places. See "Source(s) of Data to Complete Workform C9" if you need more information on how to collect the data needed.

2. The information on Workform C9 will be most valuable if it is reviewed in the context of the document delivery times for the whole library collection (or the entire collection of a specific library unit). See "Source(s) of Data to Complete Workform C9" if you need more information on how to collect document delivery data for the whole library (or library unit) collection.

3. To determine document delivery times for the materials you are using as a basis for comparison (for the entire library or for the collection of a unit of the library):

   Tabulate all of the requests for materials not available during the data collection period, including those for portions of the collection that support the activity under review

   Enter that data on a separate copy of Workform C9.

Factors to Consider When Reviewing the Data on Workform C9

1. What are the library policies pertaining to reserves? How long is the reserve period? How many reserves can be placed on a title before an additional copy is purchased? Can users place reserves on new books?

2. What are the library interlibrary loan policies? What is the average time required to obtain an item requested through interlibrary loan? Are there policies in place to review interlibrary loan requests occasionally to see if there are patterns in the requests that indicate areas of the collection that need enhancement?

3. Can users request that the library purchase specific titles? If so, is there a procedure in place to ensure that the user who requested the title is notified when it arrives?

4. See appendix G for additional considerations regarding the analysis and use of document delivery data.

Collections **165**

WORKFORM C9 Access: Document Delivery

Activity _____

Collection All _____ Adult _____ Juvenile _____ YA _____

Subject/call numbers _____

Month/year data collected _____

Library unit _____

Availability		Reserves	Interlibrary Loans	Intrasystem Loans	Purchases	Other	All
0–7 days	#						
	%						
8–14 days	#						
	%						
15–30 days	#						
	%						
More than 30 days	#						
	%						
TOTAL	#						
	%						

Completed by _____ Date completed _____

Source of data _____ Library _____

WORKFORM C9 Access: Document Delivery Tally Sheet

Library _____   Date Begun _____   Date Ended _____

Request Number	ID for Item	Date Requested (Month/Day)	Date Available (Month/Day)	Response Time (Days)	Code*

*Code for source of material (fill in after material arrives):

R = Reserve (on your library's copy)
B = Borrowed from another branch (intrasystem loans)
I = Interlibrary loan
O = Purchase
X = Other (e.g., canceled, does not exist)

Completed by _____   Date completed _____

Source of data _____   Library _____

WORKFORM C10 Access: Materials Availability

Instructions

Purpose of Workform C10

Use this workform to record information about the availability of print, media, and electronic items in your collection that support the activity under review.

Source(s) of Data for Workform C10

Materials availability is one of the output measures included in *Output Measures for Public Libraries: A Manual of Standardized Procedures*, second edition. Complete instructions for gathering the data to determine author, title, subject, and browsers' fill rates have been reprinted in appendix H. These instructions are intended to be used to measure the fill rates for all items of the library's collection. If the activity under review relates to children, follow the instructions for collecting data about in-library use of materials found in *Output Measures for Public Library Services to Children: A Manual of Standardized Procedures*, also in appendix H. If the activity under review is focused on young adults, follow the instructions for collecting data about in-library use of materials found in *Output Measures and More: Planning and Evaluating Public Library Services for Young Adults* in appendix H.

To determine the author, title, subject, or browser's fill rate for the specific portions of your collection that support the activity:

1. Follow the instructions for administering the materials availability survey reprinted from *Output Measures for Public Libraries* in appendix H.

2. At the end of the data collection period, review all of the surveys and mark those in which the user was looking for materials in the subject areas that support this activity. These might be specific titles and/or specific authors as well as subject areas. Following the instructions from *Output Measures for Public Libraries* in appendix H, tabulate the responses on the surveys you have marked separately from the other surveys.

Factors to Consider When Completing Workform C10

1. *Materials availability* is "a measure of the success library users have in obtaining materials they want when they come to the library."

2. Complete a copy of the workform for each activity for which you checked the "Access: Materials Availability" column on Workform C1.

3. If the library has multiple units, you will probably want to complete a copy of the workform for each unit and then create a summary copy of the workform that shows the entire library's resources.

4. Be sure to count the same things in each column. If you recorded information on "Title Fill Rate" in the columns above the double line, you need to count "Title Fill Rate" below the double line as well.

To Complete Workform C10

1. **Column A** In the numbered rows, indicate the specific sections of the collection that support the activity under review. Be sure to put both the call number and the subject area in this column because the workform may be used by people who are not familiar with the call number.

2. **Columns B–E** Enter the numbers for items sought and found in the appropriate rows. See "Source(s) of Data to Complete Workform C10" if you need more information on where to find the data.

3. **Row F** Total all of the columns and enter that data in row F.

4. **Row G** Calculate the fill rates for this activity by dividing the number *found* by the number *sought*. Enter that number in row G. (For example, if library users sought a total of 200 titles and found 40 of them, the fill rate would be 20% [200 ÷ 40 = .2 = 20%].)

5. **Rows H–I** This section will help you compare the availability of materials that support the activity under review with the availability of materials in other parts of the collection.

   First determine which portion of the collection you want to use as the basis of comparison.

   Row H Enter the fill rates (%) in row H for that portion of the collection you specified at the top of the workform.

   Row I Determine the difference between the fill rates for the portion of the collection used for comparison and the fill rates for the materials that support this activity by subtracting the percent in row G from the percent in row H.

Factors to Consider When Reviewing the Data on Workform C10

1. Is the portion of the collection being reviewed an area in which it is reasonable to expect that specific titles will be difficult to obtain (for example, new books)?

2. Is the portion of the collection under review usually used for browsing, or is it normally searched by author or subject?

3. Are the materials availability statistics for the portion of the collections under review considerably different from other parts of the collections? If so, why?

WORKFORM C10 Access: Materials Availability

Activity _____

Month/year data collected _____

Collection All _____ Adult _____ Juvenile _____ YA _____   Library unit _____

A. Call Number/ Subject Area	B. Title Fill Rate		C. Author Fill Rate		D. Subject Fill Rate		E. Browsers' Fill Rate	
	Sought	Found	Sought	Found	Sought	Found	Sought	Found
1.								
2.								
3.								
4.								
5.								
6.								
7.								
8.								
9.								
10.								
F. Total								
G. Fill rate for this activity	%	%	%	%	%	%	%	%
H. Fill rate for all	%	%	%	%	%	%	%	%
I. Difference (+ or –)	%	%	%	%	%	%	%	%

Completed by _____   Date completed _____

Source of data _____   Library _____

Instructions

Purpose of Workform C11

Use this workform to record information about the level of access provided to electronic resources that support the activity under review.

Source(s) of Data for Workform C11

1. Electronic databases can be divided into three groups:

   those that provide only citations to various print-based articles

   those that include both indexes and an abstract of each of the articles indexed

   those that include the full text of the indexed articles or resources that are full-text documents, such as electronic encyclopedias, atlases, or phone books

2. Remember that a single electronic index product often provides access to multiple titles and that within a single electronic product you may find all three types of access.

3. To determine the number of titles in each of the three categories, refer to the product literature from the vendor of each of the electronic products in the collection that support the activity.

Factors to Consider When Completing Workform C11

1. Complete a copy of the workform for each activity for which you checked the "Access: Electronic Text" column on Workform C1.

2. If the library has multiple units and those units provide access to different electronic resources, complete a copy of the workform for each unit. Then create a summary copy of the workform that shows the entire library's resources.

3. Be sure to count the same things in each column. If you recorded information on "Indexed Databases" in the boxes above the double line, you need to count "Indexed Databases" below the double line as well.

4. Do not enter data in the shaded sections.

To Complete Workform C11

1. **Column A**   In the numbered rows, indicate the specific sections of the collection that support the activity under review. Be sure to use both the call number and the subject area because the workform may be used by people who are not familiar with the call number.

2. **Columns B–D**   Complete the columns for each of the numbered rows of the workform. See "Source(s) of Data to Complete Workform C11" if you need more information on where to find the data you need.

3. **Column E**   Total the rows for columns B–D and write the sum in the appropriate row in column E.

4. **Row G**   (See the sample on page 171.)

   # Titles   To determine the number of titles of each type that support the activity, total the data in the "#Titles" column in each of the three categories and write those totals in the appropriate places in row G marked #.

   Total the numbers in column E and record the number in row G of that column.

   %   To determine the percent of the titles in columns B–D, divide the number of titles in columns B–D by the total number of titles (column E, row G). (For example, you might find that of the electronic titles that support this activity, 20 are in databases that provide only indexes, 25 are in databases that include both indexes and abstracts, and 35 are in databases that provide full-text access. The Total # of Titles is 80 [20 indexed + 25 indexed and abstracted + 35 full-text]. To determine the percent of titles in databases that provide only indexes, you would divide 20 by 80 to discover that 25% of the titles that support this activity are available in databases that provide only index information.)

   Column F   You will complete column F for row G after completing the # sections for row H.

5. **Row H**   To put the data you collect into a context, compare it with data about the type of access available to all of the electronic resources in the portion of the library's collections you marked on the "Collection" line at the top of workform C11. (See the sample on page 171.)

   #   Determine the total number of titles in the portion of the library's collection you marked at the top of the workform for each of the three categories and record that number in the appropriate column in row H marked #.

   Add the numbers in the row H # spaces and record the total in column E, row H.

   Column F, row G   Determine the percent of the total number of electronic titles that support the activity by dividing the number in column E row G by the number in column E row H (in the example, 80 ÷ 500 = 16%).

   %   To calculate the percentage of titles in each of the three categories, divide the number in the # box in row H by the number in the # box in column E, row H. (For example, you might find that of all of the electronic titles available in the library unit, 75 are in databases that provide only indexes, 150 are in databases that include both indexes and abstracts, and

(Continued)

WORKFORM C11 Access: Electronic Text Availability (Cont.)

275 are in databases that provide full-text access. The Total # Titles is 500 [75 indexed + 150 indexed and abstracted + 275 full-text]. To determine the percent of titles in databases that provide only index information, you would divide 75 by 500 to discover that 15% of the titles available in the unit are in databases that provide only index information [75 ÷ 500 = .15 = 15%].)

6. **Row I** Determine the difference between the types of access for electronic titles in the portion of the collection you marked in the "Collection" line on Workform C11 and the types of access for the electronic titles that support this activity. Subtract the percent numbers in row H from the percent numbers in row G. (For example, 44% of the library's full-text electronic resources support the activity under review. The library provides 11% less full-text electronic resources for this activity than it does for the same type of access in other areas [44% − 55% = −11%]. Given that the activity under review is a priority for the library, this negative percentage would indicate that the library needs to put additional resources into providing access to full-text electronic resources for this activity.)

Factors to Consider When Reviewing the Data on Workform C11

1. For the index-only electronic resources, does the library have subscriptions to the materials indexed, or must the patron use interlibrary loan to request these items?

2. Are the abstracts in the index/abstracts products sufficiently detailed to substitute for the full article or to help the user identify specifically which articles to borrow/request in full text?

3. Do the full-text resources expand the library's print collection, or do they simply duplicate it in another format? What percentage of overlap is there between the library's print and electronic full-text collections?

A. Call Number/Subject Area	B. Electronic Indexes		C. Electronic Indexes with Abstracts		D. Full-Text Electronic Resources		E. Total # of Titles	F. Total % of Titles
	#Titles	%	#Titles	%	#Titles	%		
G. Total for this activity	# 20	25 %	# 25	31 %	# 35	44 %	# 80	16 %
H. Total for all electronic resources	# 75	15 %	# 150	30 %	# 275	55 %	# 500	
I. Difference (+ or −)		+10 %		+1 %		−11 %		

WORKFORM C11 Access: Electronic Text Availability

Activity _____

Month/year data collected _____

Collection All _____ Adult _____ Juvenile _____ YA _____

Library unit _____

A. Call Number/Subject Area	B. Electronic Indexes		C. Electronic Indexes with Abstracts		D. Full-Text Electronic Resources		E. Total # of Titles	F. Total % of Titles
	#Titles	%	#Titles	%	#Titles	%		
1.								
2.								
3.								
4.								
5.								
6.								
7.								
8.								
G. Total number of titles for this activity	#	%	#	%	#	%		%
H. Total number of titles for all electronic resources	#	%	#	%	#	%	#	
I. Difference (+ or –)		%		%		%	#	%

Completed by _____ Date completed _____

Source of data _____ Library _____

Instructions

WORKFORM C12 Age: Copyright—Print

Purpose of Workform C12

Use this workform to record information about the age of the print titles in the collection that support the activity under review.

Source(s) of Data for Workform C12

You may be able to get this copyright date information from the library's automated circulation system. If the library does not have an automated system or can't get the data from the system, you can determine the age of the titles in the collection that support the activity using the shelf list.

1. Mark the beginning and ending of the sections in the shelf list that represent the call numbers/subject areas that support the activity.

2. Estimate the number of titles in the sections of the shelf list you marked. Measure the number of cards in the marked section. If the cards measure less than one inch, count all of the cards in the section. If there is more than one inch of cards in the section you marked, use the following method:

   Measure one inch of cards.

   Count the number of cards in that inch.

   Multiply the number of cards in one inch of cards by the total number of inches of cards (for example, 100 cards per inch × 2.75 inches = 275 cards = 275 titles).

3. If there are fewer than 100 cards in the section of the shelf list that represents titles that support the activity, use the Tally Sheet portion of this workform to tally the copyright date for all of the titles in that section.

4. If there are more than 100 cards in the section of the shelf list that represents titles that support the activity, you can tally the copyright dates for a sampling of those cards. The recommended sample size for all but the very largest collections is 100 titles. To determine the sample, divide the number of cards in the section of the shelf list you are evaluating by 100. (For example, if there are 600 cards in the section of the shelf list being evaluated, divide 600 by 100. Based on the example, you would tally the copyright date for every sixth card in the portion of the shelf list under review.)

Factors to Consider When Completing Workform C12

1. Age is determined by the copyright date of the item.

2. Complete a copy of the workform for each activity for which you checked the "Age: Copyright—Print" box on Workform C1.

3. If the library has multiple units, complete a copy of the workform for each unit. Then create a summary copy of the workform that shows the entire library's resources.

4. If you are collecting this data through sampling, it may be worth the effort to gather the data required to make comparisons (rows H, I, and J).

5. Do not enter data in the shaded sections.

To Complete Workform C12

1. **Column A** In the numbered rows, indicate the specific sections of the collection that you have determined support the activity under review. Be sure to put both the call number and the subject area in this box because the workform may be used by people who are not familiar with the call number.

2. **Columns B–D** Enter the numbers in the appropriate spaces. See "Source(s) of Data for Workform C12" if you need more information on how to find the data.

3. **Column E** Add the numbers for each row and record the total in column E.

4. **Row F** Add the numbers for each column (B–E) and enter the totals in row F.

5. **Row G** Determine the percent of the titles supporting this activity that fall into each of the three age categories. Divide the number in row F for each age category (columns B–D) by the number in row F column E. (For example, if 150 titles are less than five years old, 275 titles were published between five and ten years ago, and 175 titles are more than ten years old, you have a total of 600 titles. To calculate the percent of titles less than five years old, divide 150 by 600 to determine that 25% of the titles supporting the activity are less than five years old [150 ÷ 600 = .25 = 25%].)

(Continued)

WORKFORM C12 **Age: Copyright—Print (Cont.)**

Factors to Consider When Reviewing the Data on Workform C12

1. Is the percent of newer materials available in the subject areas under review greater than that of the portion of the collection used for comparison?

2. Do the materials in the sections of the collections under review contain information that becomes dated quickly?

3. Do library users often request that the library obtain newer materials through interlibrary loan in the subject areas under review? (See Workform C9: Document Delivery for more information on interlibrary loan.)

4. What is the condition of the older volumes in the portion of the collections under review? Often older volumes show significant signs of wear. (See Workform C16: Worn or Damaged—Print for more information on condition.)

6. **Row H** Determine what portion of the collection you want to use as the basis of comparison. In most cases, this will be the part of the collection you indicated in the "Collection" section at the top of the workform. Use your automated system to determine the total number of titles in each age group in this comparison portion of the collection and enter that number in the appropriate boxes in row H.

7. **Row I** Determine the percent of the portion of the collection used for comparison that falls into each of the three age categories by dividing each number in row H, columns B–D, by the number in row H column E.

8. **Row J** Determine the difference between the percent of titles in each of the three age categories that support the activity under review and the percent of the titles in the three categories in the portion of the collection used for comparison by subtracting the percents in row G from the percents in row I (I − G).

WORKFORM C12 Age: Copyright—Print

Activity _____

Collection All _____ Adult _____ Juvenile _____ YA _____

Month/year data collected _____

Library unit _____

| A. Call Number/Subject Area | Print Titles (including microforms) | | | E. Total Titles |
	B. Less Than 5 Years	C. 5–10 Years	D. More Than 10 Years	
1.				
2.				
3.				
4.				
5.				
6.				
7.				
8.				
9.				
10.				
F. Number of titles supporting activity				
G. Percent of titles supporting activity	%	%	%	
H. Total number of titles in the portion of the collection used for comparison				
I. Percent of titles in the portion of the collection used for comparison	%	%	%	
J. Difference (+ or −)	%	%	%	

Completed by _____

Source of data _____

Date completed _____

Library _____

Subject area/call number _____

Less Than 5 Years Old	5–10 Years Old	More Than 10 Years Old

Completed by _____ Date completed _____

Source of data _____ Library _____

WORKFORM C13 Age: Copyright—Media

Instructions

Purpose of Workform C13

Use this workform to record information about the age of the media titles in your collection that support the activity under review.

Source(s) of Data for Workform C13

You may be able to get this copyright date information from the library's automated circulation system. If the library does not have an automated system or can't get the data from the system, you can determine the age of the titles in the collection that support the activity using the shelf list.

1. Mark the beginning and ending of the sections in the shelf list that represent the call numbers/subject areas that support your activity.

2. Estimate the number of titles in the sections of the shelf list you marked. Measure the cards in the marked section. If the cards measure less than one inch, count all of the cards in the section. If there is more than one inch of cards in the section you marked, use the following method:

   Measure one inch of cards.

   Count the number of cards in that inch.

   Multiply the number of cards in one inch of cards by the total number of inches of cards (for example, 100 cards per inch × 2.75 inches = 275 cards = 275 titles).

3. If there are fewer than 100 cards in the section of the shelf list that represents titles that support the activity, use the Tally Sheet portion of this workform to tally the copyright date for all of the titles in that section.

4. If there are more than 100 cards in the section of the shelf list that represents titles that support the activity, you can tally the copyright dates for a sampling of those cards. The recommended sample size for all but the very largest collections is 100 titles. To determine the sample, divide the number of cards in the section of the shelf list you are evaluating by 100. (For example, if there are 600 cards in the section of the shelf list being evaluated, divide 600 by 100. Based on the example, you would tally the copyright date for every sixth card in the portion of the shelf list under review.)

Factors to Consider When Completing Workform C13

1. Age is determined by the copyright date of the item.

2. Complete a copy of the workform for each activity for which you checked the "Age: Copyright—Media" box on Workform C1.

3. If the library has multiple units, complete a copy of the workform for each unit. Then create a summary copy of the workform that shows the entire library's resources.

4. If you are collecting this data through sampling, it may be worth the effort to gather the data required to make comparisons (rows H, I, and J).

5. Do not enter data in the shaded sections.

To Complete Workform C13

1. **Column A** In the numbered rows, indicate the specific sections of the collection that you have determined support the activity under review. Be sure to put both the call number and the subject area in this box because the workform may be used by people who are not familiar with the call number.

2. **Columns B–D** Enter the numbers in the appropriate spaces. See "Source(s) of Data for Workform C13" if you need more information on where to find the data you need.

3. **Column E** Add the numbers for each row within each media grouping and record the total in column E for each type of media.

4. **Row F** Add the numbers for each column (B–E) and enter the totals in row F.

5. **Row G** Determine the percent of the titles supporting this activity that fall into each of the age categories. Divide the number in row F by the number in column E of row F for each type of media. (For example, if 150 videos are less than five old, 275 videos were published between five and ten years ago, and 175 videos are more than ten years old, you have a total of 600 videos. To calculate the percent of videos less than five years old, divide 150 by 600 to determine that 25% of the videos supporting the activity are less than five years old [150 ÷ 600 = .25 = 25%].)

(Continued)

Instructions

6. **Row H**   Determine what portion of the collection you want to use as the basis of your comparison. In most cases, this will be the part of the collection you indicated in the "Collection" section at the top of the workform. Use your automated system to determine the total number of titles in each age group in that comparison portion of the collection and enter that number in the appropriate boxes in row H.

7. **Row I**   Determine the percent of the portion of the collection used for comparison that falls into each of the three categories. See the direction for row G for more information on calculating percents.

8. **Row J**   Determine the difference between the percent of titles in each of the three age categories that support the activity under review and the percent of the titles in the three categories in the portion of the collection used for comparison by subtracting the percentage numbers in row G from the percentage numbers in row I.

Factors to Consider When Reviewing the Data on Workform C13

1. Do the media items in the sections of the collections under review contain information that becomes dated quickly?

2. Does the collection contain popular titles that lose their appeal as new titles become available?

3. What is the condition of the older items in the portion of the collections under review? Often older media items show significant signs of wear. (See Workform C17: Worn or Damaged—Media for more information on condition.)

Activity _____

Month/year data collected _____

Collection All _____ Adult _____ Juvenile _____ YA _____

Library unit _____

Media Titles

A. Call Number/Subject Area	B. Video				C. Audio				D. Other			
	Less Than 5 Years	5–10 Years	More Than 10 Years	E. Total Titles	Less Than 5 Years	5–10 Years	More Than 10 Years	E. Total Titles	Less Than 5 Years	5–10 Years	More Than 10 Years	E. Total Titles
1.												
2.												
3.												
4.												
5.												
6.												
7.												
8.												
9.												
10.												
F. Number of titles supporting activity												
G. Percent of titles supporting activity	%	%	%		%	%	%		%	%	%	
H. Total number of titles in the portion of the collection used for comparison												
I. Percent of titles in the portion of the collection used for comparison	%	%	%		%	%	%		%	%	%	
J. Difference (+ or –)	%	%	%		%	%	%		%	%	%	

Completed by _____

Source of data _____

Date completed _____

Library _____

Age: Copyright—Media Tally Sheet

Subject area/call number _____

Less Than 5 Years Old	5-10 Years Old	More Than 10 Years Old

Completed by _____ Date completed _____

Source of data _____ Library _____

Purpose of Workform C14

Use this workform to record information about the coverage of the print and microform periodical titles that support the activity under review.

Source(s) of Data for Workform C14

1. The library's periodical holding records provide the data needed to complete this workform.

2. If you completed Workform C3 for the activity under review, you will find the data you need in column C of that workform. If you have not completed that workform, you will need to do so before completing Workform C14.

Factors to Consider When Completing Workform C14

1. *Coverage* is defined as "the number of years a particular periodical title is available."

2. Complete a copy of the workform for each activity for which you checked the "Age: Periodicals—Print and Microform" column on Workform C1.

3. If the library has multiple units, complete a copy of the workform for each unit. Then create a summary copy of the workform that shows the entire library's resources.

To Complete Workform C14

1. **Column A**   In the numbered rows, list the periodical titles in the collection that support the activity under review.

   If you have more than fifteen titles that support the activity, use a second copy of the workform.

   If there are too many titles to list, you might wish to group these titles by years of coverage and count the number of titles in each group. (For example, the library has five years of coverage for ten business periodicals.)

2. **Columns B–D**   Enter the numbers in the appropriate columns. See "Source(s) of Data for Workform C14" if you need more information on where to find the data required.

3. **Column E**   Calculate the total coverage in years for each title. Remember to subtract any missing years.

Factors to Consider When Reviewing the Data on Workform C14

1. What is the coverage of the periodicals under review? Are there significant breaks in coverage (months or years for which there are no holdings)?

2. Does the library purchase the periodicals under review in more than one format (print, microform, electronic)? If so, why? If not, should that option be considered?

3. Does the library maintain the same coverage for all of the periodicals in the subject areas under review? If yes, is that necessary or desirable? If no, why not?

WORKFORM C14 Age: Periodicals—Print and Microform

Activity _____

Collection All _____ Adult _____ Juvenile _____ YA _____

Month/year data collected _____

Library unit _____

A. Titles	B. Beginning Year	C. Ending Year	D. Missing Years (if any)	E. Total Coverage
1.				
2.				
3.				
4.				
5.				
6.				
7.				
8.				
9.				
10.				
11.				
12.				
13.				
14.				
15.				

Completed by _____ Date completed _____

Source of data _____ Library _____

WORKFORM C15   Age: Periodicals—Electronic

Instructions

Purpose of Workform C15

Use this workform to record information about the coverage and timelines of the electronic periodical titles that support the activity under review.

Source(s) of Data for Workform C15

1. Vendor(s) from whom you lease or purchase electronic periodicals should be able to provide the data needed to complete this workform.

2. If you completed Workform C4 for the activity under review, you will find the data you need for column B on that workform. If you have not completed that workform, you will need to do so before completing Workform C15.

Factors to Consider When Completing Workform C15

1. *Coverage* is defined as "the number of years a particular periodical title is available." *Timeliness* is measured by the frequency with which an electronic database is updated.

2. Occasionally a database may provide different coverage for different titles. If so, enter in column A the different titles that support the activity. Leave column B blank, and complete the rest of the workform according to the instructions.

3. Complete a copy of the workform for each activity for which you checked the "Age: Periodicals—Electronic" column on Workform C1.

4. If the library has multiple units, complete a copy of the workform for each unit. Then create a summary copy of the workform that shows the entire library's resources.

To Complete Workform C15

1. **Column A**   In the numbered rows, list the library's databases that provide access to one or more periodicals supporting the activity under review. If there are more than twelve databases, use a second copy of the form.

2. **Columns B–D**   Enter the numbers in the appropriate rows. See "Source(s) of Data for Workform C15" if you need more information on where to find the data.

3. **Column E**   Calculate the total coverage for each title.

Factors to Consider When Reviewing the Data on Workform C15

1. Is timeliness an important factor in the subject areas under review? (For example, it might be less important to update children's periodical holdings than to update scientific journals or new magazines.)

2. How current is the data being added to the electronic resources with each update? If the resource is updated daily, is it with today's or yesterday's data? If the resource is updated weekly, monthly, or quarterly, what is the cut-off point for data incorporated in the update? How long after the cut-off point does the library receive the product?

3. Do the years of coverage for electronic resources change between editions of the product, or are the years of coverage changed from time to time on the Web site? Do library managers have any say in the years of coverage available to patrons, or do they accept whatever the vendor is currently offering?

WORKFORM C15 Age: Periodicals—Electronic

Activity _____

Month/year data collected _____

Collection All _____ Adult _____ Juvenile _____ YA _____ Library unit _____

A. Database	B. Number of Titles in Database That Support Activity	C. Timeliness Frequency of Updates	D. Coverage Beginning Year	D. Coverage Latest Year	E. Total Coverage
1.					
2.					
3.					
4.					
5.					
6.					
7.					
8.					
9.					
10.					
11.					
12.					

Completed by _____ Date completed _____

Source of data _____ Library _____

Purpose of Workform C16

Use this workform to record information about the condition of the print items including microforms in the collection that support the activity under review.

Source(s) of Data for Workform C16

The only way to get this information is to look at the actual books or microforms. Follow these instructions to determine the condition of the items in a specific portion of the collection.

1. For the items in the collection that are on the shelves:

   Go to the shelves housing the items in the portion on the collection you are reviewing.

   Evaluate the condition of each book on the shelf and mark the Tally Sheet for Workform C16 in the appropriate column.

2. If the section of the collection being reviewed is very large (more than 100 items), evaluate a *sample* of the collection rather than the entire collection.

   First determine the sample size. Your base sample size should be 100 items. However, this is a judgment call and depends on the size of the collection under review. You might decide to look at every fifth book, at every other shelf, or (in very large collections) at one shelf in each range.

   See "Factors to Consider When Completing Workform C16" to determine the condition of the books in your sample that are not checked out, and record your findings on the Tally Sheet for Workform C16.

   Determine the approximate percent of the items on the shelf included in the sample. (For example, if you evaluated every fifth book, you included about 20% of the collection in the sample. If you evaluated all of the books on every other shelf, on the other hand, you included 50% of the collection in your sample.)

3. For the items in the collection that are circulating during the sample period:

   During the circulation period following the day(s) you evaluated the items in a specific section of the collection, place items from that portion of the collection on a separate book truck as they are checked in.

   To determine the number of books to evaluate that were checked out during the time you did the sample, use the sample size (see item 2, above). If your sample included 20% of the collection being reviewed, you will eval-

uate every fifth book on the book truck. Don't worry if you have few returned materials; this just means you evaluated most of the collection during your initial efforts.

Use the Tally Sheet for Workform C16 to record the condition of the items being checked in.

Factors to Consider When Completing Workform C16

1. Condition is determined by inspecting these items. See figure 10 in the text for more instructions.

   excellent: mint condition; looks new

   good: shows light wear; has plastic jacket, clean pages, no marks

   fair: shows considerable wear; has plastic jacket, unbroken spine, yellowed or lightly marked pages, minor damage to cover, etc.

   very worn/damaged: shows extensive wear or is damaged; has no plastic jacket; has broken spine, torn or heavily marked pages, etc.

2. Complete a copy of the workform for each activity for which you checked the "Condition: Worn or Damaged—Print" column on Workform C1.

3. If the library has multiple units, complete a copy of the workform for each unit. Then create a summary copy of the workform that shows the entire library's resources.

4. Do not enter data in the shaded sections.

To Complete Workform C16

1. **Column A** In the numbered rows above the double line, indicate the specific sections of the collection that support the activity under review. Be sure to put both the call number and the subject area in this column because the workform may be used by people who are not familiar with the call number.

2. **Columns B–E** Enter the numbers (from the tally sheets, if used, for items on the shelf and for items in circulation) in the appropriate columns. See "Source(s) of Data for Workform C16" if you need more information on where to find the data.

3. **Column F** Add the numbers across each row, and record the total in column F.

4. **Row G** Add the numbers in columns B–F, and enter the totals in row G.

(Continued)

Instructions

5. **Row H**   Determine the percent of the items supporting this activity that fall into each of the four condition categories by dividing the number in row G for each column, B–E, by the number in row G, column F. (For example, if 50 items are in excellent condition, 250 items are in good condition, 150 items are in fair condition, and 50 items are in very worn/damaged condition, you have a total of 500 items. To calculate the percent of items in very worn/damaged condition, divide 50 by 500 to determine that 10% of the items supporting the activity are in very poor or damaged condition [50 ÷ 500 = .10 = 10%].)

6. **Rows I–K**   The data below the double lines will help you determine how the condition of the items that support the activity under review compares with the condition of items in other parts of the collection.

   Row I   Determine what portion of the collection you want to use as the basis of your comparison. In most cases, this will be the part of the collection you indicated in the "Collection" section at the top of the workform. You will have to determine the condition of the items in this portion of the collection. To do that, use the same sampling process described in "Source(s) of Data for Workform C16" and enter the total number of items in each condition group in the appropriate columns in row I.

   Row J   Determine the percent of the portion of the collection used for comparison that falls into each of the four categories. (See the directions for row H for more information on calculating percents.)

   Row K   Determine the difference between the percent of items in each of the four condition categories that support the activity under review and the percent of the items in the four condition categories in the portion of the collection used for comparison by subtracting the percentage numbers in row H from the percentage numbers in row J.

Factors to Consider When Reviewing the Data on Workform C16

1. Are the materials in the subject areas under review usually selected through browsing, or are they selected as the result of a search in the library catalog?

2. Should the worn or damaged items in the subject areas under review be replaced with new copies of the same items or with different, more-current items? Are the worn or damaged materials that you want to replace with new copies still in print?

3. Can the items under review that are in "good" or "fair" condition be easily repaired? Will they be more attractive to the user if such repairs are made? (Remember, some repairs reduce the attractiveness of materials.)

WORKFORM C16 **Condition: Worn or Damaged—Print**

Activity _____

Collection All _____ Adult _____ Juvenile _____ YA _____

Month/year data collected _____

Library unit _____

A. Call Number/Subject Area	B. Excellent	C. Good	D. Fair	E. Very Worn/Damaged	F. Total Titles
1.					
2.					
3.					
4.					
5.					
6.					
7.					
8.					
9.					
10.					
G. Number of titles supporting activity					
H. Percent of titles supporting activity	%	%	%	%	
I. Total number of titles in the portion of the collection used for comparison					
J. Percent of titles in the portion of the collection used for comparison	%	%	%	%	
K. Difference (+ or –)	%	%	%	%	

Completed by _____

Source of data _____

Date completed _____

Library _____

Condition: Worn and Damaged—Print
Tally Sheet

Subject area/call number _____

Excellent	Good	Fair	Very Worn/Damaged

Completed by _____   Date completed _____

Source of data _____   Library _____

Purpose of Workform C17

Use this workform to record information about the condition of the media items in your collection that support the activity under review.

Source(s) of Data for Workform C17

The only way to get this information is to look at the actual media items. Follow these instructions to determine the condition of the media items in a specific portion of the collection.

1. For the items in the collection that are on the shelves:

   Go to the shelves housing the items in the portion of the collection you are reviewing.

   Evaluate the condition of each media item on the shelf and mark the Tally Sheet for Workform C17 in the appropriate column.

2. If the section of the collection being reviewed is very large (more than 100 items), evaluate a *sample* of the collection rather than the entire collection.

   First determine the sample size. Your base sample size should be 100 items. However, this is a judgment call and depends on the size of the collection under review. You might decide to look at every fifth media item, at every other shelf, or (in very large collections) at one shelf in each range.

   See "Factors to Consider When Completing Workform C17" to determine the condition of the items in your sample that are not checked out, and record your findings on the Tally Sheet portion of Workform C17.

   Determine the approximate percent of the items on the shelf included in the sample. (For example, if you evaluated every fifth item, you included about 20% of the collection in the sample. If you evaluated all of the items on every other shelf, on the other hand, you included 50% of the collection in your sample.)

3. For the items in the collection that are circulating during the sample period:

   During the circulation period following the day(s) you evaluated the items in a specific section of the collection, place items from that portion of the collection on a separate book truck as they are checked in.

   Use the sample size (see item 2, above) to determine how many of the items (that were checked out during the time you did the sample) to evaluate. If your sample included 20% of the collection being reviewed, you will eval-

uate every fifth item on the book truck. Don't worry if you have few returned materials; this just means you evaluated most of the collection during your initial efforts.

Use the Tally Sheet for Workform C17 to record the condition of the items being checked in.

Factors to Consider When Completing Workform C17

1. Condition is determined by inspecting the item. See figure 10 in the text for more information.

   excellent: like new.

   good: all parts available and in good working order; software loads and runs under the intended operating system; all supporting documentation, booklets, etc. are complete; cases and display bags may be showing slight wear but remain usable

   fair: shows wear, but still operational; all parts are available; audio and visual tapes may need cleaning; cases and display bags need replacing or repair; supporting documentation may have torn or missing pages

   very worn/damaged: sound or visual quality diminished or distorted

2. Complete a copy of the workform for each activity for which you checked the "Condition: Worn and Damaged Items—Media" column on Workform C1.

3. If the library has multiple units, complete a copy of Workform C17 for each unit. Then create a summary copy of the workform that shows the entire library's resources.

4. Do not enter data in the shaded sections.

To Complete Workform C17

1. **Column A**   In the numbered rows above the double line, indicate the specific sections of the collection that support the activity under review. Be sure to put both the call number and the subject area in this column because the workform may be used by people who are not familiar with the call number.

2. **Sections B–D**   Enter the numbers (from the tally sheets, if used, for items on the shelf and for items in circulation) in the appropriate rows. See "Source(s) of Data for Workform C17" if you need more information on where to find the data you need.

(Continued)

Instructions

3. **Column E**   Within each media grouping, add the numbers for the rows, and record the sum in column E for each type of media.

4. **Row F**   Add the numbers for each column, B–E, and enter the totals in row F.

5. **Row G**   Determine the percent of the items supporting this activity that fall into the condition categories. Divide the numbers in row F for each type of media by the number in Row F, column E. (For example, if 50 video items are in excellent condition, 250 video items are in good condition, 150 items are in fair condition, and 50 items are in very worn/damaged condition, you have a total of 500 video items. To calculate the percent of videos in very poor/damaged condition, divide 50 by 500 to determine that 10% of the video items supporting this activity are in very poor or damaged condition [50 ÷ 500 = .10 = 10%].)

6. **Rows H–J**   The data below the double lines will help you determine how the condition of the items that support the activity under review compares with the condition of media items in other parts of the collection.

   Row H   Determine what portion of the collection you want to use as the basis of your comparison. In most cases, this will be the part of the collection you indicated in the "Collection" section at the top of the workform. Enter the total number of items in each condition group in that portion of the collection in the appropriate columns in row H.

   Row I   Determine the percent of the portion of the collection used for comparison that falls into each of the categories. (See the directions for row G for more information on calculating percents.)

   Row J   Determine the difference between the percent of items in each of the four condition categories that support the activity under review and the percent of items in the four condition categories in the portion of the collection used for comparison by subtracting the percentage numbers in row G from the percentage numbers in row I.

Factors to Consider When Reviewing the Data on Workform C17

1. Are the materials in the subject areas under review usually selected through browsing, or are they selected as the result of a search in the library catalog?

2. Should the worn or damaged items in the subject areas under review be replaced with new copies of the same items or with different, more-current items? Are the worn or damaged materials that you want to replace with new copies still available?

3. Can the items under review that are in "good" or "fair" condition be easily repaired? Will they be more attractive to the users if such repairs are made?

WORKFORM C17 Condition: Worn or Damaged—Media

Activity _____

Collection All _____ Adult _____ Juvenile _____ YA _____

Month/year data collected _____

Library unit _____

A. Call Number/ Subject Area	B. Video					C. Audio					D. Other (software, etc.)				
	Excellent	Good	Fair	Very Worn/ Damaged	E. Total	Excellent	Good	Fair	Very Worn/ Damaged	E. Total	Excellent	Good	Fair	Very Worn/ Damaged	E. Total
1.															
2.															
3.															
4.															
5.															
6.															
7.															
8.															
F. Number of items supporting activity															
G. Percent of items supporting activity	%	%	%	%		%	%	%	%		%	%	%	%	
H. Total number of items in the portion of the collection used for comparison															
I. Percent of items in the portion of the collection used for comparison	%	%	%	%		%	%	%	%		%	%	%	%	
J. Difference (+ or –)	%	%	%	%		%	%	%	%		%	%	%	%	

Completed by _____

Source of data _____

Date completed _____

Library _____

Condition: Worn or Damaged—Media Tally Sheet

Subject area/call number _____

Excellent	Good	Fair	Very Worn/Damaged

Completed by _____ Date completed _____

Source of data _____ Library _____

Chapter 4

Managing Your Library's Facilities

MILESTONES

By the time you finish this chapter you will know how to

- understand the relationship between activities to be performed and the facilities required to perform them

- determine what facilities the library currently has and how those facilities are being used

- determine what facilities the library needs to support its goals and objectives

- make plans to reallocate space in facilities to support the library's goals, objectives, and activities

Virtually every service a library staff offers will both affect and be affected by the library's facilities. Collections require shelving or storage. Programs require space for public seating as well as space to store equipment and supplies. Many services that people use in library buildings require places for the public to sit and work; those, in turn, require environmental controls such as heat and air-conditioning. Technology-based services require electricity and data cabling. Even electronic services intended for off-site users will affect the library's facilities. At the very least, electronic services require the space and electrical power needed to operate a server and data cabling for a telecommunications connection. The staff who support all of these services also have facilities requirements in both public and private work areas as well as places for breaks and meals.

Changes in library priorities probably require changes in the way in which library facilities are currently used. Most libraries are unable to make major changes to existing buildings every time new priorities are identified or new services are initiated. Adding on a room or undertaking a major remodeling project to support changing services is usually not an option. Instead, you will probably change the way existing facilities are used. For instance, you might decide to reduce the amount of shelving for books so that you can increase the amount of shelving available for video or audio materials. You may make room for more public access PCs by converting some of the furniture in the reference area from tables to PC carrels. If Internet training is to be an important new service, you might reconfigure the public meeting rooms to provide data cabling, more electricity, and a digital projector to support that training.

This chapter will help you think about the facilities implications of the library's chosen service responses/priorities and activities. Each library's facility issues are unique. The workforms included here can provide some general space-planning guidelines, but only you can determine how those guidelines should be applied to the library's present facilities. In essence, these workforms provide a starting place for the review of your existing facilities. Where you go and what data you need to collect beyond that starting point will be determined solely by local conditions.

Considering Facilities as a Resource

The term *facility* as used here means "the space and furnishings needed to support the library's service priorities." The definition encompasses space allocation, furniture, equipment (other than computer equipment, which is addressed in the following chapter), shelving, requirements to meet the standards set forth in the Americans with Disabilities Act (ADA), lighting, heating and air-conditioning, electricity, and data cabling needed for technology-based services. All such facility considerations will have an impact on the success of library services.

When library staff begin to plan for a new library facility, the first step is to identify the programs and services that will be offered from that building. The architect then uses those program descriptions to design spaces that will support the library's service responses/priorities. In most cases, new library buildings are functional and spacious. They truly support the staff in their efforts to serve the public. However, as time goes on, library priorities shift. The audiences the library serves change, new tools become available to serve those audiences, and the services and programs the library provides evolve. The building, once a close match for the services, becomes less functional. However, most library staff take the physical spaces in which they work for granted. Staff are far more likely to try to "make do" in an inadequate facility than they are with inadequate staff, collections, or technology.

Actually, in many cases staff can no longer actually "see" the facility they work in at all. Familiarity has the effect of making the environment largely invisible. Humorist Erma Bombeck once wrote that if someone in the family leaves a sock on the mantle and it isn't moved in a week or so, no one in the family will see it any more. It will become a part of the expected landscape. Certainly, one sees this "sock on the mantle" situation in public libraries across the country. There are libraries with dead plants scattered about, with magazines and newspapers stacked in the corners, with supplies piled haphazardly behind service desks, and with paper signs curling with age and covered with graffiti. These things may become invisible to staff through long exposure, but they are very visible to the public. They send a message to library users that this library is not organized or efficient, and they create a less than welcoming environment.

Although it is often done unconsciously, every library also signals to the public and the staff what services are considered to be most important by the amount and type of facility support devoted to each service. A bright, cheerful children's room with child-sized furniture, comfortable places for parents and children to sit together, and plenty of materials storage low enough to be accessible to children tells users that library services to children matter. By contrast, a young adult area that is nothing more than a range or two of shelving or a couple of paperback racks tucked in the back of the adult fiction area does not invite teens to use the library and its services. Thus, it sends a clear message that the library places a low priority on serving teenagers.

The intent of this chapter is to stimulate thinking about what facilities resources will be required to support the library's planned activities and how the current facility might be reconfigured to provide that support. You and your colleagues are encouraged to use the information in this chapter with two workforms from the *Planning for Results* process. The Current Resource Allocation Chart Workform can be used to organize information about how the library facilities are currently being used. (See appendix E.) The Gap Analysis Workform (appendix B) provides a process to help answer three basic questions:

- amount of space needed to accomplish the library's service responses/priorities
- furnishings needed to accomplish the library's service responses/priorities
- lighting/environmental requirements to accomplish the library's service responses/priorities

As you work with these two workforms and the workforms included at the end of this chapter, you will consider such factors as the square footage of space devoted to various programs and services including shelving, meeting rooms, individual study spaces, and computer laboratories. You will probably calculate the linear feet of shelving allocated for certain parts of the collection and the capacity of specialized shelving for materials such as CD-ROMs. You may count the number of seats available for people to work in the library or the number of comfortable chairs available for recreational readers. An inventory of the equipment the library owns (video players, audio players, microtext readers, photocopiers, etc.) or loans will provide another indication of the facilities available to support some service responses/priorities.

Once the current allocation is determined, you will identify facilities required to accomplish the priorities in the library's service plan. Finally you will identify the gap between the available facilities and the facilities that are required to accomplish the library's service responses/priorities. Knowing that you need more, or different, space or furnishings isn't enough. Most libraries don't have the option of adding space; they have to live within the boundary of existing walls. Even adding furniture, additional storage space for new formats of materials, or expanding collections of existing formats can be problematic. For many libraries, reallocation of existing space, furnishings, and shelving will be the key to supporting the library's service responses/priorities.

Collecting Data

The six workforms at the end of this chapter will help quantify the capacity of your facilities and determine the facilities implications of the technology decisions you have made. These workforms are listed in figure 12. The workforms are divided into four groups.

The first workform, F1, will help you determine what aspects of the library facility will be affected by the activities that support the library's service responses/priorities. Once you have decided what areas are likely to be affected, use the appropriate workforms to gather the data required.

The next group of workforms is concerned with capacity issues. You can use copies of Workforms F2 through F4 to record both current capacity and desired capacity. It is not necessary to inventory every item listed on the forms. You will list only those items that are relevant to the planned activities. Workform F2 will help you determine the number of feet of shelving or storage devoted to materials supporting various activities. Workform F3 will help you inventory and assess the condition of the furnishings and equipment that may be needed to achieve specific library activities. Workform F4 can be used to record information about capacity of public spaces and to assess the suitability of those spaces to accomplish the activities under review. Workform F5 focuses on utilization and is used to determine how the library's public spaces are currently used. The last workform, F6, deals with technology issues. It can be used to help determine the facilities implications of the library's technology decisions. Note, however, that you may want to complete some workforms from the technology chapter in conjunction with this workform.

FIGURE 12

Facilities Workforms Summary

Workform	Title	Purpose
		OVERVIEW
F1	What's Important?	To determine what data is needed to complete the gap analysis process
		CAPACITY
F2	Materials Storage	To assess the storage space available to house materials to support intended activities
F3	Equipment and Furniture	To inventory the equipment and furniture the library has to support intended activities and to indicate the condition of the furniture and equipment
F4	Space	To assess the capacity of the spaces in the library that support specific activities
		UTILIZATION
F5	Space	To assess the utilization of spaces in the library that support specific activities
		TECHNOLOGY
F6	Facility Requirements	To assess the impact of technology on the library's facilities used for an activity

General guidelines for the space needed to support various types of furniture and functions are not included in this chapter. The following references are good space-planning tools that can provide that type of information.

Brawner, Lee B., and Donald K. Beck Jr. *Determining Your Public Library's Future Size: A Needs Assessment & Planning Model.* Chicago: American Library Assn., 1996.

Dahlgren, Anders C. *Planning the Small Library Facility.* Chicago: American Library Assn., 1996.

————. *Public Library Space Needs: A Planning Outline/1998.* Madison, Wisc.: Wisconsin Department of Public Instruction, 1998.

Dancik, Deborah, and Emelie J. Shroder, eds. *Building Blocks for Library Space: Functional Guidelines—1995.* Chicago: Library Administration and Management Assn., 1995.

Issues to Consider When Making Facilities Decisions

Five key elements should be considered when evaluating existing facilities and making decisions about how to reallocate those facilities to support specific service responses/priorities:

- capacity of facilities to support library service responses/priorities
- ways in which existing facilities are being utilized
- condition of the facilities
- effect of technology on facilities
- ways in which facilities can be changed to better support service responses/priorities

Capacity of Existing Library Facilities

The capacity of a library's facilities refers to the ability of the facility to physically house and support the space and equipment needed to achieve the library service responses/priorities. In the past decade considerable debate has centered around the need for library buildings in the future. Some people state that the proliferation of electronic information means that soon we won't need library buildings at all. We will all use a virtual library in cyberspace. In fact, the opposite seems to be happening. The proliferation of electronic information has led to an increase in the number of people who use libraries, not a decrease. Even though many library users are connecting with library resources electronically from off-site, most library services are still delivered in specific buildings. Therefore, it continues to be necessary to consider the capacity of each building or specific area within a building where the activities connected with the selected service responses/priorities will be provided.

Capacity includes such elements as the linear feet of shelving available; the square footage of public and staff work space; the number of seats in meeting rooms, at study tables, and in individual study or PC carrels; and the number of casual seats for adults and children. It may also include the number of photocopy machines or parking spaces available, the amount of exhibit space or the number of display racks, the number of audio and video players available for use by the public, and even whether the library provides kitchen facilities for selected events.

Each of the service responses presented in *Planning for Results* included specific information about the resources that might be required to accomplish that service response. Figure 13 is a composite list of facility recommendations for the thirteen service responses/priorities. If you look at the actual facilities recommendations for specific service responses in *Planning for Results* you will find that some require many more facilities than others do. For example, the recommended facilities support for Cultural Awareness is both more extensive and more expensive than the facilities support suggested for Current Topics and Titles. That does not automatically mean, however, that it is going to be less expensive to support the activities associated with Current Topics and Titles because much of the expense for Current Topics and Titles will be for collection resources.

FIGURE 13
Facility Requirements for Service Responses/Priorities

Activity room	Kiosks	Sound system
Adaptive technologies equipment	Kitchen facilities/catering space	Storage cabinets
Audio players	Meeting rooms	Study rooms
Bulletin board	Microtext reader	Tables
Classroom	Parking space	Vault—climate controlled
Coffee bar or restaurant	Performance space	Vehicles
Comfortable chairs	Phones	Video conferencing facility
Computer laboratory	Photocopy machine	Video players
Display racks	Seats	Video production equipment
Exhibit space	Shelving	
Fax machine	Signage—multilingual if needed	

Figure 13 provides you with a starting point as you consider how to balance the facilities requirements of the library's service responses/priorities. The list in figure 13 is suggestive rather than prescriptive. If there are other facilities resources you can identify that are not included in figure 13, be sure to include them in your assessment. If all the library's service responses/priorities require many more facilities resources than the library is likely to obtain in the near future, then the service choices may need to be reconsidered in light of financial realities.

ADA Requirements

The Americans with Disabilities Act (ADA), passed in 1990, requires libraries to accommodate the access requirements of all users. When considering the capacity of the existing library facilities, you will want to assess the level of compliance with ADA requirements. To comply with the act, library facilities that have been built or substantially remodeled since 1990 must meet the Americans with Disabilities Act Accessibility Guidelines (ADA-AG). These guidelines are available at www.access-board. gov/bfdg/adaag.htm. Library facilities built before 1990 must have a plan for providing nondiscriminatory services to all users. For more information about the Americans with Disabilities Act, refer to the ADA Web page at the United States Department of Justice (www.usdoj.gov/crt/ada/adahom1.htm). Use Workforms F2–F4 to gather data about the capacity of your current facilities.

Utilization

Understanding the library's capacity to support specific services does not provide the whole picture of your facilities. Unless you are engaged in designing a new building or have unused space or equipment in the existing building(s), all of the capacity that exists today is already being used in some way. To make informed decisions about the reallocation of existing space, you will have to know how that space is being utilized.

You will start by trying to estimate the percentage of the library facility's capacity that is being utilized to provide specific services today. The easiest and most effective way to assess capacity is to look at the activities that support the library's service responses/priorities. For example, if one of the library's priorities is to enhance cultural awareness in the community, one of your activities might be to present a series of events that highlight the contributions or history of various cultural groups in the community. To accomplish this activity you will need access to a meeting room. If you find that the library meeting room is already booked for use every night that the library is open (100 percent utilization), you will have to obtain the space you need elsewhere or change your activity. You might decide to cut back on serving some of the groups already using the meeting room, or you might decide to find alternate space for the cultural awareness programs. You might even decide to change the focus of your activity and make your presentations to various local organizations and groups rather than hosting programs in the library. On the other hand, if the meeting room is typically used only three of the five nights the library is open (60 percent utilization), you are ready to begin planning programs.

Utilization of Multipurpose Facilities

Many of the library's service responses/priorities have similar facilities requirements. For example, when you review the list of the recommended facilities resources for the service responses set forth in *Planning for Results,* you will note that a large number of facilities requirements listed in figure 13 are included in more than one service response. As you review the facilities requirements for the various service responses in *Planning for Results,* you cannot assume that they include all the facilities that might be needed to offer any given service responses. For example, all of the service responses except Commons will have shelving requirements, but shelving was only specifically listed in four of the service responses. Nor can you assume that lack of a particular facility (such as performance space) will prevent the library from offering a particular service response. There are a variety of ways to fashion a service. Each library will select its own way based on the activities identified to accomplish the service. Those activities will largely determine the facilities needed, though in some cases the facilities will influence the nature of the activity. For example, it is not realistic to plan an ethnic fair to be held in the library's parking lot if the lot is miniscule.

It is also important to remember that multipurpose facilities easily can become overused. Libraries are accustomed to stretching limited resources to "make do." Sometimes a particular resource gets stretched so thin that the resource detracts from, rather than enhances, the service it was intended to support. In considering facilities needs, remember that the library's physical capacity can be oversubscribed if you select activities that all use the same set of resources.

CASE STUDY

In earlier chapters it was noted that the Anytown Public Library is focusing on services intended to introduce children to a love of books and reading, services to the business community, services to new readers, and homework help services. The Anytown Public Library has only one meeting room and it must be used for activities that support all of these priorities.

The schedule for the meeting room on Thursday reflects the multipurpose nature of the use of the room:

9:00–10:00	Storytime for two-year-olds
10:30–11:30	Storytime for three- and four-year-olds
12:00–1:00	Staff birthday party
1:00–3:30	Literacy tutoring
3:30–6:30	Homework help volunteers
7:00–9:00	Program on investing for the small business owner

The day begins with the story programs, and the storytellers bring in their flannel boards and craft supplies. Today the program is about nature, and the two-year-olds are going to color leaves. The three- and four-year-olds are going to go out to the library yard to gather leaves and learn how to press them. At 11:30 when the story program is over, there are bits of leaves all over the room, but the storyteller is due back on the desk and doesn't have time to clean up.

The staff birthday party includes a cake and sodas. The staff clean up after themselves, but they fill the only trashcan in the room with empty glasses and gooey plates. Because the maintenance staff work at night, the trash can won't be emptied until early Friday morning.

The literacy tutors and students are a little early and have to wait for the end of the party before they can start. They are still working when the homework helpers come on duty. Students from the local junior high school are working on a difficult science unit, and they bring Internet printouts and books into the meeting room as they work. By 6:30, the homework help volunteers are exhausted and leave everything as it is to go home and start dinner for their families.

At 6:45 the speaker for the investment program arrives and finds a room that needs to be vacuumed, a full trash can, and tables covered with papers and books. This is not the impression the library staff want to give to business leaders in their community. However, the tight scheduling of the room made this situation almost inevitable.

Best Use of Facilities

When reviewing utilization of facilities you will want to consider "highest and best use." Is the existing space being used for those activities that are most important to library goals? Are items of minor importance taking up space simply because they occupied the space first? For example, how much shelf space and, ultimately, floor space could be freed up for other uses simply by weeding the collection? Is obsolete furniture or equipment being stored in areas that could be converted for higher and better use? Have activities that are done behind the scenes expanded to fill the space available? If any of these situations exist, you need to study how space can be rearranged or changed to meet the library's current service responses/priorities.

Access

Access is also a factor in utilization. Do users have to wait for what they consider to be unreasonable amounts of time for OPAC or Internet terminals, seats, use of the photocopier, or any other facility that is crucial to service? If so, library managers need to consider whether utilization has overwhelmed capacity for that item or facility and make some conscious decision about how to respond. Workform F5: Utilization: Space will help you gather data about the current utilization of your facilities.

Condition

The building and its furnishings create an image of the library in the minds of users. Although some users are more sensitive to their physical surroundings than are others, most users will form their first impressions of the library based on the level of cleanliness, signage, state of repair of furnishings and equipment, appropriateness of the facilities for their intended purpose, and comfort of the facilities.

Cleanliness, Organization, and Signage

Libraries are public places, and they normally have a lot of traffic. As a result, they can be difficult to keep clean and orderly. Because public desks are staffed by several different people over the course of a day or week, sometimes those spaces become stacked with the work-in-progress of each staff member. Some libraries are operating in very cramped quarters, and staff find it difficult to keep things in order because there is simply no place to put everything away. As noted earlier, sometimes staff members become so used to the way things look that they no longer really see their surroundings. It can be helpful to consciously walk through the library facility and look carefully at the physical spaces. Figure 14 suggests some things to look for in a walk-through.

As you walk through the library, pay particular attention to the signage. Many people who use public libraries are occasional users who are not familiar with how the library is organized. These users rely heavily on library signs to find what they are seeking. In some libraries, the signage is excellent, and users can find what they need with ease. In other libraries, signage is nonexistent or, even worse, inaccurate, and users can find things only if they are lucky and persistent. Signs should be clear, visible from a distance, and unambiguous. There should be no handwritten signs in a public space because even the smallest libraries have computers and printers. Signs that are not laminated tend to get dirty and stained over time. As you review the library signs, note which signs need to be replaced.

Repair and Maintenance

Activities that rely on computer terminals, fax machines, photocopiers, and audio-visual equipment must be supported by funds to keep this equipment in good operating condition or to purchase replacements. "Out of order" signs hanging on equipment send a negative message to

FIGURE 14
Library Walk-Through

Exterior

Do library grounds and exterior appearance meet or exceed community standards?

Is there a sign with the library name clearly visible from the street?

Are the library hours posted on the exterior of the building?

Is the exterior lighting adequate?

Does the lawn need mowing?

Are there weeds in the flowerbeds?

Does the building need painting?

Does the building need repair?

Is the sidewalk cracked or broken?

Is the building easily accessible to persons with disabilities?

Interior

Does the library smell musty or smoky or is there an aroma of food?

Is the entryway clean and inviting?

Are bulletins and announcements current?

Are the floors clean?

Is the main service desk easily visible from the door?

Does the main service desk present a neat, organized appearance?

Are there clear signs to help people find various library departments?

Are the restrooms clearly marked?

Are the restrooms clean and stocked with appropriate supplies?

Are all visible plants healthy?

Is artwork hung straight?

Are there stacks of newspapers or magazines in public areas?

Are surfaces dusty or dirty?

Are the walls clean and in good repair?

Are the windows clean?

Are the shelves in reasonable order?

Are book displays attractive and inviting or have they been picked over?

Are keyboards and screens clean?

If there is a kitchen facility, is it clean?

    Are there dirty dishes?

    Is there food that has not been properly disposed of?

    Does the kitchen have an odor?

users and hinder the accomplishment of the library's activities. If equipment needed for a particular activity is known to be unreliable, and if the funds for replacement or for equipment maintenance are limited, then that activity may need to be reconsidered.

Appropriateness

The condition of facilities refers to more than just their cleanliness and state of repair. You also need to give some thought to how appropriate the facilities are for their intended purpose. Who will be using the facilities? What are their expectations about the service? What limitations might those users face? For example, a meeting room intended for use by senior citizens probably should not require that they climb stairs to reach it. How "boisterous" will the use be? Preschoolers may need more sturdy furniture than older children require. What type of lighting is appropriate to the tasks to be accomplished? Are heat or air-conditioning important? Simply having the floor space to support an activity is not enough. For example, suppose you have a 12,500-square-foot building with a 500-square-foot story program area but no other public meeting room. You will find it difficult to fulfill a goal to provide space for people "to meet and interact with others in the community and to participate in public discourse about community issues" unless the story location can do double duty and provide a reasonable environment for adult usage as well. In the same vein, a 200-square-foot meeting room without data cabling or electrical service will not function as a computer lab.

Ergonomics

No one wants to experience discomfort. As you analyze the condition of the library's facilities and equipment, consider the ergonomic factors—the relationship between individuals and their physical environment. For example, will those students using the homework help center have to contend with glare on the computer monitor? Can the height of chairs in the computer lab be adjusted to accommodate both tall and short people? Are the chairs in the meeting room sufficiently padded for comfortable prolonged sitting? If people are expected to take notes, is there a flat surface on which they can write? Are the local history and genealogy buffs who are using microfilm comfortable with the illumination? Are staff who provide telephone reference equipped with headsets that allow them to move from place to place, or must they scrunch their necks to cradle the phone receiver between shoulder and ear?

Don't assume that the facilities are satisfactory. You and the staff might test them out for yourselves. Better still, ask the users about the ergonomic conditions in the library and what they find comfortable and uncomfortable. You might be surprised by the answers.

For more information on ergonomics, you might want to use an Internet search engine such as Yahoo or Alta Vista, searching under the term *ergonomics*. Several sites are devoted to the topic and include descriptions of common ergonomic problems, checklists, recommendations, and links to other online and periodical resources on ergonomics.

Impact of Technology on Facilities

These days, library managers must think not only about the life expectancy of buildings, furnishings, and equipment but also about obsolescence. In the past, most of us used something until it wore out. For some facility elements, such as roofs and carpeting, this still holds true. However, the electronic revolution has created a new situation—technological obsolescence. Think of all the equipment that has been superseded over the past few decades—film projectors, record turntables, card catalogs, and typewriters to name a few. The difference today is not that replacement is required but that things become obsolete more quickly. It doesn't matter that the computers purchased three years ago continue to operate their three-year-old software just as well as they did when new. They are now a generation or two behind the current standard and are not sufficiently powerful to run new software, and they are considered too slow and out of date for most staff and public uses.

Libraries are now expected to provide state-of-the-art equipment. At present, the public wants access to color printers and portable computer projectors. In the future, patrons will want whatever is cutting-edge. Technology changes constantly, and users expect libraries to continue to replace the old with the new. Unfortunately, replacing the old with the new often affects more than just the item to be replaced: the new item will probably require new or different furniture or electrical wiring or data cabling or lighting.

Because of this rapid pace of change, and in view of most libraries' limited funds, it may seem prudent to buy the least expensive model of equipment or furnishings. This is rarely a good decision because the least expensive model usually lacks features that users want and because its durability is probably inadequate to withstand heavy use by a variety of users. For example, a photocopier that cannot enlarge and reduce as well as make copies from books and periodicals is not up to the standard expected for top-notch service to the business community.

Advances in information technology and equipment are unlikely to slow down, and libraries are going to continue to have to spend a larger and larger portion of the library's budget on technology and equipment each year. It is a fact of life that technological change will be constant for some time and that you must plan to replace the equipment that is important to the library's service responses/priorities as it becomes outdated.

When you consider how the technology you need to accomplish the library's priorities will affect your facilities, you will want to review the library's electrical, heating, ventilation, and air-conditioning systems and its data cabling infrastructure. You will also want to consider what furniture and storage will be required. Finally, you will want to give some thought to the space needed to manage the technology—perhaps a secure server room or a staging area for handling new and repaired PCs. Each of these topics is addressed in the sections that follow. Although each topic is addressed separately, you will note that there is considerable overlap among them. For instance, the issues surrounding electricity and data cabling also affect computer furniture. To get the full picture of the effect of technology on the library's facilities, you will need to review the status of the facilities in each of these areas and then you will have to look at how effectively the areas interconnect. Workform F6 can be used to record data about the effect of technology-based activities on your facilities.

Electricity and Heating, Ventilation, and Air-Conditioning

The demands that new technologies place on electricity are many and varied. For example, every added piece of equipment will need at least one electrical outlet, and many will require two or three outlets. Furthermore, some equipment includes a transformer on the power cord that is so large that it covers more than one outlet in a duplex or quadraplex outlet. In addition, digital equipment often must be isolated on its own electrical circuit. Sharing a circuit with other devices, particularly devices with large power draws upon start-up such as photocopiers, can cause problems with the operation of computer equipment.

Separate circuits are also absolute requirements for servers and telecommunications equipment. A twenty-amp circuit will typically support four PCs. Mission-critical servers often require their own dedicated circuits and a UPS (universal power supply) to even out power fluctuations and allow time for a "graceful" shutdown of the equipment in the event of a power outage.

Remember that any major electrical upgrade will lead to an increase in the library's electric bills and budget accordingly. (Electricity is an ongoing cost item.) Whenever you are making electrical changes to a building, try to project your needs for at least the next three years. The labor involved is the primary cost element in a wiring project, so it is better to limit the number of times the work must be done.

With any major upgrade of electrical capacity or plans to dramatically increase the number of computers supported in the library, it is crucial to involve the heating, ventilation, and air-conditioning (HVAC) experts in the planning process. These experts may be library staff members, city or county employees, or outside personnel hired to assist the library staff. They will ask you to identify the types and numbers of devices to be supported as well as the intended location of those devices.

Data Cabling

Every device meant to share data with or access to another device needs data cabling to support the connection. Data cable connects terminals and PCs to the library automation system's host server, PCs to the Internet, and PCs to networked resources such as a CD server or networked printer. A small, discrete grouping of devices that "talk" only to each other and are located close together can be connected with well-managed (that is, protected in cable chases or by PVC cable covers) local data cable. More typically, you will need to have data cable run through walls, floors, or ceilings to a central "punch down block" usually located in a computer room or a telecommunications closet. In a large building the cable runs may be too long (greater than 300 feet) to comply with cabling standards and will need interim termination points to a device that boosts the signal.

As with electricity, in any data cabling project it is important to project the cabling needs for the next three to five years to avoid redoing this work. It is much less expensive to lay all the data cable at one time, especially if it is necessary to install conduit or to pull the data cables through walls or ceilings. Once the data cabling is in place, the wires can be connected as needed.

Computer Furniture

Computers, printers, and other specialized equipment have unique furniture requirements. These include mechanisms to manage wires and cables, sufficient size to hold a computer, and convenient storage for supplies. A PC carrel for the public has a larger footprint than a typical desk. It needs to include space for a monitor, a mouse, and a keyboard and space for the users to place books, purses, backpacks, etc., while still leaving room for users to write. In addition, some library technology users have special needs that require special furniture configurations.

MANAGING WIRES

Personal computers and servers are connected to each other and to worldwide networks through an amazing assortment of wires, both data cables and electrical connections. Not only is the management of these wires important for compliance with local fire and safety codes, it is critical to the long-term health and successful operation of the equipment. Libraries need to purchase specialized furniture for public and staff PCs with integral "cable chases," or housing for wire management; secure housing for CPUs; panels behind the desktop equipment to protect peripheral cables (monitor, mouse, keyboard, and printer); and network or telecommunications connections.

If one or more of the library's activities require that facilities be usable by patrons who bring in their own laptop computers, then you will need carrels or desks with built-in electrical outlets. These outlets give users access to power while keeping their laptop power cords off the floor. Adding electrical outlets to desk space enables laptop users to bring their own word processing or other applications into the library for taking notes or working on projects. At this time security concerns and support issues keep many public libraries from providing data cables for laptop users. It is entirely possible that these concerns will be addressed and resolved over time. Therefore, public furniture can also provide the option of adding plugs for network or laptop connections in the future.

PRINTERS

Printers have their own furniture and space requirements. After determining what type of printer access the library will support (one printer per workstation or networked printers), you will need to provide space and a flat surface (printer stand, tabletop, etc.) to house printers. Convenient storage is needed for supplies and paper. If this storage is not a part of the computer stand, it must be close to the printer. Faster printers that are used as networked printers are typically larger than "personal" printers and need more space. You may also need storage space for centrally printed jobs waiting to be picked up. If the library intends to use some type of cost-recovery mechanism that involves patrons queuing up for a machine or a centralized place to pick up printed materials, be sure to allow space for people to stand while waiting.

SPECIALIZED EQUIPMENT

Some activities could also involve specialized equipment for public or staff uses. These include digital scanners, digital projectors, or fax machines. Each of these devices requires a surface area to sit upon and a work area around it to hold materials. In some cases, particularly for scanning projects, staff also need a nearby "staging area" to prepare materials.

OTHER SPECIAL CONSIDERATIONS

Some planned activities may need to be conducted in private locations in the library because of the noise associated with the activity (group training, for instance) or because of privacy requirements (for adult literacy classes, for example). If the library has only one room available for such activities and that room has to be used for both technical and nontechnical events, you might consider buying computer carrels with wheels that can be moved in and out of the meeting room as needed. However, remember that you will need a place to park the carrel when it is not in use.

In public service areas you may need to plan for multiple users sharing a single device. For example, parents often want to surf the Web with their children. This ability to share a terminal will be especially important if library objectives include services to students. Group work is an important component of formal education, and you should expect that groups might want to work together on classroom projects.

Secure Server Room

Although large computer rooms with controlled environments seem to be a thing of the past, many organizations, libraries included, are discovering the return of the computer room under the guise of the "server room." This is a room containing the multitude of computer servers needed to run a modern medium- to large-scale library. Most libraries don't need a classic, environmentally controlled computer room with raised floors, but as the number of servers in a library grows, security and support issues are making the advantages of having a server room increasingly obvious. Housing servers together eases administration and keeps them all in a secure place. Doors that lock and an area that is out of the line of traffic patterns for access to other areas are important features of a room selected to house the servers. The room also can serve as the termination point of a building's data cabling and telecommunication services.

As the number of servers increases, so does the heat they generate. At some point the BTU output of the assembled equipment will exceed the HVAC system's capacity to dissipate the heat. When planning a server room or planning to add servers to an existing area, be sure to involve the HVAC people to assess the air-conditioning requirements.

Specialized racks and shelving for servers and telecommunications equipment have been developed for use in a computer or server room. Some equipment, especially network and telecommunications equipment, is designed to be "rack-mounted" in specially designed racks that incorporate cable management and ease-of-access features and that supply power through a single connection. Server racks include stacked shelves especially designed to house multiple servers and their monitors and keyboards in small spaces. Not only is this an efficient use of space, it makes managing the servers much easier for staff. Some server racks are even designed with wire shelving to reduce the potential for dust accumulation near the equipment.

Staging Area and Help Desk

Any library with a large number of PCs will need an area where they can be stored, configured, and then distributed throughout the organization. Spare PCs, those to be sent to or returned from repair, and PCs being diagnosed and repaired on site all require space. Space for both staff and the equipment to set up new PCs, test them, and load software is also needed.

Libraries supporting multiple outlets in a wide area network with an ever-increasing number of PCs and software applications may also need a centralized "help desk" operation. Help desk staff need a space that has multiple telephone lines, individual desktop PCs, and access to the server room as necessary.

Effect of New Service Responses/Priorities on Facilities

As noted earlier, when an architect designs a library, the first question is: "How will this building be used?" The architect then designs a building that supports the service responses/priorities of the library. Over time the library's service responses/priorities change, but the building does not. We certainly cannot build a new building or even remodel an existing building every time our priorities, or the activities that support those priorities, change. Therefore, many of the space utilization decisions you will be making will involve *re*allocation and not just allocation of facility resources.

Reallocation is always a challenge because it means changing "the way it always has been." This is often particularly true with facilities, which seem somehow more immutable than other resources. It is important to involve staff early on in the process when discussing how facility spaces might be reallocated. Change is usually easier for people who helped define the change.

Reallocating Space

We are all aware of the need for extra wiring and phone connections to allow access to the burgeoning electronic resources. However, electronic resources are changing our facilities in another way—they are gradually reducing the space needed for the stack areas. As more information becomes available in electronic format and as publishers replace print titles with electronic ones, the need for shelving and for space to house that shelving will decline or at least cease to grow. Similarly, as more periodicals migrate to electronic format, licensing agreements will replace subscriptions and, hence, the need to house back issues. As another example, consider the impact of technology on phone directories and newspapers. Many libraries once devoted literally dozens of feet of shelving to phone directories from cities across the country. Now the information in those print directories is available both in CD-ROM format and also on the World Wide Web. Major newspapers such as the *New York Times,* the *Washington Post,* and the *Los Angeles Times* have on-line editions. Over time, as more content appears in electronic format, the need for paper copies and racks to hold them will diminish. People will still want to read newspapers and periodicals and will still want phone numbers of people and businesses in other cities. However, the way they obtain access to those materials will continue to change.

The migration of many reference and information resources to electronic format will also provide libraries with some flexibility in reconfiguring space. Fewer printed resources might mean freeing up space that could be allocated to meeting rooms, group study areas, or storage of nonprint materials. Of course, it also means allocating more space to PCs and printers and designing public service desks at which a staff member and a client can jointly use a PC during a reference session.

Each library's facilities are unique, and most are currently being fully utilized. Therefore, reallocation is an exercise in trade-offs. As you work on space allocation issues, keep in mind all of the information you gathered about the current use of the facilities. The space or furnishings needed for one activity may become available when you implement another activity. For example, by adding PCs in the reference department, you may be able to recover reference shelving from print resources that will be purchased in electronic format in the future and use it to expand the circulating business collection. Stay flexible when considering facilities issues and be willing to consider a range of options. If the reference shelving isn't near the business collection's current location, could you develop a "business service center" in the space to house the materials and publicize the library's new efforts to increase business services?

Remodeling Space

Occasionally a library has the opportunity to reconfigure its space through a remodeling project. Remodeling projects can range from cosmetic changes (such as painting and new furniture) to structural changes (such as adding or removing walls, rewiring for electrical and data transmission, or adding windows and skylights to increase natural lighting). Library staff who have the opportunity to remodel a building often feel an enormous pressure to "get it right," to use this seemingly one-time opportunity to create the perfect building.

As emphasized in every chapter of this book, change is constant. There are no "perfect" buildings; there are only buildings that work in today's environment, providing today's clientele with access to the formats of materials and information available now. Five years from now, the clients may be different, the material formats may have changed, even the types of services desired may be significantly altered. Any remodeling project needs to allow for the continuing evolution of the public's needs and the library's responses to those needs.

The most important objective of a remodeling project is to build in flexibility by designing space that can be reconfigured with relative ease. Ensure that conduit for electrical, telephone, and data services includes room for future growth. Select furniture that can be upgraded to include wire management features and can be adjusted to support new types of equipment. At every decision point in a remodeling project ask yourself,

"If the library's service priorities change, can this product or space be easily reconfigured to meet new conditions?" Do everything in your power to ensure that the answer to the question is "Yes."

ATMOSPHERICS

Every library activity is designed to attract a specific target audience. The audience may be seniors, children, new readers, businesspeople, students, or members of a particular cultural group. Each of these audiences affects the library environment differently and wants different things from that environment. According to William Sannwald, if the target audiences are varied, then the decisions about space utilization become more complex.[1] For example, children's programs commonly involve music, art projects, and noise. Some people who prefer the old-fashioned "quiet please" library might consider such programs noisy and messy. Businesspeople want quick and easy service, preferably in a location near the entry doors. Cultural and commons activities are likely to involve meeting rooms with kitchen facilities. Seniors are concerned with parking and easy access to facilities.

Atmospherics is the "conscious designing of space to create certain effects. It represents the interface between the user and the organization and is directly related to the feeling that people have about an organization."[2] Sannwald recommends that we think of the library in sensory terms—sight, sound, scent, and touch. You might think about the planned activities in these terms. Can you capture the attention of one of these senses in a positive way to enhance an activity? Will any activity have a negative effect on the senses of the target audience or other library users?

The Envirosell company videotapes customer behaviors in retail establishments to provide insight into what stores might do to stimulate sales. Envirosell has learned that shoppers will not conform to the desires of sellers, that shoppers' behaviors are quite complicated, "and that retailers need to know more and more about them simply to keep pace."[3] The same holds true for libraries. The key to success is discovering what people want in library facilities and then providing it. What library users want may not always conform to the way facilities have been designed and used in the past or to the ways that staff think facilities should be designed and used in the future.

Interpreting and Deciding

The issues discussed in this chapter and the data you collect on the facilities workforms will provide you with a framework for assessing how effectively your current facilities support the service priorities you have identified. In particular, the lists of factors to consider, which appear at the end of the instructions for each workform, will help you organize and analyze the data you have collected.

You can use this data to complete the gap analysis process illustrated in *Planning for Results* and included in appendix B. As noted earlier, the gap analysis process suggests that you determine what resources the library currently has that support the intended outcomes, what resources are needed to achieve those outcomes, and how you plan to address the gap between the two.

However, that is just the beginning of using your resources effectively. Don't forget that there is often a big difference between what we plan and what we actually end up with. You have been encouraged throughout *Managing for Results* to "estimate, implement, check, and adjust" and then "check and adjust" again. This continual monitoring is the critical final step required to ensure that the library's facilities continue to change to support new and evolving priorities.

NOTES

1. William Sannwald, "Espresso and Ambiance: What Public Libraries Can Learn from Bookstores," *Library Administration & Management* 12, no. 4 (fall 1998): 203.

2. Sannwald, 203.

3. Malcolm Gladwell, "The Science of Shopping," *The New Yorker* (4 Nov. 1996): 66–75.

WORKFORM F1   What's Important

Instructions

Purpose of Workform F1

Use this workform as the basis for deciding what information you need to determine about your facilities to implement the goals and objectives of your plan.

Source(s) of Data for Workform F1

The goals, objectives, and activities in the library plan are the sources of data for this workform.

Factors to Consider When Completing Workform F1

The facilities issues you must deal with are different for each of the 13 service responses in *Planning for Results* or for the priorities you identified in any other planning process. Some of your goals and objectives may lead to activities that will change the size or composition of the library's collections; other activities will require new types of equipment or additional space to accommodate more users.

To Complete Workform F1

1. **Activity column**   List the activities that will have an impact on the library's facilities in the left column headed Activities. Use additional copies of the workform if needed.

2. Review the activities to determine which data elements are most important for that activity, and place an *X* in those boxes.

> *Completed by*   Enter the name of the person or people who completed the workform.
>
> *Source of data*   Indicate the source of the data used to complete the workform.
>
> *Date completed*   Enter the date the workform was completed.
>
> *Library*   Enter the library name.

Factors to Consider When Reviewing the Data on Workform F1

1. Have you reviewed all of the goals and objectives in the library plan or project to be sure that you understand the results expected from the activities?

2. Have you identified all of the activities that will have an effect on the library's facilities?

WORKFORM F1   What's Important?

Workform Number	F2 Capacity: Materials Storage	F3 Capacity: Equipment and Furniture	F4 Capacity: Space	F5 Utilization: Space	F6 Technology: Facility Requirements
Activity					
1.					
2.					
3.					
4.					
5.					
6.					
7.					
8.					
9.					
10.					
11.					
12.					

Completed by _____   Date completed _____

Source of data _____   Library _____

General Instructions

At the Top of Workforms F2–F6

1. **Activity**   Indicate the activity being reviewed.

2. **Month/year data collected**   Indicate the month and/or the year the data being recorded on the workform was collected.

3. **Library unit**   If the data on this workform is from an individual library unit, indicate the name of the unit. If the data is from the whole library, write the library's name.

At the Bottom of All Facilities Workforms

1. **Completed by**   Enter the name of the person or people who completed the workform.

2. **Source of data**   Indicate the source of the data used to complete the workform.

3. **Date completed**   Enter the date the workform was completed.

4. **Library**   Enter the library name.

Instructions

WORKFORM F2   Capacity: Materials Storage

Purpose of Workform F2

Use this workform to assess the storage space available to house materials needed to support the intended activities.

Source(s) of Data for Workform F2

1. A tally of the number of storage units or length of shelving provides data for line 2.
2. Sampling or manufacturer's specifications for specialized storage with specific capacities can provide the data for line 3.
3. A comfort factor can be just a reasonable guess. To estimate it in a more precise fashion, completely fill a unit of storage and count the number of items it contains. Remove items until the storage unit becomes easy to use. Count the number of items removed. Divide the number of items removed by the total. The resulting percent is the comfort factor. (For example, if 100 books completely fill a unit of shelving and you find that by removing 20 books the books are easier to use, your comfort factor would be 80% [100 − 20 = 80; 80 ÷ 100 = 80%].)

Factors to Consider When Completing Workform F2

1. *Storage* includes linear feet of shelving or display space or the capacity of specialized shelving for materials such as CDs, paperbacks, or multimedia kits. Storage may also include the capacity of space to store program support materials such as story hour materials or PCs used for staff or public training.
2. Complete a copy of the workform for each activity for which you checked the "Capacity: Materials Storage" column on Workform F1. If the activity requires more than one type of storage (for example, books, CDs, and program supplies), complete a separate copy of the workform for each type of storage required.
3. Each type of space has its own unit of measurement. Shelving is generally measured in linear feet; specialized storage is often measured by the number of bins, hooks, or drawers available to hold materials. Be sure to use the same units of measure in all parts of the workform.
4. If the library has multiple units, complete a copy of this workform for each unit in which the activity is to take place. If the activity requires more than one type of storage, complete a separate copy of the workform for each unit and each type of storage. Then complete a summary copy of the workform that shows the entire library's resources for that activity and type of storage.

5. Concern yourself only with the capacity of storage related to the activity being assessed. (For example, if you are considering expanding the adult circulating CD collection, assess only the CD storage capacity in the adult services area.)
6. With some types of storage, completely filling some types of storage to capacity makes use difficult. Full book shelves, for example, are much more difficult to use than shelves that are only 80% full. The unused space makes it easier to remove and return materials to the shelves. Other types of storage, such as CD racks, are designed to be usable when filled to capacity. Be sure to think about whether the unit of measure needs a "comfort factor" of unused capacity to be user-friendly.

To Complete the Workform

1. **Line 1**   List the type of storage being considered.
2. **Line 2**   Determine the appropriate unit of measure for the type of storage being assessed and enter that unit of measure on line 2. Examples of units of measure include, but are not limited to

    linear feet of shelving

    racks (paperbacks, CDs, etc.)

    bins (phonograph records)

3. **Line 3**   Determine the total number of units available by counting the number of racks or bins or by measuring the linear feet of shelving available.
4. **Line 4**   Calculate the capacity of one unit of measure either from the specifications of the unit (for example, the number of CD slots in the rack) or through sampling. To use sampling:

    Count the number of materials in a single unit of measure. (For example, if your measure in line 2 was linear feet of shelving, you would measure a one-foot area of shelving in the portion of the collection being counted and count the number of books shelved in that one-foot space. If your measure in line 2 was hooks to store media kits, you would count the number of media kits hanging on a single hook.)

    Repeat this procedure twice more. (For instance, in the shelving example, you would measure two more one-foot areas in the same section of the collection and again count the number of books shelved in each.)

    Determine the average number of items stored in the unit of storage by adding the three results together and dividing that total by three.

(Continued)

WORKFORM F2 Capacity: Materials Storage (Cont.)

Instructions

5. **Line 5** Multiply line 3 by line 4 to determine the total capacity of the existing materials storage. This is the *maximum* number of items of this type you can store with your current facilities.

6. **Line 6** Estimate, if appropriate, a comfort factor for this type of storage. (For example, fully loaded shelves are difficult to use, both for browsing and for reshelving. Therefore, you might decide that you only want to fill 80% of each shelf. In that case, you would write 80% on line 6.) See "Source(s) of Data for Workform F2" for more information.

7. **Line 7** Multiply line 5 by line 6 to determine the comfortable capacity of your facilities for this type of material.

Factors to Consider When Reviewing the Data on Workform F2

1. If capacity/comfort are tight, can some materials from this collection be weeded?

2. If capacity/comfort are tight, can materials in other collections be weeded to provide more space for these materials?

3. Are funds available to buy more storage facilities? If not, how will the needed storage space be obtained?

4. Is floor space available to house more storage facilities? If not, where will the needed storage facilities be housed?

WORKFORM F2   **Capacity: Materials Storage**

Activity _____

Library unit _____

Month/year data collected _____

1. Type of storage _____

2. Appropriate unit of measure for the storage type _____

3. Total units of measure available _____

4. Capacity of one unit of measure _____

5. Total capacity _____

6. Comfort factor to be applied _____

7. Comfortable capacity _____

Completed by _____   Date completed _____

Source of data _____   Library _____

Instructions

WORKFORM F3 Capacity: Equipment and Furniture

Purpose of Workform F3

Use this workform to inventory the equipment and furniture the library has to support the intended activities and to indicate the condition of that equipment and furniture.

Source(s) of Data for Workform F3

A tally of the number of pieces of equipment or furniture provides the information for this workform.

Factors to Consider When Completing Workform F3

1. Complete a copy of this workform for each activity for which you checked the "Capacity: Equipment and Furniture" column on Workform F1.

2. If the library has multiple units, complete a copy of this workform for each unit in which the activity is to take place. Then create a summary copy of the workform that shows the entire library's resources for that activity.

3. Estimate the condition of the equipment from observation. If this workform will be completed for more than one unit, it may help to discuss and agree on a common definition of the terms *good, fair,* and *poor* prior to completing the workform.

4. Concern yourself only with the equipment and furniture related to the activity being assessed. (For example, if you are considering expanding the amount of community information distributed from the library, you need to assess only the number of bulletin boards, display racks, or kiosks available.)

5. The list of equipment and furniture on the workform is not exhaustive. Add any other equipment or furniture you have identified in the rows under "Other."

6. Do not enter data in the shaded sections.

To Complete Workform F3

1. **Column A** Mark the equipment and furniture needed for the activity you are assessing by putting a check mark in column A.

2. **Columns B–F** Count the number of pieces of equipment or furniture the library has and assess the condition of each piece. In columns B–E, enter the number of pieces in good, fair, poor, or broken condition. Enter the total number of pieces in column F.

Factors to Consider When Reviewing the Data on Workform F3

1. Does each designated branch or unit have sufficient facilities to engage in the proposed activity?

2. Look at the items required for all the activities planned in each branch or unit. Can the facilities to be shared simultaneously among activities accommodate all of them?

3. If many of the facilities required are in poor condition or broken, how will that condition affect the successful implementation of the activity under review?

Activity _____

Library unit _____

Month/year data collected _____

A. ✓	Equipment	Condition				F. Total
		B. Good	C. Fair	D. Poor	E. Broken	
	Adaptive technology (list)					
	Audio player					
	Bulletin board					
	Display rack					
	Fax machine					
	Kiosk					
	Microtext reader					
	Phone					
	Public					
	Staff					
	Photocopy machine					
	Sound system					
	Vehicle to transport staff or materials					
	Video conferencing equipment					
	Video player					

(Continued)

WORKFORM F3 **Capacity: Equipment and Furniture (Cont.)**

A. ✓	Equipment	Condition				
		B. Good	C. Fair	D. Poor	E. Broken	F. Total
	Video production equipment					
	Other (list)					
	Furniture					
	Comfortable chair					
	Individual study desk					
	PC workstation/terminal carrel					
	Stand-up					
	Sit down					
	Seat					
	Signage					
	Storage cabinet					
	Table					
	Other (list)					

Completed by _____ Date completed _____

Source of data _____ Library _____

Instructions

Purpose of Workform F4

Use this workform to assess the capacity of the spaces in the library that support specific activities.

Source(s) of Data for Workform F4

A tally of the seats or room capacity standards, such as fire standards, provides the information for this workform.

Factors to Consider When Completing Workform F4

1. Complete a copy of this workform for each activity for which you checked the "Capacity: Space" column on Workform F1.

2. If the library has multiple units, complete a copy of this workform for each unit in which the activity is to take place. Then create a summary copy of the workform that shows the entire library's resources for that activity.

3. Concern yourself only with the type of space related to the activity being assessed. (For example, if the activity requires public meeting space, you need to assess only the general meeting and conference room space.) Six types of space are identified in the workform:

    Seating includes the general space used by patrons and staff for their own purposes.

    General meeting space is an auditorium or multipurpose area that can be used for a variety of events.

    Conference space is meeting space designed for group work, such as a classroom or group study room.

    Storytime space is configured for specific audiences, usually children.

    Special purpose space is customized space that is usable only for its intended purpose.

    Parking space includes bike racks and handicap spaces.

4. Do not enter data in the shaded sections.

To Complete Workform F4

1. **Column A** Mark the type of space needed for the activity being assessed by placing a check mark in column A.

2. **Column B** Note the number of people the space will support at capacity for each type of space you are assessing. For parking, you will count spaces for vehicles or bicycles.

Factors to Consider When Reviewing the Data on Workform F4

1. In what building or units will the activity take place?

2. In what areas of the building/unit will the activity take place?

3. Is this space shared with other activities? If so, is it shared simultaneously or sequentially?

4. Remember that capacity reflects the *maximum* number that can be accommodated. When a facility or equipment is used to capacity, the level of comfort usually declines significantly

WORKFORM F4 Capacity: Space

Activity _____

Month/year data collected _____

Library unit _____

A. ✓	Space Needed	B. Number of Users			
	Seating				
	Adult				
	Juvenile				
	Young adult				
	Staff				
	Public areas				
	Workroom				
	Other (list)				
	General meeting				
	Multipurpose				
	Performance				
	Conference				
	Classroom				
	Study rooms				

(Continued)

A. ✓	Space Needed (cont.)	B. Number of Users
	Special purpose	
	Coffee bar/restaurant	
	Computer lab	
	Exhibit space	
	Kitchen	
	Video conference	
	Video production	
	Storytime	
	Story area	
	Activity area	
	Parking	
	Regular parking spaces	
	Handicapped spaces	
	Bike parking	
	Other (list)	

Completed by _____   Date completed _____

Source of data _____   Library _____

WORKFORM F5 · Utilization: Space

Instructions

Purpose of Workform F5

Use this workform to assess the utilization of spaces in the library that support specific activities.

Source(s) of Data for Workform F5

1. Observations or documents such as room rental/sign-up sheets provide the information needed to determine the use of specific spaces.

2. The data in column B of Workform F4 is used to complete the capacity information on Workform F5.

Factors to Consider When Completing Workform F5

1. Complete a copy of this workform for each activity for which you checked the "Utilization: Space" column on Workform F1.

2. If the library has multiple units, complete a copy of this workform for each unit in which the activity is to take place. Then create a summary copy of the workform that shows the entire library's resources for this activity.

3. To understand utilization, observe the usage of the facilities over a period of time. Plan on collecting data for at least a week. If the usage varies widely from one week to another, you may want to gather data for as long as a month. If usage varies during the year, you might want to gather data several different times during the year.

4. Concern yourself only with the type of space related to the activity being assessed. If the activity being assessed requires public meeting space, assess only the utilization of general meeting and conference room space. Six types of spaces are identified in the workform:

   Seating includes the general space used by patrons and staff for their own purposes.

   General meeting space is an auditorium or multipurpose area that can be used for a variety of events.

   Conference space is meeting space designated for group work, such as a classroom or group study room.

   Storytime space is configured for specific audiences, usually children.

   Special purpose space is customized space that is usable only for its intended purpose.

   Parking includes space for specialized parking needs.

5. Although space is provided for observing utilization over an entire day, for many activities only certain times are relevant. (For example, programming targeted to working adults will probably be scheduled at night and on weekends; therefore, assess only nighttime meeting space utilization.)

6. Do not enter data in the shaded areas.

To Complete Workform F5

1. **Column A**   Place a check mark in this column if the type of space is needed for the activity being assessed.

2. **Row B**   Enter the time at which observations will be recorded.

3. **Section C**   Enter the capacity for each type of space being assessed. This figure will come from Workform F4, column B.

4. **Sections D–I**   At the designated times listed in row B, record the number of people using each type of space under review.

Factor to Consider When Reviewing the Data on Workform F5

To understand the utilization of the facilities, you will need to compare the usage data and the capacity of the space under review. Divide the capacity (column C) by the number of people observed to be using a resource during any recorded time period (sections D–I) to determine the percentage of utilization of that resource at that time. (For example, if you have seating for 30 adults and you observed 9 seats in use at 10:00 A.M., you had 30% utilization of your adult seating at 10:00 A.M.)

WORKFORM F5 Utilization: Space

Activity _____

Library unit _____

Month/year data collected _____

A. ✓	B. Hours									C. Capacity
D. Seating										
	Adult									
	Juvenile									
	Young adult									
Staff										
	Public areas									
	Workroom									
Other (list)										
E. General Meeting										
	Multipurpose									
	Performance									
F. Conference										
	Classroom									
	Study rooms									

(Continued)

A. ✓	B. Hours							C. Capacity
G. Storytime								
Story area								
Activity area								
H. Special Purpose								
Coffee bar/restaurant								
Computer lab								
Exhibit space								
Kitchen								
Video conference								
Video production								
I. Parking								
Regular parking								
Handicapped spaces								
Bike parking								
Other (list)								

Completed by _____   Date completed _____

Source of data _____   Library _____

WORKFORM F6 Technology: Facility Requirements

Instructions

Purpose of Workform F6

Use this workform to assess the impact of the technology required to accomplish an activity on the library's facilities.

Source(s) of Data for Workform F6

The library's technology plan or information on Workforms T13, T14, and T15 in chapter 5 can provide the information needed for this workform.

Factors to Consider When Completing Workform F6

1. Complete a copy of this workform for each activity for which you checked the "Technology: Facility Requirements" column on Workform F1.

2. If the library has multiple units, complete a copy of this workform for each unit. Then create a summary copy of the workform that shows the entire library's resources for this activity.

3. Concern yourself only with facilities for the technology related to the activity being assessed.

To Complete the Workform

1. **Column A** In the numbered spaces, list the technology equipment you need to support the activity under review.

2. **Columns B–F** Circle either yes or no under each heading for each type of equipment listed in column A.

   Column B Does the equipment require electricity or HVAC?

   Column C Will the equipment be linked to other equipment in a network? If so, it will require data cabling.

   Column D Will the equipment require special computer furniture to house it?

   Column E Is the equipment a server or telecommunications equipment? Should it be put in a secure server room?

   Column F Will the receipt, distribution, or on-going maintenance of this equipment require a staging area to facilitate the handling of the equipment, or will the activity require a help desk?

Factors to Consider When Reviewing the Data on Workform F6

1. Will the electrical service need to be upgraded?

2. Will the building need to be rewired?

3. Does the data cabling in place now meet the required standards for transmission?

4. Will these activities require climate control?

WORKFORM F6 **Technology: Facility Requirements**

Activity _____

Library unit _____

Month/year data collected _____

A. Equipment by Type	B. Electricity/ HVAC		C. Data Cabling		D. Computer Furniture		E. Secure Server Room		F. Staging Area/ Help Desk	
1.	Yes	No	Yes	No	Yes	No	Yes	No	Yes	No
2.	Yes	No	Yes	No	Yes	No	Yes	No	Yes	No
3.	Yes	No	Yes	No	Yes	No	Yes	No	Yes	No
4.	Yes	No	Yes	No	Yes	No	Yes	No	Yes	No
5.	Yes	No	Yes	No	Yes	No	Yes	No	Yes	No
6.	Yes	No	Yes	No	Yes	No	Yes	No	Yes	No
7.	Yes	No	Yes	No	Yes	No	Yes	No	Yes	No
8.	Yes	No	Yes	No	Yes	No	Yes	No	Yes	No
9.	Yes	No	Yes	No	Yes	No	Yes	No	Yes	No
10.	Yes	No	Yes	No	Yes	No	Yes	No	Yes	No

Completed by _____ Date completed _____

Source of data _____ Library _____

Chapter 5

Managing Your Library's Technology

MILESTONES

By the time you finish this chapter you will know how to

- identify the technology needed to accomplish the library's goals and objectives

- determine what technology the library currently has

- understand the difference between the capacity of this technology and its utilization

- determine how the library's current technology is being utilized

- calculate the cost of the additional technological capacity needed to accomplish the library's goals and objectives

- prepare a plan to reallocate existing technology and acquire new technology as needed

Assessing your technology investments on the basis of the library's chosen service priorities can be difficult. For instance, only one of the service responses in *Planning for Results*—that of Information Literacy—explicitly requires technology. Yet we all know that technology is an integral component of service delivery in a modern public library and that most of the other twelve service responses will be supported by activities that require technology. In fact, recognizing that technology is a means of delivering service and not an end in itself is the key to effectively allocating your technology resources.

The basic question you need to answer in allocating resources for technology expenditures is, Do we have enough of the right type of technology to achieve the library's goals and objectives? There are three assumptions in this question:

- you have clearly defined objectives
- you can identify the type of technology needed
- you can define "enough" in the context of the library's service objectives

These are fairly big assumptions. Most of you reading this book have clearly defined objectives. Many of you have made a start in identifying the types of technology needed. The big challenge we all face is defining "enough." In fact, some librarians question whether there ever can be enough technology. This chapter will help you gather and analyze the data needed to identify and meet the library's technology requirements.

Considering Technology as a Resource

The term *technology* as used here includes hardware, software, telecommunications services, electrical circuits, and data cabling or wiring. These are the basic elements of technology that are used by most libraries to provide service to their customers and to support staff in accomplishing their tasks.

The budget for library technology is often managed somewhat differently from the budgets for the other resources discussed in this book. The monies for staff, materials, and facility maintenance tend to be clustered into individual budget categories. Money for technology, however, is generally spread throughout the library's budget. In many libraries, the money for hardware is included in the capital line on the budget and considered to be a one-time expenditure. Some libraries have a special line item for software; others include it in their collection development budgets. Money for electrical circuits and data cabling or wiring is usually included in the building budget, and the funds for telecommunications services are normally lumped with other telephone costs. The disbursed nature of these technology resources can make it difficult for library managers to stay aware of the total impact of technology on the library's budget.

On the other hand, in some ways dealing with the allocation and re-allocation of resources for technology may be easier than dealing with those same issues in staffing, materials, and space allocation. Technology is the newest major category of expenditure for public libraries, and it has been a constantly moving target for most of the past decade. Staff have not had a chance to become as committed to the status quo in technology as they have in other areas of library resources. In fact, there has been no status quo in library technology for ten years, unless one chooses to define continual change as a status quo. Therefore, some of the issues that library managers will face when attempting to change long-standing practices and priorities in staffing, materials allocations, and space utilization will not apply here. Staff expect change in this area and are likely to be quite supportive of efforts to use technology more effectively.

As a reminder, this chapter is not intended to be used to design the basic technology infrastructure in your library nor is it intended to help significantly change or upgrade the library's current infrastructure. As noted in the Introduction, you should use *Wired for the Future: Developing Your Library Technology Plan* as the basis for making those fundamental decisions about the library infrastructure.[1] The intent of this chapter is to provide you with information about the availability and use of the library's technology and to help you determine what technology you will need to allocate or reallocate to accomplish the library's goals and objectives.

You are encouraged to use the information in this chapter in conjunction with the *Planning for Results* Gap Analysis Workform (see appendix B). That workform was designed to help you analyze data to answer three basic questions:

- equipment needed [to accomplish the library's service priorities]
- software needed [to accomplish the library's service priorities]
- telecommunications/electrical/wiring requirements [to accomplish the library's service priorities]

The Gap Analysis Workform encourages you to define the technology needed to accomplish the library's service priorities, to identify the technology currently owned, to determine the gap between the two, and then to decide how to fill that gap or reallocate the surplus.

Collecting Data

The fifteen workforms at the end of this chapter will help you gather the data needed to complete a gap analysis to determine what, if any, equipment and telecommunications capacity will be required to accomplish the library's service priorities. Those workforms are listed in figure 15.

The technology workforms will be used somewhat differently from the workforms in the other chapters in this book: They are intended to be used together, and data from some forms will be required to complete other forms. The forms are divided into five sections that correspond to the gap analysis process.

The first step in the gap analysis process is to define the technology needed to accomplish the library's service priorities. Workforms T1–T5 in the "Needs Estimates" group will help you gather this data.

The second step in the gap analysis process is to identify the technology currently owned. To gather this data you will start by completing Workforms T6–T8 in the "Capacity Available" group. You will then complete Workform T9 *or* T10 in the "Utilization" group. If library users

FIGURE 15

Technology Workforms Summary

Workform	Title	Purpose
NEEDS ESTIMATE		
T1	Equipment, Software, and Dial Capacity	To estimate the technological capacity needed to support a planned activity
T2	Printers	To estimate how many and what types of printers are needed to support a planned activity
T3	Summary of Equipment, Printers, Software, and Dial Capacity	To summarize the capacity of technology needed to support a specific activity in each library unit
T4	Leased Lines	To determine the leased line capacity needed to support a specific activity
T5	Summary of Needs Estimates: Leased Lines	To summarize the leased line capacity needed in each library unit
CAPACITY AVAILABLE		
T6	Workstation and Terminal Functions	To record information on the number of single and multifunction workstations and terminals in each library unit
T7	Workstation and Terminal Condition	To record information on the condition of the workstations and terminals in each library unit
T8	Equipment, Software, and Telecommunications	To record information about the equipment, software, and telecommunications capacity in each library unit

(Continued)

FIGURE 15 Continued

Workform	Title	Purpose
	UTILIZATION	
T9	Utilization: Observation	To collect utilization data through observation
T10	Utilization: Public Services Sign-Up Analysis	To analyze utilization data obtained from sign-up sheets in library units that allow users to reserve a specific time to use equipment or to sign up on a first-come, first-served basis
T11	Utilization: Summary	To summarize the utilization data gathered using Workforms T9 and T10
	COMPARISON OF CAPACITY REQUIRED TO UNUSED CAPACITY	
T12	Comparison of Capacity Required to Unused Capacity Available	To compare the capacity needed with the capacity available in each library unit
	ADDITIONAL EQUIPMENT AND LINES NEEDED	
T13	Technology Needed	To determine the number of additional devices to be purchased to reach needed capacity in each library unit
T14	Leased Line Capacity Needed	To determine the additional leased line capacity to be acquired to reach needed capacity in each library unit
T15	Costs of Needed Technology	To translate the number and types of devices needed and the dial and leased line telecommunications capacity required into estimated costs

do not have to sign up to use the library's computers, you will complete Workform T9. If library users are required to sign up to use computers, either in advance or on a first-come, first-served basis, you will complete Workform T10. Then you will summarize the data gathered in the "Utilization" section on Workform T11.

The third step in the gap analysis process is to determine the gap between what you need and what you have. You will complete Workform T12 in the "Comparison of Capacity Required to Unused Capacity" group and Workforms T13 and T14 in the "Additional Equipment and Lines Needed" group to do this. The final workform, T15, will help translate the additional capacity needed into costs. This will identify the money you need to allocate to technology purchases to achieve the library's objectives. As you can see, most libraries will complete fourteen of these fifteen forms, selecting only between forms T9 and T10 in the "Utilization" group.

Issues to Consider When Making Technology Decisions

The information in this chapter will help you understand and analyze the data you will gather on the technology workforms. The chapter focuses on five issues that library managers should consider as they make decisions about allocating resources for technology. These issues include

- defining technology needs based on service priorities
- identifying the types of technology a library needs
- understanding the current capacity, utilization, and condition of the library's technology
- determining the technology required to meet current and anticipated needs
- converting capacity to cost

Technology Needs Based on Service Priorities

Determining if the library has enough technology begins by determining how much service you want to deliver. Therefore, you need to have defined the library's intended outcomes as goals and expressed the library's objectives in measurable terms. Then you need to consider the objectives carefully. How many units of service do these objectives imply? How many people do you expect to serve? How long will each of these service transactions take?

You may only be able to make "informed guess" answers to these questions, but those informed guesses are basic elements in assessing the adequacy of the library technology to meet library objectives. Estimating the number of service transactions to be supported and the average length of time each is expected to take will help you determine how many hours of access to the supporting technology are needed. Once you have made that determination, you can decide if the current technology is adequate. If the library doesn't have enough technology, you will have the information you need to identify how much more technology is required.

When you are estimating hours of access needed, you will most likely be working at the level of activities selected to accomplish the library's service goals and objectives.

CASE STUDY PART 1

Let's return to the Anytown Public Library and look at one of its priorities—Business and Career Information. One of the library's goals is "Business owners in Anytown will have the information they need to run their businesses in an efficient and effective manner." The three objectives for this goal are as follows:

1. At least 20 percent of the small-business owners in Anytown will indicate on a survey that they used the library for business-related information in the past year.
2. At least 75 percent of the small-business owners in Anytown who reported that they used the library to find business-related information in the past year will say that information was available to them in a convenient location.
3. The number of business reference questions answered will increase from *XX* to *XX* during the fiscal year.

The library staff have selected the following activities to help them achieve their goals and objectives:

1. Increase the number of reference sources available that provide answers to business questions (to increase the number of questions you can answer).
2. Distribute more business reference materials to Anytown's branch libraries (to enhance the convenience of the service to business owners).
3. Develop a marketing campaign focused specifically on services to small-business owners (to encourage use by small-business owners).

It is at the activity level that the library staff can begin to answer questions about the types of technology needed and whether the library currently has enough.

Types of Technology Needed

As noted earlier, a library's technology includes its hardware, software, telecommunications services, electrical circuits, and data cabling or wiring. Examples of each are included in the following sections.

Hardware

Hardware includes printers, servers, and workstations or personal computers.

printer Mechanical device for printing a computer's output on paper

> *networked printer:* single printer that accepts output for printing from multiple workstations connected by a local area network

> *stand-alone printer:* printer connected to and used with a single workstation

server Computer that shares its resources and information with other computers, called "clients," on a local or wide area network

> *local area network (LAN):* connects computers in a work group, department, or building; requires data cabling that serves as the medium for message-passing between the devices

wide area network (WAN): communications system that connects geographically dispersed computers or LANs, usually in two or more separate buildings; typically uses telephone lines between sites to serve as a message-passing medium

workstation   Also known as a personal computer; a computer that provides access to resources to a single user at a time

Often libraries also invest in adaptive equipment for persons with disabilities. Sometimes additional hardware is added to meet special needs, for example, a scanner for digitizing local documents or historical collections.

Software

Libraries use many types of software. For the purposes of this book software is divided into four broad categories by type and purpose: applications software, development software, management software, and navigation software.

applications software   The commercial software packages libraries offer for the public to use in library computers, including office automation packages such as word processing or desktop publishing software available to the public

development software   Generally licensed for staff use; examples include development tools such as HTML authoring packages or programming tools to assist with the development of local electronic resources such as Web pages or creating databases of local information

management software   Software that libraries use to manage their business operations; examples include a library's automated system, its Web and e-mail server software, and internal office automation software

navigation software   Supports searching for and connecting to electronic information resources; examples include a Web browser, a Telnet application, an FTP client, and special clients developed by a library automation vendor to access a library's online catalog, such as PAC for Windows or Kids Cat©

Software in this chapter of *Managing for Results* does not include commercial databases. Databases are included in the Collections chapter.

Telecommunications

Telecommunications includes dial-up phone lines, Internet services, leased telephone circuits, and wireless technology.

dial-up lines   Both the telephone circuits in the library that support outbound access to external resources and the phone lines for patrons to dial in to the library's electronic services

Internet services Support for the library's connection to the Internet: it is not enough to have a phone line, that line has to connect to an Internet service provider who accepts the library's incoming and outgoing electronic traffic and routes all messages to their intended destinations; includes access *to* the Internet for staff and public in the library's buildings and access to the library's server or Web pages *from* the Internet; may also include electronic mailboxes for staff or the ability to mount the library's Web pages on a server owned and maintained by the library's Internet service provider

leased circuits Dedicated lines between library facilities and the site of the online system or primary Internet connection point; also the dedicated line(s) to the library's Internet service provider

wireless technology Used to transmit data locally (LAN) and over limited distances (WAN) at fixed cost with little or no recurring monthly charges; at present, examples include infrared, radio frequency, and microwave

Electrical Circuits and Wiring

Strictly speaking, the electricity and internal wiring needed to operate workstations and servers are facilities issues. However, most libraries think about those two issues when assessing their technology needs because it is the technology that drives the need to add more electric outlets and service or to install data cabling throughout the library.

As discussed in chapter 4, each piece of equipment you add will require both space to house it and electricity to power it. You may also need furniture to hold the equipment as well as furniture for the staff or patron who will use the equipment. If the equipment is meant to interact with any other equipment, such as with a library automation system or your Internet connection, it will probably also need data cable. After working through this technology chapter, you may want to review chapter 4 to be sure you have thought through the facilities requirements of the technology you have identified.

Current Capacity, Utilization, and Condition

As you and your colleagues review the technology the library currently has in place, you will consider capacity, utilization, and condition. Each of these issues is discussed in detail in the following sections.

Current Capacity

Capacity is the total hours of service the library can provide with the equipment, software, wiring, and telecommunications it now has. In other words, capacity refers to the amount of access offered to or through the library's technology. Capacity is expressed in time increments, usually hours, that can be extended to weekly, monthly, or annual figures, as needed. For example, if the library has 4 public access PCs and is open 40 hours per week, it has the capacity to provide the public with 160 hours per week of PC-based services. If the library has 2 circulation terminals available for staff use, it has the capacity to provide 80 hours a week of circulation services.

Capacity can also be reported as the number of hours of work that can be accomplished by the available equipment. In this way capacity measures the staff's access to the tools they need to do their jobs, as can be seen in the second part of the technology case study.

CASE STUDY PART 2

As described in the first part of the case study, the Anytown Public Library decided to "develop a marketing campaign focused specifically on services to small-business owners (to encourage use by small-business owners)."

To determine if the library currently has the capacity to accomplish this activity, staff first have to decide how much computer time will be required to develop the marketing campaign and what software will be required. Then they need to learn how the existing computer equipment is being used and whether that equipment has the desired software. If the desired software is not available, they will also have to learn if the software can be added to the available equipment.

Let's say the people developing the marketing campaign decide they need access to a PC ten hours per week to produce flyers, mailings, Web pages, etc. The Anytown Library business office has a PC with the needed software that is used Monday through Friday from 8 A.M. to 5 P.M. to maintain budget records and administrative files. However, at least one of the staff members who is developing the campaign works 10 A.M. to 7 P.M. Monday through Friday. Since the staff member's hours overlap with unscheduled hours on the PC by ten hours a week, and the right software is loaded on the PC, the library could have 100 percent of the technical capacity needed to support this marketing activity.

TELECOMMUNICATIONS CAPACITY

Capacity takes on a special meaning when it refers to telecommunications connections. The capacity of dial phone connections can be calculated, like the capacity of other equipment, on the basis of the number of hours of access. Leased line phone and wireless connections are different.

Wireless and leased line phone connections are available twenty-four hours a day, seven days a week; hours of access are not a determining issue in the capacity of wireless or leased lines. However, wireless technologies and leased lines supplied by the phone company have specific limits on the amount of data they can carry. The throughput, or capacity, of a wireless connection or a leased line refers to the number of bits of data per second that can be transferred through the line. The two most common capacities for leased lines are 56,000 bits per second (56K) and 1,544,000 bits per second (T1). (Some very large libraries use T3 lines that can transfer up to 45 million bits per second.) It is also possible in some areas of the country to contract for capacities between these two rates. To get some idea of the difference in these two types of lines, see figure 16.

Each device that transmits data over a leased line uses some number of the bits-per-second capacity of the line. Because it is impossible to predict exactly when a device will transmit data, or how much data it will send and receive, capacity planning is based on average usage figures. These usage estimates vary based on whether the device is transmitting primarily text data or graphic data. A workstation accessing a library's circulation system, or the Internet via Telnet or Lynx, is primarily a text device. A workstation accessing the Internet via a Web browser is a graphic device.

The rule of thumb for telecommunications capacity planners is that 30 to 40 text devices or 2 to 5 graphic devices can be supported on a 56K leased line. A T1 line has 24 times the capacity of a 56K line, so it can support 700 to 950 text devices or 45 to 120 graphic devices. A T3 line has 28 times the capacity of a T1 and can support proportionally more devices.

Utilization

Utilization tracks how much capacity is actually being used to deliver services or accomplish work. Utilization figures also help you determine how much unused capacity can be applied to new or expanded services. Like capacity, utilization is expressed in time increments, usually hours, and these too can be extended to weekly, monthly, or annual figures as needed.

FIGURE 16
Data Transfer Speeds

Type of File	Number of Bits	Transfer Time at 56K Speed	Transfer Time at T1 Speed
Circulation transaction	300	.005 of a second	Too fast to calculate
Typical OPAC display	2,400	.04 of a second	Too fast to calculate
MARC record	8,000	.14 of a second	.005 of a second
Thumbnail graphic	400,000	7 seconds	.33 of a second
30-second sound file	1.8 million	32 seconds	1.2 seconds
Half-screen, high-quality photograph	2.4 million	43 seconds	1.6 seconds
3-minute video clip	200 million	59.5 minutes	2 minutes 9 seconds

It is important to remember that utilization figures cannot be evaluated by themselves. They must be tempered with what sailors call "local knowledge," an understanding of the unique local environment. The numbers may indicate that a given branch is utilizing only 70 percent of its technical capacity to serve the public. Therefore, it should theoretically be possible to add another service that will increase the usage of the machines without adding equipment because there are unused hours available.

This, however, may not be at all true. For example, let's say that you want to add electronic homework help resources, which would be used primarily from 2:30 P.M. until closing. However, when you examine the availability of the equipment more closely, you find that most of the 25 percent of the unused capacity occurs during the morning hours. It may be that 100 percent of the technical capacity is fully utilized from 2:30 P.M. to closing. If that is the case, adding electronic homework helper resources to existing machines and expecting those resources to attract new, additional users without adding equipment won't work. You don't have sufficient technology available after school for students to access the new resources. The equipment is already serving as many people as it can during the times the students need to use it.

Of course, if you add the homework helper resources, the people who are being served will have more services to choose from in meeting their needs. However, if the measurable objective is an increase in the number of people served, you won't be successful. At 100 percent utilization, the library lacks the capacity to serve additional people. Any new resources added to equipment that is fully utilized will offer only wider choices.

Condition

The condition of the technology is an important factor in determining if capacity is sufficient for the library's objectives. Answering the question "Can I do what I want to with the equipment I have?" is dependent in large part on the condition of the equipment.

Condition covers a host of factors including the processor type and speed of the library's computers, the amount of memory the computers have, and the operating system(s) used. Electronic products change constantly. Each new product, or upgraded version of an old product, is typically designed to need more computer memory and faster processing power than earlier products. As operating system upgrades are introduced, software becomes less available for older operating systems. Think of how hard it is now to find products written to run under Windows 3.1.

Condition also covers the repair status of equipment. As equipment ages, it wears out from use and becomes harder to repair. Breakdowns are more frequent, and repairs usually take longer. This, in turn, reduces capacity—if the equipment is out of order, it can't be used. If the average time taken to repair equipment is quite long or the percentage of equipment needing repair is high, the library may well have less capacity than you think.

Technology Capacity Needed

Determining how much technical capacity is required to accomplish a particular activity is not an exact science. It is just as important to "estimate, implement, check, and adjust" when making decisions about technology as it is when making staffing, collection, or facility decisions.

In the second part of the case study, the Anytown Library staff were able to determine with some degree of accuracy the capacity needed to support the marketing campaign. Because they also were able to identify the period of time in which that capacity could be utilized, 5 P.M. to 7 P.M. Monday through Friday, they could say with confidence that the necessary capacity would be available to accomplish their activity.

However, even in a fairly clear-cut case such as that of the Anytown Library, it is important to check and make sure that things are going as planned. It is possible that staff underestimated the computer time needed to develop the marketing program. Perhaps the equipment being used is unreliable, resulting in long down-time periods when it is being serviced. Maybe the library administrators are developing the budget or writing a grant proposal or doing some other activity that requires use of the office equipment after 5 P.M. If any of these conditions (or the dozens of other things that might have come up) have happened, then the people responsible for completing the activity will have to reassess capacity and utilization again to identify new technology resources to accomplish their activity.

Technical Requirements for Public Service Activities

Estimating the technical requirements for public service activities can be far more complicated that the simple example in the case study. While it is possible that the public service activities you develop will translate easily into hours of access needed, it is equally possible they may not.

Let's start with an example of a public service activity that is relatively easy to translate into hours of access. If your library used *Planning for Results* and selected the Cultural Awareness service response, one library objective might be "The library will introduce at least 200 recent immigrants to library services specifically designed to meet their needs during FY__." An activity selected to help meet that objective might be "Provide Internet training on accessing Web sites in the immigrants' native languages in neighborhood cultural centers." The technology required to support this activity can be reliably quantified in several steps.

First, you will determine the type of equipment needed. To go to neighborhood cultural centers you will need a laptop PC with a modem, the right software, and a large screen display device that can connect to the laptop. Also, don't forget about access to a telephone line at the demonstration site.

Second, you will determine the hours of access required. You expect to hold 10 meetings. Staff will require a total of 4 hours of PC time to plan for the PowerPoint presentations for the meetings, and each meeting will take 2 hours of PC time to deliver. Therefore, achieving this objective requires 24 hours of laptop PC capacity.

Not all activities can be so easily translated into technology requirements. For example, let's say another objective states that 75 percent of the immigrants who use the library will indicate they were able to find Internet resources in their native language. Library activities might include providing the equipment, developing a Web page to help the immigrants get to sites they want, and providing Internet training. Determining the type of equipment, software, and telecommunications needed seems to be straightforward at first glance: PCs with Web browsers and an Internet connection. But do you also need special foreign language keyboards or display devices capable of displaying non-Roman characters?

Utilization of Public Service Activities

Estimating utilization is even more challenging than estimating technical requirements. If the objective is not easily quantifiable in terms of the desired utilization, you will probably begin your assessment of how much technology is needed based on an informed estimate.

If the library is considering a new service or introducing an existing service to a new audience, how many people might use the service? How long will each usage take? How do those estimates translate into hours per week of additional utilization? Is the new service likely to be used during specific times of day, such as during story hour times or primarily in the hours after school and before closing? If so, be sure to apply your "local knowledge" to the utilization model.

If the objective is to increase the use of an existing service by some percentage, keep in mind that the equation for relating capacity to service transactions is

capacity ÷ utilization per transaction = number of transactions possible

For example, if one PC is available to the public during the 40 hours the library is open each week, you have 40 hours of capacity. If people are allowed to sign up for one-hour time slots and each person uses the PC for that one hour, you have one hour of utilization per transaction. Therefore, the formula is 40 hours of capacity ÷ 1 hour per transaction = 40 transactions possible. Capacity and utilization per transaction need to be expressed in the equation in the same time increment, such as minutes or hours.

To increase the number of transactions possible requires a change in one of the other two variables, either capacity or utilization per transaction. What if there is no space for more equipment or no money for the additional telecommunications services needed to increase capacity? If capacity has reached its maximum, then you need to consider changing the time spent on each transaction if you want to increase the number of service transactions that can be supported.

For example, let's say that you want to double the number of people who can access the Internet at the library. However, the four existing public PCs take all the space available in the building and they are utilized 100 percent of the time now. One way to increase the number of transactions without increasing the capacity is to reduce the time of utilization per transaction. Changing the forty hours of capacity being utilized in one-hour increments to thirty minutes per transaction doubles the transaction potential even when capacity remains unchanged.

When you plan to change the time of utilization per transaction, it is important not to reduce the access time to the point at which the service is no longer practical. Limiting people to ten minutes of time on the Internet to achieve a target for service transactions doesn't really meet the objective of offering excellent service to your users. It is necessary to balance the number of people served with the quantity and quality of the service those people get. It is better not to plan to increase service than it is to achieve that increase by unreasonably limiting users' time.

SPECIAL CONSIDERATIONS

Probably some of the library's servers and workstations are single-purpose devices that can access only one product or service. Some CD-ROM-based products that include both the hardware and the database are examples of single-purpose products. A workstation or character-based terminal used solely to access a library's online catalog is another example of a single-purpose device.

It is not uncommon for libraries to intentionally use a part of their technology to offer limited or restricted access to specific resources. For example, a library may have a small local area network with workstations that can access only CD-ROMs that are offered on that network. Some workstations may provide general access to the Internet while others do not allow Internet access. Most libraries have one or more PCs dedicated solely to office/management applications.

When assessing capacity to support new or expanded services, be sure to recognize the limitations of these dedicated devices. A single-purpose workstation specifically designed to access a single database cannot be counted among the resources available to be allocated to other purposes. You can factor in the unused capacity of that workstation; however, in any plans you have to increase access to that resource.

Converting Capacity to Costs

If you have determined that the library does not have the capacity needed to support the service objectives, you will need to allocate some of that scarcest of resources—money—to address the problem. You *may* find that the library is already spending some money on technology that can be reallocated to funding new purchases or expanded services. It is more likely that money will have to be reallocated from other budget areas to fund enhanced technical capacity. Before making the hard decisions about how to reallocate resources, you need to develop estimates of the likely costs.

You can use Workform T15: Converting Capacity Needed to Costs to develop these estimates. The workform is not meant to give you definitive budget figures. Rather, it is intended to provide general estimates of the types of equipment/software and telecommunications expenses your plans entail. A more detailed process for developing explicit cost estimates can be found in *Wired for the Future: Developing Your Library Technology Plan.* As you complete Workform T15, you might want to consider the following cost issues.

Purchase or Lease

Technology costs consist of both one-time costs and ongoing costs. Unfortunately, as we become more and more dependent on technology to support our services, "one-time" in the world of technology means only "for the next couple of years." In fact, many libraries have switched their strategy from buying equipment to leasing equipment, thus recognizing the need to continually upgrade (particularly staff workstations and public workstations). This moves much of their equipment cost from the capital expenditure budget to the operating budget and ensures regular refurbishment of these important service delivery tools.

Whether using capital or operating monies, you still need to estimate how much the library's purchase and support costs will be for the technologies required. These estimated costs should include both the cost of purchasing or leasing equipment and software and the costs of installing them. If you will be paying a vendor for the installation, you probably will want to include that cost in the technology allocation. If library staff will be doing the installation, you will want to indicate that technical staff will be required to complete the activity when you consider the staffing requirements for the activity. Do this by placing a check mark in column H of Workform S1 in Chapter 2.

Maintenance, Repair, and Replacement

In addition to purchase or lease and installation, the library will also incur monthly or annual costs for equipment maintenance and for required services, such as monthly telephone line costs and monthly or annual service fees from your Internet service provider. Be sure to include these costs in budget planning as well. If you are adding more equipment similar to equipment the library already has, you can use the equipment's repair history to estimate the allowance for annual repairs. If you are adding new equipment, the supplier or one of the supplier's references should be able to give you an estimate of the possible annual repair expense.

Reallocation of Maintenance Money

One possible source of technology monies that could be reallocated to purchasing new equipment may be found in existing allocations for maintenance and repair. Many libraries carry maintenance contracts with vendors on all of their equipment. This was a common practice in the early years of library automation, when library staffs had little experience with maintaining equipment and the options for local maintenance were not as widespread as they are today. Most of these contracts renew automatically and have escalation clauses. However, you may find that the library is paying a premium price to maintain highly reliable equipment. It can often be less expensive to pay for maintenance on a time-and-materials basis rather than purchasing a full-service maintenance contract.

The maintenance costs for some equipment, such as character-based terminals, are so high that it may be less expensive to replace the equipment than to pay for a contract to maintain it. In other cases, the cost of replacing a piece of equipment is so low that it would be less expensive to replace it than to repair it with or without a maintenance contract. This is certainly true for many printers. It is probably a good idea to determine the replacement cost of any piece of equipment before having it repaired.

Not all equipment can be maintained locally, nor should it be. However, terminals and PCs used by the staff and the public can often be maintained locally for less than would be charged by a library vendor. Be sure to investigate if you can reallocate some dollars in this area. If the library's server is more than four years old and under a maintenance contract, check to see if you could lower the annual costs for maintenance by upgrading the equipment. In the world of technology, it costs more to maintain old equipment—often a lot more. Many libraries have funded upgrades to systems entirely through maintenance cost savings.

Interpreting and Deciding

A lot of time and energy will go into completing the technology workforms in this chapter. If the data collected is not adequately analyzed, much of that time and effort will have been wasted. However, the information on the workforms is unique to your library, so no standard instructions can be given on what to do with that data.

Many library managers find making decisions pertaining to technology resources more difficult than decisions in other areas of the library's resources. This is at least partly due to having less educational and experiential background in this area than in the areas of collection management, staffing, or library facilities. However, this is also an area in which most managers have access to outside experts. These experts include the technical or computer support staff of city or county governments, technical or computer support staff at one of the local schools or from the school district office, and local software or hardware user groups. Any of these people could be asked to help review and analyze data.

Remember, this whole process is intended to help you determine what technology resources will be required to accomplish the library's service priorities and then to help you decide where to get those resources. It does no good to gather and analyze data if you do not act upon that information. Although this is true for all four of the resources under review in this book, it is particularly true for the library's technology resources. Because the number of programs and services that libraries offer using technology continues to grow geometrically, it is critical that library managers clearly understand the current capacity, utilization, and condition of the library's technology to be able to manage that growth effectively.

NOTE

1. Diane Mayo and Sandra S. Nelson, *Wired for the Future: Developing Your Library Technology Plan* (Chicago: American Library Assn., 1999).

General Instructions   WORKFORMS T1–T15   Managing Your Library's Technology

At the Top of Technology Workforms

1. **Activity** Where applicable, indicate the activity being reviewed.

2. **Library unit** If the data on this workform is from an individual library unit, indicate the name of the unit. If the data is from the whole library, write the library's name.

3. **Month/year data collected** Where applicable, indicate the month and/or year the data being recorded on the workform was collected.

At the Bottom of All Technology Workforms

1. **Completed by** Enter the name of the person or people who completed the workform.

2. **Source of data** Indicate the source of the data used to complete the workform.

3. **Date completed** Enter the date the workform was completed.

4. **Library** Enter the library name.

WORKFORM T1 Needs Estimates: Equipment, Software, and Dial Capacity

Instructions

Purpose of Workform T1

Use this workform to record information about the capacity of the technology equipment, software, and dial telephone lines you estimate the library will need to support each planned activity.

Source(s) of Data for Workform T1

The goals, objectives, and activities in the library plan are the sources of the data for this workform.

Factors to Consider When Completing Workform T1

1. Some of the activities you are considering will have requirements for technology to support public service; some will have requirements for technology to support staff; and others will require technology for both groups. Equipment on staff desks is generally not available for public use, and staff should not have to compete with the public to access the technology they need to complete their jobs. Therefore, you will want to use separate copies of the workform to assess the public and staff technology needs.

2. If the library has multiple units, complete a copy of the workform for each unit that will be involved in the activity. Then create a summary copy of the workform that shows the entire library's resource estimates.

3. Some equipment might be used by more than one unit. (For example, a single Web server may serve the needs of all library units.) In that case, you may want to complete a separate workform for "system-wide" equipment, software, and dial capacity as well as individual unit workforms.

4. You will need to determine the time period for which you are measuring capacity. In most cases, the logical time period is one week. However, for some activities you may want to measure capacity by day or month.

5. The capacity required for servers is usually the number of hours the library is open for service. Servers that support Internet services or services for off-site users are generally expected to have the capacity to provide 24-hour service.

6. The equipment section lists the most common equipment used by libraries to achieve their objectives.

   A *server* is a computer that shares its resources and information with other computers, called "clients," on a network.

A *workstation* is a personal computer, either a client computer or a stand-alone computer.

A *terminal* is a character-based device, often called a "dumb" terminal, that accepts keyboard input from a user and displays output on the computer monitor to which the keyboard is attached.

Adaptive equipment is any special equipment designed to ease access for persons with disabilities. (Voice synthesis equipment, large-type screens, and Braille keyboards are examples of adaptive equipment.)

7. The activity you are assessing most likely will require one of four types of software:

   navigation software supports searching for and connecting to electronic information resources (such as Web browser, helper applications, Telnet, FTP, OPAC, etc.)

   applications software includes the commercial software packages libraries offer for the public to use in library computers (such as graphics, word processing, desk top publishing, etc.)

   development software includes tools such as HTML authoring packages or programming tools to assist with the development of local electronic resources such as Web pages or publicly accessible databases of local information

   management software is used to manage library business operations (such as a library's automated system, its Web and e-mail servers, and internal office automation functions)

8. The Telecommunications section of this workform focuses solely on dial telephone lines. Other lines are addressed in Workform T4.

   Incoming dial lines are the lines with modems the library provides to off-site users to access the library's electronic resources.

   The *baud rate* of a dial line is the speed at which the modems can transfer data over the line. Modem speeds typically range from 2,400 to 56,000 bits per second, represented as 2400 bps to 56 kbps.

   Outgoing dial lines are those phone lines used by PCs with modems in the library to access electronic resources external to your library. The most common use of outgoing dial lines is accessing the Internet.

9. Do not enter data in the shaded sections.

(Continued)

To Complete Workform T1

1. **Line A** Place a check mark on one of the lines to indicate if the data on this workform describes public or staff needs estimates.

2. **Line B** Place a check mark on one of the lines to indicate what period of time is covered in the column F and column H estimates.

3. **Section C**

   Row C1 Enter in column H the number of hours any server needed for this activity must be available. (If the server is meant to be available only to users inside the library, these will probably be the number of hours you are open for public service. If the server will be used to provide off-site service via the Internet, for example, this will probably be 24 hours a day.)

   Items C4–C5 List the specific equipment needed in the spaces provided under "Adaptive equipment" or "Other" if the activity will require adaptive equipment or equipment other than that included on the workform.

   Column F Estimate the number of people to be served or searches to be done during the period of time you are considering.

   Column G Enter the average amount of time you think each person will use the service or each search will take.

   Column H Multiply column F by column G to calculate the hours of capacity required.

   Column I Note any special requirements for the equipment needed to support this activity in column I. (For example, you may need headphones or speakers on the workstation, or the server might need the Windows NT operating system.)

4. **Section D** Follow the same procedure for completing columns F–I as outlined for section C.

5. **Section E**

   Items E1–E2 Record the highest speed the library's dial line modems can support in the first column.

   Columns F–I Follow the same procedure for completing these columns as outlined for Part C.

Factors to Consider When Reviewing the Data on Workform T1

1. Have you used separate workforms for the needs of the staff and the needs of the public?

2. Did you duplicate "Hours of Capacity Needed" when estimating software needs? Remember that although a single machine can offer more than one type of software, only one type is likely to be in use at one time. Therefore, the "Hours of Capacity Needed" for software should not exceed the total "Hours of Capacity Needed" for equipment.

WORKFORM T1 Needs Estimates: Equipment, Software, and Dial Capacity

Activity _____

Library unit _____

Month/year data collected _____

A. Users   Public _____   Staff _____

B. Time span   Day _____   Week _____   Month _____

	F. Number of Service Transactions	G. Time per Service Transaction	H. Hours of Capacity Needed	I. Description/Comments
C. Equipment				
1. Servers				
2. Workstations				
3. Terminals				
4. Adaptive equipment (list)				
5. Other (list)				
D. Software				
1. Navigation				
2. Application				
3. Development				
4. Management				
5. Other (list)				
E. Telecommunications				
Dial lines				
1. Incoming Baud rate: _____				
2. Outgoing Baud rate: _____				

Completed by _____   Date completed _____

Source of data _____   Library _____

WORKFORM T2 Needs Estimates: Printers

Instructions

Purpose of Workform T2

Use this workform to estimate how many and what type of printers the library will need to support its planned activities.

Source(s) of Data for Workform T2

1. The goals, objectives, and activities in the library's plan are the sources of the data for this workform.

2. Any experience you have with printers may be used to help you estimate the number of pages per day that may be printed or the time needed to support the printers.

Factors to Consider When Completing Workform T2

1. A *stand-alone printer* is a printer connected to and used with a single workstation. A *networked printer* is a single printer that accepts output for printing from multiple workstations connected by a local area network (LAN).

2. Some activities require technology to support public service functions; some require technology to support staff functions; and others will require technology for both groups. Equipment on staff desks is generally not available for public use, and staff should not have to compete with the public to access the technology they need to complete their jobs. Therefore, you will want to use separate copies of the workform to assess the public and staff technology needs.

3. If the library has multiple units, complete a copy of the workform for each unit that will need printers. Then create a summary copy of the workform that shows the entire library's printer resource estimates.

4. There is no "standard" answer to the question of how many printers a library should offer to the public. Each library needs to decide on the type and number of printers it will offer based on the library's service objectives. However, some issues to be considered when determining what type of printing strategy to support include cost recovery, printer capacity, printer location, and staffing.

5. The *capacity* of a printer is calculated in the number of pages per minute (ppm) it can print.

6. If you use stand-alone printers, you will need one printer for each workstation that offers printing capability.

7. A key issue in assessing how many networked printers a library needs is the location of the printer relative to the location of the workstations. Anecdotal evidence demonstrates that workstation users will generally not travel any significant distance to retrieve printouts. This means they will not go up or down stairs

to get a printout, nor will they travel from one department to another. Although they are far more likely to retrieve printouts from a distant location if they have paid for those printouts, the distance they must travel will have a serious impact on users' level of satisfaction with the service. A distant printer will also quite likely increase the number of directional questions staff will be asked as patrons attempt to figure out where their printouts are.

A networked printer should be located within the line of sight of the workstations it serves. Proper signage clearly indicating where to pick up printouts will reduce the number of directional questions staff will be asked.

8. Supporting printers is a staff-intensive process. The steps involved include

loading paper

changing ink cartridges

fixing paper jams

distributing printouts, if printers are behind staff desks

If networked printers are located behind staffed desks, loading paper, changing cartridges, and fixing jams can be handled by the staff at that service point. However, if you locate the printer at the reference desk, realize that this means the professional staff may be spending their time servicing the printer (and collecting money?), not providing reference service.

If the library chooses to use stand-alone printers or self-service networked printers in public service areas, you will need to allocate staff time to checking and maintaining the printers. Try not to use your professional staff to support your printers; designate and train pages or clerical staff in each unit or facility to proactively manage the printers.

To Complete Workform T2

1. **Line A**   Place a check mark on one of the lines to indicate if the data on this workform describes public or staff needs estimates.

2. **Section B**   The library's plans for recovering the costs of printer supplies will have an impact on the type of printers it chooses to use.

   Item 1   Circle *yes* or *no* to indicate the library's cost recovery intentions.

   Item 2   Select the type of cost recovery to be used.

   Honor system means trusting patrons to voluntarily pay after they print.

   Controlled distribution means putting the printer behind a desk and collecting money before the patrons get their printouts.

   Electronically controlled printing includes coin-operation, stored-value cards, credit card, and other nonmediated payment options.

(Continued)

Instructions

Item 3   Circle the type of printers to be used. You may decide that you need both types of printers. If so, circle both.

If you use an honor system, you can use either stand-alone or networked printers.

If you use controlled distribution, you will need networked printers.

If you use electronically controlled printing, you will need to conform to the requirements of the vendor that provides the controlling mechanism, for example, software, coin boxes, or card readers. Electronically controlled cost recovery systems usually require networked printers.

3. Section C

Item 1   Complete the estimates for lines a and b for each stand-alone workstation. Then calculate on line c the number of pages printed each day (line a × line b).

Item 2   Enter on line a the number of pages printed by the stand-alone printer calculated in C1 above. Enter on line b the minutes per day the service point where the printer is located will be open. Then calculate the pages-per-minute requirements for the networked printer (a ÷ b).

Item 3   Complete the estimates for lines a and b for each networked printer. Then enter the number of workstations you expect to support with each printer. Calculate on line c the number of pages printed each day (line a × line b).

Item 4   Enter on line a the number of pages printed by the networked printer calculated in C3c above. Enter on line b the minutes per day the service point where the printer is located will be open. Then calculate the pages-per-minute requirements for the networked printer (a ÷ b).

4. Section D

Line 1   Enter the number of stand-alone workstations that will require stand-alone printers.

Line 2   Enter the number of locations within the library or unit that will need networked printers.

Line 3   Enter the total number of networked printers that will be required.

5. Section E

Line 1   Enter the number of times per day you think printers should be checked. It is best to check printers on a regular schedule.

Line 2   Estimate the amount of time you think each check will take.

Line 3   Calculate the number of minutes it will take to service each printer each day (E1 × E2).

Line 4   Enter the number of printers needing to be checked.

Line 5   Calculate the number of minutes of staff time per day you will need to devote to printer support (E3 × E4).

6. Section F

Item 1   Copy the number of stand-alone printers you will need from item D1 to line a. Copy the capacity requirements for those printers from item C2c to line b.

Item 2   Copy the number of networked printers you will need from item D3 to line a. Copy the capacity requirements for those printers from item C4c to line b.

Factors to Consider When Reviewing the Data on Workform T2

1. Have you completed separate workforms for the needs of the staff and for the public?

2. Have you investigated the requirements of any electronically controlled cost-recovery system you may be planning?

3. Do you have enough staff to support the number of printers planned? Remember it is easier to identify and solve problems when there are no patrons waiting to use the device. Proactively checking printers for problems on a regular basis, rather than waiting for the public to report problems, may reduce the time spent on printer support in the long run.

4. Does the library have a network linking PCs into which you can add a networked printer?

5. Do you have the space and staff needed for controlled distribution of printouts?

6. Is there sufficient space to support patrons queuing for printouts from a networked printer?

WORKFORM T2 Needs Estimates: Printers

Library unit _____

Month/year data collected _____

A. **Users**   Public _____   Staff _____

B. **Cost Recovery**

1. Do you intend to use some form of cost recovery with printers?   Yes   No

2. If yes, which of the following type or types of cost recovery will you use?

   honor system   Yes   No
   controlled distribution   Yes   No
   electronically controlled   Yes   No

3. Type of printers needed   Stand-alone   Networked

C. **Printer Capacity**

1. Average number of pages to be printed each day by each stand-alone workstation

   a. Number of pages printed per user _____

   b. Number of users printing per day _____

   c. Number of pages printed per day _____

2. Printer capacity of each stand-alone workstation

   a. Number of pages printed each day by each stand-alone workstation _____

   b. Number of minutes open during service period _____

   c. Page-per-minute (ppm) capacity required of printer _____

3. Average number of pages to be printed each day by each networked printer

   a. Number of pages printed per day per workstation _____

   b. Number of workstations supported by printer _____

   c. Number of pages printed per day by printer _____

4. Printer capacity of networked printers needed

   a. Number of pages printed per day by networked printer _____

   b. Number of minutes open during service period _____

   c. Page per minute (ppm) capacity required of printer _____

(Continued)

WORKFORM T2   Needs Estimates: Printers (Cont.)

D. Number and location of printers needed

1. How many workstations will need stand-alone printers? _____

2. How many physical locations within the library or unit will need networked printers?

3. How many networked printers will you need? _____

E. Staffing

1. Number of times per day each printer should be checked _____

2. Number of minutes each check takes _____

3. Number of minutes needed to check each printer _____

4. Number of printers to be checked _____

5. Number of minutes per day needed to service printers _____

F. Summary

1. Stand-alone printers
   a. Number needed _____
   b. Capacity of each _____

2. Network printers
   a. Number needed _____
   b. Capacity of each _____

Completed by _____ Date completed _____

Source of data _____ Library _____

WORKFORM T3 Summary of Needs Estimates: Equipment, Printers, Software, and Dial Capacity

Instructions

Purpose of Workform T3

Workforms T1 and T2 helped you estimate the equipment, software, dial capacity, and printers the library will need to support each of the *activities* you are considering. Use this workform to summarize those requirements for each library *unit*.

Source(s) of Data for Workform T3

The copies of workforms T1 and T2 for each activity provide the sources of data for this workform.

Factors to Consider When Completing Workform T3

In addition to summarizing the requirements for each unit, you may also want to complete a summary sheet for the library as a whole.

To Complete Workform T3

1. **Line A** Place a check mark on one of the lines to indicate if the data on this workform describes public or staff needs estimates.

2. **Line B** Place a check mark on one of the lines to indicate what period of time was covered in Workform T1.

3. **Section C** List each activity in the "Activity" column for which you completed a copy of Workform T1.

   Columns G–K Transfer the "Hours of Capacity Needed" that were calculated on Workform T1 for each type of equipment in each activity.

   Row C11 Total the columns for each type of equipment to determine the total hours of capacity required for all the activities under consideration.

4. **Section D** Transfer the number of stand-alone and networked printers needed in this library unit from the "Summary" section of Workform T2.

5. **Section E** List each activity in the "Activity" column for which you completed a copy of Workform T1.

   Columns L–P Record the "Hours of Capacity Needed" that were calculated on Workform T1 for each type of software in each activity.

   Row E11 Total the columns for each type of software to determine the total capacity required for all the activities under consideration.

5. **Section F** List each activity in the "Activity" column for which you completed a copy of Workform T1.

   Columns Q–R Transfer the "Hours of Capacity Needed" that were calculated on Workform T1 for each type of dial line.

   Row F11 Total the columns for each type of dial line to determine the total capacity required for all the activities under consideration.

Factors to Consider When Reviewing the Data on Workform T3

1. Remember that you are summarizing the hours of capacity needed, not the number of devices of each type. Later in the process you will find forms that help you translate hours of capacity into the number of devices.

2. The "Total Hours of Capacity Needed" for software should not exceed the "Total Hours of Capacity Needed" for equipment. Although a single machine can offer more than one type of software, only one type is likely to be in use at a time.

WORKFORM T3 Summary of Needs Estimates: Equipment, Printers, Software, and Dial Capacity

Library unit _____

Month/year data collected _____

A. Users Public _____ Staff _____

B. Time span Day _____ Week _____ Month _____

C. Equipment

Activity	G. Server	H. Workstation	I. Terminals	J. Adaptive Equipment	K. Other
1.					
2.					
3.					
4.					
5.					
6.					
7.					
8.					
9.					
10.					
11. Total hours of capacity					

D. Total number of printers

1. Networked _____

2. Stand-alone _____

(Continued)

WORKFORM T3 Summary of Needs Estimates: Equipment, Printers, Software, and Dial Capacity (Cont.)

E. Software

Activity	L. Navigation	M. Application	N. Development	O. Management	P. Other
1.					
2.					
3.					
4.					
5.					
6.					
7.					
8.					
9.					
10.					
11. Total hours of capacity					

F. Telecommunications

Activity	Q. Incoming Dial Lines	R. Outgoing Dial Lines
1.		
2.		
3.		
4.		
5.		
6.		
7.		
8.		
9.		
10.		
11. Total hours of capacity		

Completed by _____ Date completed _____

Source of data _____ Library _____

WORKFORM T4   Needs Estimates: Leased Lines

Instructions

Purpose of Workform T4

Use this workform to determine the capacity of the leased line services needed to support a specific activity.

Source(s) of Data for Workform T4

1. The library's inventory of devices is one source of data for this workform.

2. The capacity required of leased lines can be estimated by multiplying the number of devices to be supported over the line by a throughput factor. This form will help you with those calculations.

3. It may be necessary to enlist the aid of the library's technology suppliers to develop throughput factors for servers and other equipment.

Factors to Consider When Completing Workform T4

1. Use one workform for each activity you are assessing. You will also need to complete Workform T5 to understand each library unit's total leased line capacity needs.

2. Leased line capacity is one area in which staff devices and public devices should be combined in the assessment because both groups use the same leased lines to transmit and receive data.

3. If you expect off-site users to access any of the library's servers from the Internet, include the needs of those users in the calculations on the workform.

4. The type of technology column items are defined as follows.

   A *text-based workstation* is a workstation accessing a library's circulation system or accessing the Internet via Telnet or Lynx.

   Graphic workstations are workstations accessing the Internet via a Web browser.

   Servers connected to the Internet include the library's Web server, an e-mail server if you have one, and an online library system to which you offer Telnet or Web access, etc.

5. Do not enter data in the shaded sections.

To Complete Workform T4

1. **Column A**   Add under "Other" any devices you have that transmit data but are not included in the listed categories.

2. **Column B**   Record the number of staff devices and public devices of each type in use in this library unit in column B1 or B2. Add B1 and B2 in each row and enter the total in column B3.

3. **Column C**   Estimate and enter a throughput factor (number of bits per second transmitted) in column C for each device listed under "Other." (You may need assistance from your vendor to calculate the number of bits per second transmitted by some devices.)

4. **Column D**   Multiply the total number of devices of each type (column B3) by column C in that row. Enter the result in the same row in column D.

   Ask your vendors for assistance in calculating the capacity required for each server. The number and type of transactions (Web pages, e-mail messages, etc.) each server supports determines the average number of bits per second of data it will deliver. If you can't estimate these requirements, leave the box blank and see the factors to consider below.

5. **Column E**   Make any notes or comments on your analysis in column E.

6. **Row F**   Add each unshaded column and record the information in row F.

Factors to Consider When Reviewing the Data on Workform T4

1. The throughput factors for text and graphic workstations represent the average number of characters generated per second by these devices. *These numbers are estimates only.* Each library's actual throughput is based on the mix of data resources being accessed.

2. Factors affecting needs of servers include such things as the number of e-mail messages sent and received and the average size of each message or the number of Web pages served and the average size of each page. If you already have the servers, this information may be available from existing statistics. However, if you are planning for a new service, you may not even be able to estimate these numbers. In that case, put a + behind the total at the bottom of column D as a reminder that when you work with this number on Workform T14 it represents the-less-than-total capacity you need.

3. The throughput factors on this workform do not allow for the bandwidth requirements of delivering video and audio files over your telecommunications lines. If you intend to support video and audio downloading, you will probably want to use a network analyzer tool to assess the impact of these types of files on the network. There are no convenient rules of thumb for these types of files.

Needs Estimates: Leased Lines

Activity _____

Library unit _____

Month/year data collected _____

A. Type of Technology	B. Number of Devices to Be Supported			C. Throughput Factor for Each Device*	D. Capacity Required in Bits per Second	E. Description/Comments
	1. Staff	2. Public	3. Total			
Text-based workstations and terminals				1,600		
Graphic workstations				11,200		
Servers connected to the Internet						
Other (list)						
F. Total						

*Note: Based on "rule of thumb" estimates of 35 text devices or 5 graphic devices per 56K line. Note that the throughput figures are the same even if your line capacity is T1 or a fraction of a T1.

Completed by _____   Date completed _____

Source of data _____   Library _____

Instructions

WORKFORM T5 Summary of Needs Estimates: Leased Lines

Purpose of Workform T5

Workform T4 helped you calculate the leased line capacity the library will need to support each of the *activities* you are considering. Use this workform to summarize those requirements for each library *unit*.

Source(s) of Data for Workform T5

1. Multiple copies of Workform T4 are the source of data for this workform.

2. You can also use Workform T5 to compile a summary of leased-line needs for a unit housed in a single building.

Factors to Consider When Completing Workform T5

1. Leased line capacity is one area in which staff devices and public devices should be combined in the assessment because both groups use the same leased lines to transmit and receive data.

2. You will also need to include the number of devices presently installed to arrive at a complete picture of your leased line capacity requirements per library unit.

3. If you are calculating capacity requirements for separate library units housed within a building, complete an additional copy of this workform for all of the units within that building to establish the leased line requirements for the entire building.

To Complete Workform T5

1. **Column A** List each activity for which you completed a copy of Workform T4.

2. **Column B** Record the information from the corresponding total on Workform T4 for this activity.

3. **Row C** Add the entries in column B to determine the total capacity required for all the activities under consideration.

Factors to Consider When Reviewing the Data on Workform T5

1. Have you included all of your existing equipment in the calculations, including any equipment you may think of as administrative only? Every piece of equipment that accesses resources outside your local area network, even a device on a secretary's desk that sends only administrative e-mail to a city or county mail server, will use your leased line capacity.

2. The throughput of different leased line services varies among telephone companies. If your needs fall between two service offerings, plan on leasing the larger capacity lines. Throughput requirements will continue to increase for the foreseeable future.

Summary of Needs Estimates: Leased Lines

Library unit _____

Month/year data collected _____

A. Activity	B. Capacity Required in Bits per Second

C. Total capacity required	

Completed by _____ Date completed _____

Source of data _____ Library _____

WORKFORM T6 Capacity Available: Workstation and Terminal Functions

Instructions

Purpose of Workform T6

Use this workform to record information about the functions supported by the workstation and terminal equipment each library unit already has.

Source(s) of Data for Workform T6

An existing inventory of equipment and software might provide this information. If such an inventory does not exist, count the equipment and software.

Factors to Consider When Completing Workform T6

1. Some of the activities you are considering will have requirements for technology to support public service; some will have requirements for technology to support staff; and others will require technology for both groups. Equipment on staff desks is generally not available for public use, and staff should not have to compete with the public to access the technology they need to complete their jobs. Therefore, you will want to use separate copies of the workform to assess the public and staff technology needs.

2. Patrons and staff in libraries use personal computer workstations or character-based terminals to access technology-based services. Some of these devices can be used with only one service; others are multifunction devices. When you are trying to determine the library's capacity for adding or expanding services, the distinction between single-function and multifunction devices is important. Simply having unused capacity on a device is not enough; that device must also be capable of supporting the service you wish to offer.

3. If the library has multiple units, complete a copy of the workform for each unit. Then create a summary copy of the workform that shows the entire library's resource capacity.

4. Column B lists the most common equipment used by libraries.

   A *single-function workstation* is one that is limited to accessing only one product or service. A workstation that can be used only to access the online catalog is an example of a single-function workstation. A workstation dedicated to a single CD-ROM product is another example.

A *multifunction workstation* is capable of accessing more than one product or service. A workstation on a local area network offering access to multiple CD-ROM databases is an example of a multifunction workstation, as is a PC offering both access to the Internet and a selection of office automation programs.

A *terminal* is a character-based device, often called a "dumb" terminal, that accepts keyboard input from a user and displays output on the computer monitor to which the keyboard is attached.

Adaptive equipment may be used to provide the same types of services as workstations and terminals. As appropriate, note in Section C the types of services supported by the library's adaptive equipment.

5. Section C includes four types of service.

   Navigation Devices used for this service access electronic resources such as the library's online catalog, the Internet, or CD-ROM databases. A navigation workstation might have a Telnet or GUI software client used to access the online catalog, a Web browser, or an application used to access a specific database loaded on the workstation.

   Applications Devices used for this service provide public access to commercial personal computer applications. Such devices would include word processing or desktop publishing workstations available to the public.

   Development Devices for this service are used by the staff to create Web pages, scan resources into digital formats, develop local electronic databases, or write software programs to support the library's delivery of its services.

   Management Devices for this service are used for staff functions in the management of the library. They may be on a workstation used exclusively on the administrative local area network or a circulation or cataloging terminal attached to the library's integrated system. Online catalog terminals, although they are attached to the library's online system, would be recorded under navigation.

6. Do not enter information in the shaded sections.

(Continued)

To Complete Workform T6

1. **Line A**   Place a check mark on one of the lines to indicate if the data on this workform describes public or staff needs estimates.

2. **Column B**   Enter a device-specific identifier in column B for each single-function or multifunction workstation, terminal, or adaptive equipment device you have. This could be an indication of the location of the device (Reference Desk #1), an inventory number, a serial number, or any other identifier that uniquely identifies that specific device.

3. **Column C**   Place a check mark in one or more of the four columns to indicate the type of service each device supports.

4. **Column D**   Note the product or software package name(s) supported by each device in this area. (For example, you might have a CD-ROM periodical index on a single-function workstation and Internet Explorer and PAC for Windows on a multifunction workstation.)

Factor to Consider When Reviewing the Data on Workform T6

Are you offering both graphic and text access to some services? If so, you may note a strong public preference for the graphic environment. Even if you have text-based capacity available for all but the most text-oriented resources (the library's online catalog, for example), users generally prefer graphic interfaces when they are available. This is especially true if your Internet access is through a text-based Lynx browser.

WORKFORM T6 Capacity Available: Workstation and Terminal Functions

Library unit _____ Month/year data collected _____

A. Users Public _____ Staff _____

B. Equipment	**C. Type of Service**					**D. Description/Comments**
	Navigation	Applications	Development	Management		
1. Single-function workstations						
2. Multifunction workstations						
3. Terminals						
4. Adaptive equipment						

Completed by _____ Date completed _____

Source of data _____ Library _____

Instructions

Purpose of Workform T7

Use this workform to record information about the condition of the workstation and terminal equipment already in your library.

Source(s) of Data for Workform T7

An existing inventory of equipment and software might provide this information. If such an inventory does not exist, conduct an inventory of the equipment and software.

Factors to Consider When Completing Workform T7

1. Use one copy of the workform for each library unit included in the library's service plan.

2. Computer equipment evolves constantly. Each new release of a software package requires more memory or a faster processor to continue to operate with acceptable performance. Just as you need to know what functions the library's existing technology supports, you also need to have a basic understanding of the condition of the equipment.

3. As equipment ages, it wears out from use and becomes harder to repair. Breakdowns are more frequent and repairs usually take longer. Out-of-order equipment reduces capacity. If the library's "mean time to repair" for equipment is quite long or the percentage of equipment needing repair is high, capacity may be significantly less than you think.

4. Column B lists the most common equipment used by libraries.

   A *single-function workstation* is one that is limited to accessing only one product or service. A workstation that can be used only to access the on-line catalog is an example of a single-function workstation. A workstation dedicated to a single CD-ROM product is another example.

   A *multifunction workstation* is capable of accessing more than one product or service. A workstation on a local area network offering access to multiple CD-ROM databases is an example of a multifunction workstation, as is a PC offering both access to the Internet and a selection of office automation programs.

   A *terminal* is a character-based device, often called a "dumb" terminal, that accepts keyboard input from a user and displays output on the computer monitor to which the keyboard is attached.

A *terminal emulation protocol* is a set of rules that govern the communication between a host computer and its terminals. Every terminal device supports one or more specific terminal emulations.

5. When entering information on workstations, use a unique identifier that indicates the function of the device if the function is tied to the technical condition of the device. (For example, if you listed a label-printing PC as TS#3 on Workform T6, you might add DOS 386/Labels to that identifier on this workform.)

6. If the library has multiple units, complete a copy of this workform for each unit. Then create a summary copy of the workform that shows the entire library's resource condition.

7. Do not enter data in the shaded sections.

To Complete Workform T7

1. **Line A** Place a check mark on one of the lines to indicate if the data on this workform describes public or staff equipment.

2. **Section B** Enter a device-specific identifier in column B for each single- or multifunction workstation you have. This could be an indication of the location of the device (Reference Desk #1), an inventory number, a serial number, or any other identifier that uniquely identifies that specific device. If you have completed Workform T6, use the same device identifiers on Workform T7.

3. **Column C** Enter in columns C1–C4 information on each device listed in column B.

   Column C1 Enter the computer chip type (for example, 386, 486, Celeron, Pentium, Cyrix, AMD, Pentium II, Macintosh) and the speed (90 MHz, 233 MHz, 400 MHz, etc.).

   Column C2 Enter the amount of random access memory (RAM) the device has (640 K, 4 MB, 32 MB, 64 MB, etc.).

   Column C3 Enter the operating system and its release level (Macintosh 8.5, DOS, Windows 3.1, Windows 98, etc.).

   Column C4 Note if the device has fixed or removable disks and the capacity or size of the disk(s) (1.4 MB floppy, 8.0 GB hard drive, 100 MB Zip drive, 2.0 GB Jaz drive, etc.).

4. **Column D** Make any special notations on the repair history and status of the device.

(Continued)

Instructions

5. **Column E** List each terminal, following the same procedure as outlined for Section B.

6. **Column F** Enter the terminal emulation(s) supported by each terminal.

7. **Column G** Make any special notations on the repair history and status of the device.

Factor to Consider When Reviewing the Data on Workform T7

Remember, some devices may be acceptable for a specific function but incapable of being used for other functions. At some point, even devices that perform one old function well may need to be replaced because the costs of keeping staff trained to operate them will outweigh the costs of replacing them.

Library unit _____

Month/year data collected _____

A. Users   Public _____   Staff _____

B. Workstations	C. Technical Condition				D. Repair History
	1. Processor Type and Speed	2. Memory	3. Operating System	4. Disk Type and Size	
Single-function workstations					
Multifunction workstations					

E. Terminals	F. Terminal Emulation	G. Repair History

Completed by _____   Date completed _____

Source of data _____   Library _____

WORKFORM T8   Capacity Available: Equipment, Software, and Telecommunications

Instructions

Purpose of Workform T8

Use this workform to record information about the capacity of the equipment and telecommunications already in the library.

Source(s) of Data for Workform T8

1. Workform T1 provides information on the time span. Workform T6 provides the source of information on your workstations and terminals.

2. An existing inventory of equipment can also provide some of this information. If such an inventory does not exist, you can conduct a physical count of the equipment and software.

3. Phone bills can provide information on number of dial-line connections and number and type of leased-line connections and their capacity.

Factors to Consider When Completing Workform T8

1. If the library has multiple units, complete a copy of this workform for each unit. Then create a summary copy of the workform that shows the entire library's resource capacity.

2. If the library has equipment other than that included on the workform, list the equipment in the spaces provided under "Other."

3. The workform distinguishes between single-function and multifunction workstations. Be sure to record the two types of workstations separately.

4. Section D of the workform records the type of dial lines available in your library.

5. Do not enter data in the shaded sections.

To Complete Workform T8

1. **Line A** Place a check mark on one of the lines to indicate if the data on this workform describes public or staff needs estimates.

2. **Line B** Place a check mark on one of the lines to indicate the period of time that is covered in the "Number of Service Transactions" and "Hours of Capacity Needed" estimates as noted on Workform T1.

3. **Section C**

   Item 1 List each server's function in the spaces provided. If the library has more than one server of a type, note the number of servers in column F.

   Skip item 1 for units without servers if all of the servers are centralized in a single location.

   Item 2 Group single-function workstations by the service they support (navigation, applications, development, or management).

   Column F, Item 2 Count each group, and enter the number of each type of workstation in column F.

   Column I, Item 2 Use column I to record specific information about the type of software (browser, OPAC client, word processing, desktop publishing, etc.) supported. You may want to note the specific function itself, (for example, OPAC access only or Internet access only).

   Item 3 Group multifunction workstations by the combination of functions they serve (navigation, applications, development, or management). Write the groups under "Multifunction workstations" in the spaces provided.

   Column F, Item 3 Count the number of workstations in each group and enter it in column F. (For example, if the library has two workstations that offer access to the Internet and word processing software to the public, you would enter Navigation/applications under Multifunction workstations and 2 in column F for that row.)

   Column I, Item 3 Use column I to record specific information about the types of software (browser, OPAC client, word processing, desktop publishing, etc.) supported. You may want to record information on the functions themselves, (for example, word processing and CD network access).

   Item 4 Follow the same procedures for terminals as outlined for items 2 and 3.

   Item 5 Enter information on the type and number of adaptive devices you have. Use column I for a fuller description as needed.

   Item 6 Record the type and number of any equipment not noted elsewhere.

(Continued)

Column G   For all items in section C, enter the number of hours each type of device is available. This number will typically be the number of hours the library unit is open. If the device is used to provide off-site service (such as an Internet-connected Web server), the hours of availability are generally calculated at 24 hours per day.

Column H   For all items in section C, multiply column F by column G to determine total hours of capacity for each type of device in the library unit.

4. **Section D**

Column F   Enter the number of lines of each type in column F.

Column G   Enter the number of hours each type of line is available in column G. For outgoing lines, this number will typically be the number of hours the library unit is open. For incoming lines, the hours of availability are generally calculated as the number of hours these electronic resources are available to off-site users, usually 24 hours per day.

Column H   Multiply column F by column G to determine total hours of capacity for each type of *dial* line in the library unit.

5. **Section E**

Column J   Enter the number of lines of each type available to the library unit in column J.

Row 4   Note the capacity of the *leased* line connection to the Internet in row 4 if the library unit has a separate Internet line.

Column K – Record information on the type of line (ISDN, frame relay, etc.) or comments about the line (for example, integrated library system traffic only or Internet and integrated library system traffic mixed).

Factor to Consider When Reviewing the Data on Workform T8

The speed of a dial connection affects its value. A 56 K or 28.8 bits per second (bps) modem is far more likely to be used than a slower (14.4 bps or less) modem.

WORKFORM T8 Capacity Available: Equipment, Software, and Telecommunications

Library unit _____

_____ Month/year data collected

A. Users Public _____ Staff _____

B. Time span Day _____ Week _____ Month _____

C. Equipment/Software	F. Number of Devices	G. Hours Available	H. Total Hours of Capacity	I. Comments
1. Servers (list by function)				
2. Single-function workstations (group by function)				
Navigation				
Applications				
Development				
Management				
3. Multifunction workstations (group by functions)				

(Continued)

WORKFORM T8 Capacity Available: Equipment, Software, and Telecommunications (Cont.)

C. Equipment/Software (Cont.)	F. Number of Devices	G. Hours Available	H. Total Hours of Capacity	I. Comments
4. Terminals (group by function)				
Navigation				
Management				
5. Adaptive equipment (group by type)				
6. Other (group by type)				

D. Telecommunications—Dial lines				
Incoming				
Outgoing				

E. Telecommunications—Leased Lines	J. Number of Lines Available	K. Description/Comments
Capacity of Line		
1. 56 K (56,000 bits per second)		
2. T1 (1.5 million bits per second)		
3. Other (list)		
4. Access to the Internet (list capacity)		

Completed by _____ Date completed _____

Source of data _____ Library _____

Instructions

WORKFORM T9   Utilization: Observation

Purpose of Workform T9

Use this workform to record observed usage over the course of a day. If your library uses sign-up sheets, use Workform T10.

Source(s) of Data for Workform T9

1. Direct observation of usage provides the information for this workform.

2. Workform T8 provides the data for column F.

Factors to Consider When Completing Workform T9

1. *Utilization* is the amount of time the library's technical capacity is actually being used to provide service. There are several ways to determine the utilization of equipment, including observation of actual usage throughout the day (recorded on this workform) and an analysis of sign-up sheets used to schedule public access to resources. Use Workform T10 to analyze sign-up sheets.

2. You will probably want to record hourly usage for at least a full week to get an accurate picture of usage patterns.

3. If the same person is using equipment during two or more observation periods, record that person each time.

4. It will be easier to draw conclusions from these observations if your data-gathering efforts are consistent. If you intend to record your observations once an hour, try to do it at the same time every hour (for example, 9:15, 10:15, etc.).

5. If you want to record the mix of functions being used at multifunction workstations, observe the software in use as you are recording and note it on the workform. (For example, if you have 9 multifunction workstations offering both OPAC and Internet access, you might note on the workform for your 12:30 P.M. observation that OPAC = 3 and Internet = 6.)

6. If the library has multiple units, complete a copy of this workform for each unit. Then create a summary copy of the workform that shows the entire library's resource utilization.

7. Do not enter data in the shaded sections.

To Complete Workform T9

1. **Line A**   Place a check mark on one of the lines to indicate if the data on this workform describes observations of public or staff utilization.

2. **Row B**   Enter the times you will record your observations.

3. **Row C**   Record the initials of the staff member conducting the observations. This will help in analyzing the data if questions arise later.

4. **Section D**

   Item 1   Record the number of available single-function workstations of each type in column F. (See Workform T8.)

   Item 2   List multifunction workstations by the combination of functions they serve (navigation/applications, development/management, etc.) and record the number of workstations in each group in column F.

   Items 3–5   Count the terminals, adaptive equipment, and other equipment and record the numbers in column F.

   Section G   The columns in this section correspond to the observation times listed in row B. Make a complete survey of the equipment you are observing at the same time each hour and record the number of people using the equipment in section G under the appropriate time slot.

5. **Section E**

   Column F   Refer to Workform T8, section D and record the number of dial lines available in column F.

   Section G   Record the fact that the phone line is in use (if it is) in the appropriate time slot for section G if a workstation has a modem and an outgoing telephone line. You may be able to determine this from observing the software in use on the workstation, or you may need to ask the user. Check the modems on incoming phone lines for in-use indications and record the usage during your survey as well.

6. **Column H**   Total the number of hours each device was in use and enter that information in column H.

Factors to Consider When Reviewing the Data on Workform T9

1. Pay attention to *when* the devices are in use as well as the total number of hours in use. When you consider new activities, you must determine if there is a match between the hours the devices are unused and the hours an activity's target population is likely to use the devices?

2. Are some devices consistently underused? What factors might be contributing to that usage pattern? Can you change the usage by offering different services at these devices or relocating the devices?

WORKFORM T9 Utilization: Observation

Library unit _____

Date _____

Public _____ Staff _____

Day of the week _____

A. Users

B. Observation times

C. Observer's initials

D. Equipment/Software	F. Number of Devices Available	G. Number in Use											H. Total Hours in Use
1. Single-function workstation (group by function)													
Navigation													
Applications													
Development													
Management													
2. Multifunction workstations (group by functions)													
3. Terminals (group by function)													
Navigation													
Management													
4. Adaptive equipment (list)													

(Continued)

WORKFORM T9 Utilization: Observation (Cont.)

	F. Number of Devices Available	G. Number in Use								H. Total Hours in Use
B. Observation times										
C. Observer's initials										
D. Equipment/Software (Cont.)										
5. Other (list)										
E. Telecommunications— Dial Lines										
Incoming lines										
Outgoing lines										

Completed by _____   Date completed _____

Source of data _____   Library _____

Instructions WORKFORM T10 Utilization: Public Services Sign-Up Analysis

Purpose of Workform T10

Use this workform to analyze sign-up sheets if you sign up people for specific, reserved periods of technology use or sign up people on a first-come, first-served basis. If your library does not use sign-up sheets, use Workform T9.

Source(s) of Data for Workform T10

Data from sign-up sheets provides the information for this workform.

Factors to Consider When Completing Workform T10

1. *Utilization* is the amount of time the library's technical capacity is actually being used to provide service. There are several ways to determine the utilization of your equipment, including direct observation (recorded on workform T9) or analysis of sign-up sheets used to schedule public access to resources.

2. If library staff needs to schedule time on staff equipment, use a separate copy of this workform to record staff usage.

3. You will probably want to record your sign-ups for at least a week to get an accurate picture of your usage patterns.

4. If the library allows both scheduled and unscheduled use of equipment, use Workform T9 in conjunction with this workform to develop a complete picture of utilization.

5. It will be easier to draw conclusions if your data gathering efforts are consistent. If you intend to record your sign-ups once an hour, try to do it at the same time every hour (for example, 9:15, 10:15, 11:15, etc.).

6. If the library has multiple units, complete a copy of this workform for each unit. Then create a summary copy of the workform that shows the entire library's resource utilization.

7. Do not enter data in the shaded sections.

To Complete Workform T10

1. **Line A** Place a check mark on one of the lines to indicate if the data on this workform describes public or staff sign-ups.

2. **Row B** Enter the times you will record your sign-ups for equipment.

3. **Section C**

   Item 1 Record in column E the number of individuals that can be served by the available single-function workstations of each type. (For example, if you have four workstations that are navigation workstations and you permit customers to sign up for ½-hour periods, you can potentially serve 8 customers per hour.)

   Note on the comments line at the end of the workform any special conditions that may exist during your data-gathering period, such as a broken machine.

   Item 2 List multifunction workstations by the combination of functions they serve (navigation/applications, development/management, etc.) and record the number of individuals that can be served by each group in column E.

   Items 3–4, Column E Count and record the customers who can be served by terminals, adaptive equipment, and other equipment and record the numbers in column E.

4. **Section F** The columns in this section correspond to the sign-up times listed in row B.

   If you sign people up in advance for specific time slots, count the number of people signed up to use the equipment for each hour and record that number under the appropriate time slot.

   If you sign people up for increments of less than an hour, record the total number of people signed up during the hour. (For example, if you sign people up in 30-minute increments, record 2 people in that hour if both time slots are assigned.)

(Continued)

Instructions

If you sign people up on a first-come, first-served basis, count the number of people using the equipment and the number signed up and waiting to use the equipment. Record that number on the workform for each hour.

If you sign people up in 30-minute increments, record 2 people as users of the device in that hour if both time slots are filled.

5. **Section D**

   Column E   If single-function workstations with modems and outgoing telephone lines are in use, record that use in column E. If multifunction workstations with modems and outgoing lines are in use, ask the customer if he or she used those modems and phone lines during the session. Record the answer on the sign-up sheet, then note the usage on this workform.

6. **Column G**   Total the number of hours each device was in use and enter that information in column G.

Factor to Consider When Reviewing the Data on Workform T10

For first-come, first-served, if the number of people who sign up to use a computer consistently exceeds the number of people that can be served by that computer, you have 100 percent utilization of your existing equipment. The number of people who sign up beyond those that can be served each hour indicates how much more technology you could use just to support your present service offerings.

Utilization: Public Services Sign-Up Analysis

Library unit _____

Date _____

A. Users   Public _____   Staff _____

Day of the week _____

B. Sign-Up Times

C. Equipment/Software	**E.** **Customers** **That Can** **Be Served**	**F. Number of Sign-Ups**															**G.** **Total Hours** **in Use**
1. Single-function workstation (group by function)																	
Navigation																	
Applications																	
Development																	
Management																	
2. Multifunction workstations (group by functions)																	
3. Terminals (group by function)																	
Navigation																	
Management																	
4. Adaptive equipment (list)																	

(Continued)

WORKFORM T10 **Utilization: Public Services Sign-Up Analysis (Cont.)**

B. Sign-Up Times												
C. Equipment/Software (Cont.)	**E. Customers That Can Be Served**	**F. Number of Sign-Ups**										**G. Total Hours in Use**
5. Other (list)												
D. Telecommunications— Dial Lines												
Incoming												
Outgoing												

Special conditions during data collection period

_____

_____

_____

_____

Completed by _____ Date completed _____

Source of data _____ Library _____

Instructions

Purpose of Workform T11

Use this workform to summarize the utilization data gathered from Workforms T9 and/or T10.

Source(s) of Data for Workform T11

Workforms T8, T9, and T10 provide the information for this workform.

Factors to Consider When Completing Workform T11

1. Once you have recorded the actual usage of the library's technical capacity, using Workforms T9 or T10, you will want to determine how much capacity remains. This is capacity that might be used to support expansion of existing services or introduction of new services.

2. If the library has multiple units, complete a copy of this workform for each unit. Then create a summary copy of the workform that shows the entire library's resource utilization.

3. Do not enter data in the shaded sections.

To Complete Workform T11

1. **Line A**   Place a check mark on one of the lines to indicate if the data on this workform describes public or staff utilization.

WORKFORM T11   Utilization: Summary

2. **Line B**   Place a check mark on one of the lines to indicate the period of time covered in the data for Workforms T9 and/or T10.

3. **Section C–D**   These sections include the same categories of equipment, software, and telecommunications as the other workforms in this utilization series. Enter the functions and other types of equipment you recorded in Workform T9 or T10.

4. **Column E**   Transfer the data in the "Total Hours of Capacity" column from Workform T8 to column E.

5. **Column F**   Transfer the data from the "Total Hours in Use" column on Workform T9 or T10 to column F. If you used both workforms in gathering your data, add the hours in use from each workform before recording them here.

6. **Column G**   For each row, subtract column F from column E to determine unused hours of capacity (if any).

7. **Column H**   Record in column H important observations, particularly about usage patterns. (For example, if Workform T9 or T10 indicates that the unused capacity is available only at certain hours each day, note that here.)

Factors to Consider When Reviewing the Data on T11

1. Can you truly deploy any unused capacity identified to meet the needs?

2. Is the capacity available at the times you expect the new or added service to be in demand?

WORKFORM T11 Utilization: Summary

Library unit _____

A. Users   Public _____   Staff _____

B. Time span   Day _____   Week _____   Month _____

Month/year data collected _____

C. Equipment/Software	E. Total Hours of Capacity	F. Total Hours in Use	G. Unused Hours of Capacity	H. Comments
1. Single-function workstation (group by function)				
Navigation				
Applications				
Development				
Management				
2. Multifunction workstations (group by functions)				
3. Terminals (group by function)				
Navigation				
Management				
4. Adaptive equipment (list)				

(Continued)

C. **Equipment/Software** (Cont.)	E. **Total Hours of Capacity**	F. **Total Hours in Use**	G. **Unused Hours of Capacity**	H. **Comments**
5. Other (list)				
D. **Telecommunications— Dial Lines**				
Incoming				
Outgoing				

Completed by _____ Date completed _____

Source of data _____ Library _____

WORKFORM T12 Comparison of Capacity Required to Unused Capacity Available

Instructions

Purpose of Workform T12

Use this workform to compare the capacity needed with the capacity available in each library unit.

Source(s) of Data for Workform T12

Workforms T1 and T9–T11 provide the information for this workform.

Factors to Consider When Completing Workform T12

1. Workform T11 helped you identify the unused technical capacity the library has available to apply to new or expanded services. This workform compares the unused capacity available with the hours of capacity needed to support the library's chosen activities. Completing this workform will help you determine if you need additional capacity and how much you need.

2. If you are studying the technical requirements of more than one activity for a library unit and those activities use multifunction workstations, complete a summary copy of Workform T12. Add together the Additional Hours of Capacity Needed or Available for all the activities.

3. If the library has multiple units, complete a copy of this workform for each unit. You may also want to create a summary copy of the workform that shows the entire library's resource utilization.

4. Do not enter data in the shaded sections.

To Complete Workform T12

1. **Line A** Place a check mark on one of the lines to indicate if the data on this workform describes public or staff needs estimates.

2. **Line B** Place a check mark on one of the lines to indicate the period of time covered for column F.

3. **Sections C–D** These sections include the same categories of equipment/software and telecommunications as workforms in the Utilization series. Enter the functions and other types of equipment recorded on Workform T9 or T10.

4. **Column E** Transfer the data from "Unused Hours of Capacity" on Workform T11 to column E.

5. **Column F** Transfer to column F the "Hours of Capacity Needed" data from Workform T1 for this activity.

6. **Column G** For each row, subtract column F from column E to determine additional hours available (or needed). If the difference is a negative number, record it in parentheses to indicate that these are hours needed.

7. **Column H** Transfer to column H the observations on Workforms T9, T10, or T11.

Factors to Consider When Reviewing the Data on Workform T12

1. Pay particular attention to comments on usage patterns or technical requirements. If the activity being considered will be performed during certain hours of the day, be sure you compare those times with the hours of availability you discovered on Workforms T9 and/or T10.

2. If your activities require leased line telecommunications capacity, be sure to complete Workforms T4, T5, and T14 to assess those capacity requirements as well.

WORKFORM T12 **Comparison of Capacity Required to Unused Capacity Available**

Activity _____

Library unit _____

A. Users Public _____ Staff _____

B. Time span Day _____ Week _____ Month _____ Month/year data collected _____

C. Equipment/Software	E. Unused Hours of Capacity	F. Hours of Capacity Needed	G. Additional Hours of Capacity Available (or Needed)	H. Comments
1. Single-function workstation (group by function)				
Navigation				
Applications				
Development				
Management				
2. Multifunction workstations (group by functions)				
3. Terminals (group by function)				
Navigation				
Management				
4. Adaptive equipment (list)				

(Continued)

WORKFORM T12 Comparison of Capacity Required to Unused Capacity Available (Cont.)

	E. Unused Hours of Capacity	F. Hours of Capacity Needed	G. Additional Hours of Capacity Available (or Needed)	H. Comments
C. Equipment/Software (Cont.)				
5. Other (list)				
D. Telecommunications— Dial Lines				
Incoming				
Outgoing				

Completed by _____

Source of data _____

Date completed _____

Library _____

Instructions

Purpose of Workform T13

Use this workform to determine the number of additional devices to be purchased to reach needed capacity in each library unit.

Source(s) of Data for Workform T13

Workform T12 and the library's hours provide the information for this workform.

Factors to Consider When Completing Workform T13

1. Workform T12 identified the hours of additional capacity you have determined you need to support each of the chosen activities. Completing this workform will translate those hours of capacity into the number of devices you need. That information will form the basis of determining the costs of any additional technical capacity required.

2. In calculating the requirements for multifunction workstations, you may complete Workform T13 for each activity separately, or you may complete one copy of Workform T13 for each library unit, based on a summary copy of Workform T12.

3. Do not enter data in the shaded sections.

To Complete Workform T13

1. **Line A**   Place a check mark on one of the lines to indicate if the data on this workform describes public or staff needs estimates.

2. **Line B**   Place a check mark on one of the lines to indicate the period of time covered.

3. **Sections C–D**

    Items 1–5   Enter the functions and other types of equipment you recorded on Workform T12.

WORKFORM T13   Technology Needed

Column E   Transfer to column E only the data on *needed* additional hours of capacity from "Additional Hours of Capacity Available (or Needed)" on Workform T12.

Column F   Enter the number of hours this library unit is open in column F.

Column G   Divide column E by column F to determine the number of devices required. Note that you will need to round any fractional number resulting from this calculation to a whole number. (For example, if the period covered is one week and if the library is open 36 hours per week and the capacity needed is 72 hours, 2 devices are needed.)

Column H   Transfer any relevant observations on Workforms T9–T12 to column H.

Factors to Consider When Reviewing the Data on Workform T13

1. The number of devices you determine you need is *only an estimate*. This number must be evaluated in light of local needs and knowledge about the usage patterns in the library units and the intended audience for the service activities being evaluated. (For example, if you need 40 hours of capacity in a library unit open 40 hours a week, one additional device may meet your needs. However, if the 40 hours of capacity required is meant to serve the needs of 2 half-time staff members who work the same shift, a single device will not meet their needs unless their work hours are adjusted.)

2. If planned activities require leased line telecommunications capacity, be sure to complete Workforms T4, T5, and T14 to assess those capacity requirements as well.

3. If you need more devices than the library can physically support to accomplish the library's objectives, you will need to reassess those objectives. If the library can't provide the technical capacity needed to meet its objectives, there will be no way to accomplish the desired results.

4. Be sure to consider the facility's ability to support the number of devices needed. Electricity, data cabling, and sufficient cooling are all needed to support an increase in technology. See chapter 4 for more information on these issues.

WORKFORM T13 **Technology Needed**

Activity _____

Library unit _____

Month/year data collected _____

A. Users   Public _____   Staff _____

B. Time span   Day _____   Week _____   Month _____

C. Equipment/Software	E. Additional Hours Needed	F. Open Hours	G. Number of Devices Required	H. Comments
1. Single-function workstation (group by function)				
Navigation				
Applications				
Development				
Management				
2. Multifunction workstations (group by functions)				
3. Terminals (group by function)				
Navigation				
Management				
4. Adaptive equipment (list)				

(Continued)

C. Equipment/Software (Cont.)	E. Additional Hours Needed	F. Open Hours	G. Number of Devices Required	H. Comments
5. Other (list)				
D. Telecommunications— Dial Lines				
Incoming				
Outgoing				

Completed by _____   Date completed _____

Source of data _____   Library _____

WORKFORM T14 Leased Line Capacity Needed

Instructions

Purpose of Workform T14

If the activities you are considering will make use of leased telephone lines for transferring data, use this workform to identify the additional capacity, if any, required.

Source(s) of Data for Workform T14

Workforms T4 and T8 provide the information for this workform.

Factors to Consider When Completing Workform T14

Usually, all of the devices in a building share a leased line to transmit data outside the building. This is true regardless of whether the device is for staff or public use. It is important to ensure that the assessment of capacity requirements for a leased line takes this into account.

To Complete Workform T14

1. **Line A** Enter the number of leased lines available in the library unit being assessed. This information is available on Workform T8.

2. **Line B** Enter the capacity in bits per second of those lines. This information is available on Workform T8.

3. **Line C** Multiply line A by line B to determine the total capacity presently available and record it on line C.

4. **Line D** Transfer to line D on this workform the capacity-required total from row F, column D of Workform T4.

5. **Line E** Copy your answer from line C to line E.

6. **Line F** Subtract line E from line D to determine if additional capacity is available or more will be required. Record the answer on line F. If the difference is a negative number, record it in parentheses to indicate that it represents capacity needed.

Factor to Consider When Reviewing the Data on Workform T14

1. Have you included all the devices using your leased lines in the calculations, including any servers you are supporting or any business applications (such as electronic book orders or e-mail) that might also be utilizing the bandwidth?

2. If the number on Workform T4 includes a + at the end, you did not include the requirements of your servers in the calculations. You should adjust line F to allow for your server(s). If line F is a positive number, reduce it to allow for your server(s). If line F is a negative number, increase the negative amount (for example, from –56,000 bits to –128,000 bits).

   There is no "correct" factor to use here. Start by reducing the capacity by 56,000 bits per second per server. However, understand this is truly just an estimate. If you begin to experience response-time problems or want a more accurate measure of your requirements, you will need to do a technical assessment.

   To estimate the average bits-per-second output of a server, you need to analyze your wide area network traffic. This can be done with software and hardware tools designed for this purpose or with the help of network consultants. Sometimes your telephone supplier can provide reports on the utilization of your leased lines that will help with this as well.

WORKFORM T14 **Leased Line Capacity Needed**

Activity _____

Month/year data collected _____

Library unit _____

A. Number of leased lines available _____

B. Capacity in bits per second of installed lines $\times$ _____

C. Total capacity available $=$ _____

D. Capacity required in bits per second _____

E. Total capacity available $-$ _____

F. Additional capacity available (or needed) $=$ _____

Completed by _____ Date completed _____

Source of data _____ Library _____

WORKFORM T15　Costs of Needed Technology

Instructions

Purpose of Workform T15

Use this workform to translate the number and types of devices needed and the dial and leased line telecommunications capacity required into estimated costs.

Source(s) of Data for Workform T15

1. Workforms T13 and T14 provide some information for this workform.
2. You will also need to gather estimated cost data from suppliers of the needed equipment and from telecommunications and Internet service providers.

Factors to Consider When Completing Workform T15

1. Workforms T13 and T14 identified the number and types of devices needed and the dial and leased line telecommunications capacity required to support each of the library's chosen activities. Completing this workform will translate those requirements into estimated costs for the additional technical capacity required.

2. If you are considering multiple activities for a single unit, complete this workform for each activity. Then create a summary of the overall costs for all of the additional technology you wish to deploy in that unit. You will most likely want to complete a summary copy of this workform for the entire library as well.

3. Telecommunications costs include both hardware and service. Dial in or out lines need modems as well as phone lines. Leased lines need routers or bridges and CSU/DSU equipment. Don't forget to include these items in your cost estimates.

4. If the devices to be added are similar to ones the library already has, use your own repair cost experience to estimate maintenance costs. If you are adding new types of equipment and don't have a repair history, try to get quotes from vendors to estimate these requirements.

5. Do not enter data in the shaded sections.

To Complete Workform T15

1. **Sections A–B**　Enter the functions and other types of equipment you recorded on Workform T13.

2. **Column D**　Transfer to column D the data from column G on Workform T13.

3. **Column E**

   Column E1　Enter your estimate of the unit cost of each device in column E1.

   Column E2　Enter any installation costs associated with each device in column E2. (Many libraries choose to include these costs if they will be paid to a vendor but may not include these costs if the installation will be done by library staff.)

   Column E3　Add columns E1 and E2 (if you are using column E2) and multiply that sum by column D. Enter the result in column E3.

4. **Column F**

   Column F1　Estimate the annual maintenance cost for each device and multiply it by column D. Enter the result in column F1.

   Column F2　Enter the annual service fees for telecommunications services in column F2.

5. **Row C**　Total columns E3, F1, and F2 and enter the results in the corresponding places in row C.

Factors to Consider When Reviewing the Data on Workform T15

1. The costs you develop are *only* estimates. The costs of technology change rapidly. When you are ready to implement this plan, you will need to revise your cost estimates.

2. You may be able to reallocate some existing equipment to meet the needs you have identified, particularly if you are attempting to expand a service that can make use of terminals or single-function workstations.

Technology　**293**

WORKFORM T15   Costs of Needed Technology

Activity _____

Library unit _____

Month/year data collected _____

A. Equipment/Software	D. Number of Devices Required	E. One-Time Costs			F. Annual Ongoing Costs	
		1. Unit Cost	2. Installation Costs	3. Total	1. Maintenance	2. Service Fees
1. Single-function workstation (group by function)						
Navigation						
Applications						
Development						
Management						
2. Multifunction workstations (group by functions)						
3. Terminals (group by function)						
Navigation						
Management						
4. Adaptive equipment (list)						

(Continued)

WORKFORM T15 **Costs of Needed Technology (Cont.)**

A. **Equipment/Software** (Cont.)	D. **Number of Devices Required**	E. **One-Time Costs**			F. **Annual Ongoing Costs**	
		1. Unit Cost	2. Installation Costs	3. Total	1. Maintenance	2. Service Fees
5. Other (list)						
B. Telecommunications						
Dial lines—incoming						
Dial lines—outgoing						
Leased lines						
ISP services						
C. Total						

Completed by _____ Date completed _____

Source of data _____ Library _____

Appendixes

Activities for This Planning Cycle

GOAL: _____

_____

_____

_____

Activity	Person Responsible	Date (Start/Finish)

Completed by _____ Date Completed _____

Library Name _____

From Ethel Himmel and William James Wilson, *Planning for Results: A Public Library Transformation Process* (Chicago: American Library Assn., 1998), Z.

APPENDIX B
Gap Analysis

Service/Response/Activity			
(Resource under review)	Have	Need	Gap
	Plan for filling the gap or reallocating the surplus		
(Resource under review)	Have	Need	Gap
	Plan for filling the gap or reallocating the surplus		

APPENDIX C
Analyzing Numeric Data

Some managers will be more comfortable with a statistical approach to resource allocation than with reporting raw data from the workforms. Much of the data you will collect on the workforms is numeric. Librarians tend to report numbers about library activities as percentages or averages. Neither is sufficient for the decisions to be made about staffing. As you review current and projected staffing needs, it is important to understand if the difference between two or more numbers reported for the same activity or work performed is meaningful. To do that you need to know something about number distributions.

The numbers that are reported by different individuals or units/teams, whether derived from the workforms in this book or from the library's own statistics, represent a distribution whose values range from high to low. However, the terms *high* and *low* are relative. The important question is whether a number—either highest or lowest—falls outside what is considered reasonable in relation to the other numbers for this group.

For example, each of the branch libraries in your system submits a monthly report that totals the number of reference questions answered in that branch. Probably the numbers range from low to high, since it is unlikely that the same number of questions was answered in each branch. The total number of reference questions reported by all branches constitute a number distribution. Suppose these monthly reports indicate that one branch seems to handle far fewer questions than the others. Is the difference between this branch and the others important? To find out, you first need to calculate the average number of questions handled by all the branches as a group. (The average is calculated by adding the numbers submitted by each unit and dividing that sum by the number of branches.) It is also important to know how the numbers are dispersed—meaning how close to or how far from the average they are. Dispersion can be assessed by calculating the standard deviation. However, for your purposes, you can use the following rule of thumb—more than 25 percent above or below the average for the group. If the fewest number of questions for a branch falls more than 25 percent below the average for the group, then some investigation seems in order.[1] Determine the ratio of questions answered per staff member or per reference librarian among all branches; then determine it for the branch in question. What is the number of questions answered per hour for all branches? For the branch in question?

Other questions to consider when looking at the discrepancy in branch scores include the following:

Is the staff for the branch in question interpreting and counting reference questions the same way other branches do?

Does this branch handle questions of greater complexity?

Is the staff inexperienced compared with those in the other branches?

Is the branch location or patron security a problem?

The preceding example had only one variable—the number of reference questions. In other cases, you will want to understand the relationship between two types of measures. For example, you might want to graphically show the relationship between staff and days absent from work (not including vacation days) for a particular time period. Assuming that the library has 99 staff members, use attendance records to create something like the following table. Note that the number of days in each interval is equal until the last segment.

Days Absent	Number of Staff
1–3	10
4–6	17
7–9	28
10–12	11
13–15	9
16+	3
Staff absent	78

Seventy-eight staff had absences, but twenty-one did not. Next, plot the data onto a graph and connect the lines as shown in figure 17.

For your purposes, you will probably want to pay attention only to the extreme ends of the graph—the tails. The lowest numbers usually appear at the left side of the graph, the highest at the right side. The side of the graph that is of interest depends on how the distribution is structured. In the graph, you would probably be interested in the right side, which reflects more absences. Plotting the data in this way allows you to visualize the number distribution.

FIGURE 17
Distribution of Staff Absences

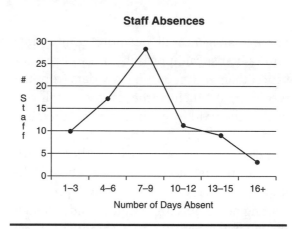

To keep things simple, you need only be concerned about numbers that are out of the norm for the data set. That is, focus on the extreme end of a side on plotted data or, as mentioned previously for averages, data that is more than 25 percent above or below the average for the group.

NOTE

1. The rule of thumb is based on P. L. Chebyshev's Theorem that at least 75 percent of any set of data must fall within two standard deviations of its mean.

APPENDIX D
Library Scan

1. Materials/Resources

How many	5 years ago	Now	In 5 years
Adult books			
Adult periodical titles			
Adult CDs, videos, tapes			
Other formats (list)			
Children's books			
Children's periodical titles			
Children's CDs, videos, tapes			
Other formats (list)			
Young Adult books			
YA periodical titles			
YA CDs, videos, tapes			
Other formats (list)			
Electronic resources for public use			
CD-ROM titles			
for Adults			
for Children			
for Young Adults			
Database licenses			
Internet access (# public workstations)			
for Adults			
for Children			
for Young Adults			

Completed by _____ Date Completed _____

Library Name _____

From Ethel Himmel and William James Wilson, *Planning for Results: A Public Library Transformation Process* (Chicago: American Library Assn., 1998), I.

APPENDIX E

Current Resource Allocation Chart

	Selected Service Response 1 ___ ___ ___	Selected Service Response 2 ___ ___ ___	Selected Service Response 3 ___ ___ ___	Selected Service Response 4 ___ ___ ___	Selected Service Response 5 ___ ___ ___	Other Service Responses ___ ___ ___	Other Services ___ ___ ___ ___	Totals = 100%
Staff								
Collections/ Resources								
Facilities								
Technology								
Other								

Completed by _____ Date Completed _____

Library Name _____

From Ethel Himmel and William James Wilson, *Planning for Results: A Public Library Transformation Process* (Chicago: American Library Assn., 1998), W.

In-Library Use of Materials

Output Measures: In-Library Materials Use per Capita

Definition:	Number of materials used in the library per person in the community served.
Calculation:	ANNUAL IN-LIBRARY MATERIALS USE divided by POPULATION OF LEGAL SERVICE AREA.
Data Collection:	Ask users not to reshelve, and for one week count all materials used.

Any item that is removed from the shelf (or from its usual location) by staff or public is considered "used." All formats of library materials are included. Just as circulation counts all items used outside the library, ANNUAL IN-LIBRARY MATERIALS USE counts all items used within the library. Each physical item (periodical issue or bound volume, microfilm reel, pamphlet file or folder, etc.) counts as one.

> *Example:* During one sample week, 6703 items were used. 6703 × 52 = an ANNUAL IN-LIBRARY MATERIALS USE of 348,556. The POPULATION OF LEGAL SERVICE AREA is 67,030. The **In-Library Materials Use per Capita** is 5.2 (388,556 divided by 67,080).

Analysis and Use of Data

Traditionally, libraries have used circulation data, and sometimes number of reference transactions, as indicators of activity levels. Adding **In-Library Materials Use per Capita** creates a more complete picture of service to the public, especially in libraries with extensive reference collections, or those where

people tend to use materials in the library rather than checking them out.

- A high **In-Library Materials Use per Capita** may be associated with a high **Reference Transactions per Capita** and/or with a large reference collection.

- A high **In-Library Materials Use per Capita** may indicate that users tend to spend time in the library. It may indicate a need for a large seating capacity and/or for many copy machines, microfilm readers, and the like.

- A low **In-Library Materials Use per Capita** may indicate a library where people stop in to pick up materials to take home, and do not stay long.

Possible approaches to increasing **In-Library Materials Use per Capita** include:

- Make the library a more inviting place to spend time
- Increase the seating and study space
- Consider whether hours are convenient for people who would like to spend time in the library
- Add more seating geared to special groups, for example, different sizes of tables and

Editor's note: Throughout this appendix, figure numbers have been changed to maintain the sequence within *Managing for Results.* Where feasible, cross references or sections irrelevant to this book were deleted.

From Nancy A. Van House and others, *Output Measures for Public Libraries: A Manual of Standardized Procedures,* 2d ed. (Chicago: American Library Assn., 1987), 44–7, 79.

chairs for children of different ages, or a homework corner for young adults.

Possible approaches to decreasing **In-Library Materials Use per Capita** are:

• Consider whether some reference materials should be made circulating

• Strengthen the circulating collection in subjects in which the reference collection is heavily used.

Collecting the Data

1. Choose a one-week "typical" period to collect data.

2. Ask users not to reshelve their materials during this period. Post signs in obvious places throughout the library: "Survey in progress. Please do not reshelve materials."

   a. It may help to place book trucks (or boxes, or laundry baskets, or whatever) throughout the library for people to leave materials on (or in). Label them prominently: "Please don't reshelve materials. Leave here." Arrange things so that it is easier for the user to leave the item than to reshelve it.

3. At least every hour on the hour throughout the sample days, collect and count materials left on tables or at collection points. Exclude those returned from outside circulation.

4. You can use the In-Library Materials Use Log, figure 18, to collect the counts; use a separate log sheet for each day. You may want separate log sheets in different parts of the library, for example, in different departments.

5. Enter the times when the counts are made across the top. If the library opens at 9:00 a.m., the first log entry would be for one hour later or 10:00 a.m., and so forth, until closing time.

6. Very busy libraries (or areas within a library) may need to collect materials more

often. Simply add more columns to figure 18.

7. The rows of figure 18 are labeled by type of material. These categories are *suggestions* only: use whatever categories make sense in your library, or you may use only the total at the bottom and not count materials by type.

8. "Controlled Materials" on figure 18 refers to materials that users must get from the staff, for example, books kept behind the reference desk. The staff responsible for those materials should have a copy of figure 18 and count each item as it is given to the user.

9. Total the number of materials used during the entire sampling week. Multiply this total by 52 to get ANNUAL IN-LIBRARY MATERIALS USE.

Pointers/Special Considerations

• An item is counted as used even if a patron looked at it and found that it wasn't what she or he wanted.

• The counting process should not interfere with library operations. Delaying reshelving in popular areas may *decrease* use because people can't find what they need when they need it. In that case, collect and count materials more often.

• In some libraries, especially small libraries, users may be reluctant to leave materials "in the way." It helps to mark a spot (e.g., a book truck) with the sign "Place materials here—please do not reshelve." This is also useful for users who want to protect their privacy—especially if the book truck is not near a service desk.

• The use of some kinds of materials may be particularly challenging to measure without inconveniencing users. For example, put magazines in strict alphabetical order and check hourly.

FIGURE 18
In-Library Materials Use Log

Library _____

Date _____

Use one tally sheet for each day. Every hour on the hour collect and count the materials left for reshelving. Enter the time at the top of the form.

Type of Material	Hour											Total
Books												
Magazines												
Pamphlet Files												
Sound Recordings												
Newspapers												
Controlled Materials[1]												
Other												
Totals												

1. Desk reserve or other materials user has to check out for in-library use.

- Some uses are almost impossible to count: for example, periodical indexes that are used continually. (Some libraries have put slips on each volume with a note asking people to make a mark every time they use it.) Other uses will go uncounted, for example, when a user looks at a book at the shelf and reshelves it. Do the best you can but know that no measure is perfect.

- It is easy to forget the collection time when staff are busy with other duties. Setting a timer or using an alarm clock will help.

Further Possibilities

- Determine **In-Library Materials Use per Capita** by type of material or subject area.

- Determine turnover rate based on in-library materials use (ANNUAL IN-LIBRARY MATERIALS USE divided by HOLDINGS).

- Analyze **In-Library Materials Use per Capita** by time of day.

- Conduct a user survey, asking people as they leave how many materials they used in the library.

Output Measures for Children:
In-Library Use of Children's Materials per Child

Definition:	Number of children's materials used in the library per person age 14 and under in the community served.
Calculation:	ANNUAL IN-LIBRARY USE OF CHILDREN'S MATERIALS divided by CHILDREN'S POPULATION OF LEGAL SERVICE AREA.
Data Collection:	For two weeks in a year (one in summer and one during the school year), ask users not to reshelve. Count all children's materials used.
Example:	During one sample week in summer, 124 children's materials were used in the library. Multiply 124 by 12 to get the Summer In-Library Use of Children's Materials count of 1488. During one sample week during the school year, 175 children's items were used in the library. Multiply 175 by 40 to get the School Year In-Library Use of Children's Materials count of 7000. Add the Summer In-Library Use of Children's Materials (1488) to the School Year In-Library Use of Children's Materials (7000) to get the ANNUAL IN-LIBRARY USE OF CHILDREN'S MATERIALS (8488). The CHILDREN'S POPULATION OF LEGAL SERVICE AREA is 5500. Divide the ANNUAL IN-LIBRARY USE OF CHILDREN'S MATERIALS (8488) by the CHILDREN'S POPULATION OF LEGAL SERVICE AREA (5500) to get the **In-Library Use of Children's Materials per Child** of 1.5. An average of 1.5 children's books were used within the library for each child age 14 and under living in the community.

$$\frac{(124 \times 12) + (175 \times 40)}{5500} = 1.5$$

Collecting the Data

1. Any item that is removed from the shelf (or from its usual location) by staff or public is considered used. All formats of library materials should be included—books, magazines, pamphlets, reference materials, computer software, CD-ROM indexes, cassettes, and so forth. Each physical item counts as one.

2. Choose a typical week in summer and a typical week during the school year to collect data.

3. Make a special effort to ask users not to reshelve children's materials during this period. It's a good idea to post signs throughout the library: "Survey in progress. Please do not reshelve materials." Make it easy for people to follow your directions. You might place book trucks or boxes or laundry baskets throughout the library with big signs on them: "Please don't reshelve materials. Leave them here." Frequent verbal reminders are also a good idea, especially with preschoolers.

From Virginia A. Walter, *Output Measures for Public Library Service to Children: A Manual of Standardized Procedures* (Chicago: American Library Assn., 1992), 37–9, 81.

4. At designated times throughout the day during the sample weeks, collect and count children's materials left on tables, on the floor, on tops of shelves, and/or at collection points. Other Children's Librarians have found that collecting and counting the materials three times during the day (at about noon, at 5:00, and at closing time) is sufficient. If your library is very busy, you may want to collect and count more often. Be sure that counted materials are removed from tables and collection points and placed elsewhere so that you won't count them twice!

5. Use the In-Library Use of Children's Materials Log (figure 19) to collect the counts; use a separate log sheet for each day. You may want to use separate log sheets for different parts of the library.

6. Enter the times when the counts are made on the Log.

7. The rows of the In-Library Use of Children's Materials Log are labeled by type of

---

FIGURE 19
In-Library Use of Children's Materials Log

Area: _____

Date: _____

Use one tally sheet each day. Enter times at the top of the form. At each time listed on the log, collect and count the children's materials left for reshelving on tables, tops of shelves, floor, etc.

Type of Material	Time:	Time:	Time:	Time:	Time:	TOTAL
Nonfiction						
Picture Books						
Fiction						
Magazines						
Sound Recordings						
Other						
Other						
Other						
TOTAL						

material. These are the most common categories that Children's Librarians have used. Use whatever categories make sense in your own library. If you don't need to know this level of detail, ignore the categories and record only the totals at the bottom.

Calculating the Measure

1. If this is a summer week, multiply the overall total by 12 to get the Summer In-Library Use of Children's Materials. If this is a school year week, multiply the overall total by 40 to get the School Year In-Library Use of Children's Materials. Keep a record and add the two totals together to get ANNUAL IN-LIBRARY USE OF CHILDREN'S MATERIALS.

2. Divide the ANNUAL IN-LIBRARY USE OF CHILDREN'S MATERIALS by the CHILDREN'S POPULATION OF LEGAL SERVICE AREA to determine **In-Library Use of Children's Materials per Child.**

Interpreting and Using the Data

1. Adding **In-Library Use of Children's Materials per Child** to juvenile circulation data gives a more complete picture of materials usage than either count alone can give.

2. A high **In-Library Use of Children's Materials per Child** may be associated with a high **Children's Information Transactions per Child.** It may also indicate a need for relatively more seating in the library or for more copy machines.

3. If you want to increase **In-Library Use of Children's Materials per Child,** consider these approaches:
   - Increase seating and study space for children.
   - Evaluate the library's service hours.
   - Make the library more attractive and inviting for children to use.
   - Establish special areas for in-library reading, such as homework centers or family reading nooks.
   - Develop special services for target populations that may find it difficult to check out materials for home use such as homeless families.

4. If you want to decrease **In-Library Use of Children's Materials per Child,** think about these strategies:
   - Convert some reference materials to circulating materials.
   - Strengthen the circulating collection in areas where the reference collection is currently used heavily. For example, you might want to acquire multiple copies of a good children's encyclopedia for home use.

Further Possibilities

1. Calculate the **In-Library Use of Children's Materials per Child** for particular subject areas or types of materials, such as Chinese-language materials or magazines.

2. Analyze the **In-Library Use of Children's Materials per Child** by time of day.

Output Measures for Young Adults:
Materials Use Measures

Materials Use measures are indicators of the extent to which the materials collection is used. Six different approaches to measuring materials use are offered here. While all are derived from *Output Measures for Public Libraries,* second edition, some involve differences in data collection techniques because of the need to make a physical link between the young adult library patrons and the material that they are using. [*Editor's note:* Only two of the measures are excerpted.]

In-Library Use of Young Adult Materials per Young Adult indicates the annual use of young adult materials within the library relative to the number of young adults in the community served.

In-Library Use of Materials by Young Adults per Young Adult measures the annual use of materials from all parts of the collection by young adults within the library relative to the number of young adults in the community served.

In-Library Use of Young Adult Materials per Young Adult

Definition:	Number of young adult materials used in the library during a given year per young adult in the community served.
Calculation:	ANNUAL IN-LIBRARY USE OF YOUNG ADULT MATERIALS divided by YOUNG ADULT POPULATION OF LEGAL SERVICE AREA.
Data Collection:	For two typical weeks during the year, ask users not to reshelve any materials. Count all young adult materials.
Example:	During a typical week in summer, staff counted 100 young adult material items that were left unshelved by patrons. Multiply 100 by 12 to find the Summer In-Library Use of Young Adult Materials; the figure is 1,200. For a typical week during the school year, staff counted 200 young adult materials left unshelved. Multiply 200 by 40 to find the School Year In-Library Use of Young Adult Materials; the figure is 8,000. Add the Summer In-Library Use of Young Adult Materials (1,200) and the School Year In-Library Use of Young Adult Materials (8,000) to find the ANNUAL IN-LIBRARY USE OF YOUNG ADULT MATERIALS (9,200). Divide the ANNUAL IN-LIBRARY USE OF YOUNG ADULT MATERIALS (9,200) by the YOUNG ADULT POPULATION OF LEGAL SERVICE AREA (2,000 in this case). The **In-Library Use of Young Adult Materials per Young Adult** is 4.6. On average, each young adult in the community used 4.6 young adult materials in the library during the year. $$\frac{(100 \times 12) + (200 \times 40)}{2,000} = 4.6$$

From Virginia A. Walter, *Output Measures and More: Planning and Evaluating Public Library Services for Young Adults* (Chicago: American Library Assn., 1995), 52–3, 56–60, 99, 100.

Collecting the Data

1. Collect data during one typical summer week and one typical week during the school year.

2. Make a special effort to ask users not to reshelve materials during this week. Have signs posted everywhere throughout the library: "Survey in progress. Please do not reshelve materials."

    Make it easy for people to follow these directions. Place boxes or baskets or book trucks throughout the library with big signs on them, "Please do not reshelve your materials; put them here." Or put signs on the tables: "Please do not reshelve your materials. Leave them here."

3. Do not make a special effort to target young adults. Ask *all* patrons to leave their materials unshelved. It will be relatively easy to calculate in-library use rates for adult and children's materials as well as young adult materials if you wish.

4. Data collection for this output measure requires that all young adult materials be labeled as such.

5. At designated times during the day, collect and count all young adult materials left on tables, on the floor, on tops of counters, and at your collection points, such as boxes and baskets. It doesn't matter how many times you take the count as long as you reshelve the materials you count each time so the items are not counted again. (They need not be reshelved on the regular shelves; they may be placed on sorting shelves.) If library staff members have a regular daily schedule for clearing off tables, the count could be taken at those times. Be sure that the staff does not clear tables without taking a count.

6. Be sure that your data collectors know to count young adult materials in all formats, including magazines and audiovisual ma-

terials. The list of kinds of material on figure 20 should help remind them. Feel free to add other categories to meet your own needs. If you do not need to know this level of detail, ignore the categories and record only the totals at the bottom.

7. Record the counts on figure 20, In-Library Use of Young Adult Materials Log. Use one form for each day of the week.

Calculating the Measure

1. Add up the totals from each day's In-Library Use of Young Adult Materials Log for a weekly total.

2. If the sample week is in the summer, multiply your total by 12 for the Summer In-Library Use of Young Adult Materials. If the sample week is a school year week, multiply your total by 40 to find the School Year In-Library Use of Young Adult Materials.

3. Add the Summer In-Library Use of Young Adult Materials and the School Year In-Library Use of Young Adult Materials to find the ANNUAL IN-LIBRARY USE OF YOUNG ADULT MATERIALS.

4. Divide the ANNUAL IN-LIBRARY USE OF YOUNG ADULT MATERIALS by the YOUNG ADULT POPULATION OF LEGAL SERVICE AREA to find the **In-Library Use of Young Adult Materials per Young Adult**.

Interpreting and Using the Data

1. A high **In-Library Use of Young Adult Materials per Young Adult** may be associated with a high **Young Adult Information Transactions per Young Adult**. It may also indicate a community in which young adults prefer or need to use materials in the library rather than taking them home.

FIGURE 20

In-Library Use of Young Adult Materials Log

Date _____

Use one tally sheet each day. Enter times at the top of the form. At each time listed on the log, collect and count the young adult materials left for reshelving on tables, tops of shelves, floor, etc.

Type of Material	Time:	Time:	Time:	Time:	Time:	TOTAL
Paperbacks						
Hardcover Fiction						
Hardcover Nonfiction						
Magazines						
Cassette Tapes; CDs						
Other						
Other						
Other						
TOTAL						

2. If you want to increase **In-Library Use of Young Adult Materials per Young Adult,** you might:
   - Increase seating and study areas for young adults
   - Make the library itself more attractive and inviting to young adults
   - Acquire more appealing or useful young adult materials
   - Make some popular browsing materials for in-library reference use only
3. If you want to decrease **In-Library Use of Young Adult Materials per Young Adult** (presumably converting some of these statistics to circulation statistics), consider:
   - Changing some of your reference materials to circulating copies
   - Acquiring additional circulating copies of heavily used reference materials, such as encyclopedias

Further Possibilities

1. Calculate the in-library use of particular kinds of young adult materials, such as magazines.
2. Analyze the **In-Library Use of Young Adult Materials per Young Adult** by time of day.

In-Library Use of Materials by Young Adults per Young Adult

Definition:	Number of materials from any part of the collection used in the library by young adults per young adult in the community served.
Calculation:	ANNUAL IN-LIBRARY USE OF LIBRARY MATERIALS BY YOUNG ADULTS divided by YOUNG ADULT POPULATION OF LEGAL SERVICE AREA.
Data Collection:	All young adult patrons complete a tally of materials they use in the library each time they visit the library during a typical week in summer and a typical week in the school year.
Example:	All young adults using the library during a typical week in summer reported using a total of 40 books in the library. Multiply 40 by 12 to find the Summer In-Library Use of Materials by Young Adults; the total is 480. All young adults using the library during a typical week during the school year reported using a total of 200 books in the library. Multiply 200 by 40 to find the School Year In-Library Use of Materials; the figure is 8,000. Add the Summer In-Library Use of Materials (480) and the School Year In-Library Use of Materials (8,000) to find the ANNUAL IN-LIBRARY USE OF LIBRARY MATERIALS BY YOUNG ADULTS; the figure is 8,480. Divide the ANNUAL IN-LIBRARY USE OF LIBRARY MATERIALS BY YOUNG ADULTS (8,480) by the YOUNG ADULT POPULATION OF LEGAL SERVICE AREA (650) to find the **In-Library Use of Materials by Young Adults per Young Adult**. The figure is 13.05. On average, each young adult in the community used 13 materials in the library during the year.

$$\frac{(40 \times 12) + (200 \times 40)}{650} = 13.05$$

Collecting the Data

1. Select a typical week in summer and a typical week during the school year in which to collect the data.

2. This measure is designed to count *all* materials from all parts of the collection in all formats used by young adults in the library. It is self-reported because there is no way of knowing the age of the patron who has used a book that is left lying on a table. Direct observation might work, but it is impractical to observe the library behavior of all young adult patrons in the library. It would also make the young adults feel very self-conscious. Self-reporting, while somewhat unreliable, at least gives an indication of young adult in-library use of the collection as a whole.

FIGURE 21
Young Adult In-Library Materials Use Tally Sheet

Please make a hash mark (/) each time you use one of these kinds of materials while you are in the library today. Place your completed form in one of the special boxes at the circulation desk or the exit when you leave the library. Thank you for your help!

Young adult books

Books from the adult or children's section

Young adult magazines

Other magazines

Reference books

Young adult cassette tapes or compact discs

Other cassette tapes or compact discs

Pamphlets

Something else?

How old are you? _____

Thanks again! Don't forget to leave your form in the box when you leave the library.

3. During the sample week, give each young adult entering the library a copy of figure 21, Young Adult In-Library Materials Use Tally Sheet. You may need to customize this form to suit the collection scope of your own library.

4. If possible, take the time to tell each young adult that you are conducting an important survey of young adult use of the library. Ask for his or her cooperation. Tell the young adults to keep the tally with them as they use the library and to make a hash mark each time they use a different item, such as a book, encyclopedia, magazine, pamphlet, etc. Ask them to turn in the form at the circulation desk or the exit as they leave the library. Have a box handy for the completed forms at the circulation desk or the exit. You should also have somebody there to remind young adults to leave the form as they exit the building. This person should have extra blank forms in case the patron has left the tally form somewhere in the library. If this happens, ask the young adult to take a minute and fill the form in before leaving.

5. The form does not measure use of electronic resources.

6. Have signs up at strategic points throughout the library reminding young adult patrons to fill in the tally. While helping young adults with materials, reference librarians and other public service staff might also discreetly remind the patrons to mark the forms.

Calculating the Measure

1. At the end of the week, count the totals from all Young Adult In-Library Use Tally Sheets that were found in the boxes. Ignore those that were left throughout the library even if they have some marks on them. You have no way of knowing whether these are duplicates or whether they are complete; it is safest to discard them.

2. If the sample week is in the summer, multiply the total from the tallies by 12; this figure is the Summer In-Library Use of Materials by Young Adults. If the sample week is during the school year, multiply the total by 40 to find the School Year In-Library Use of Materials by Young Adults.

3. Add the Summer In-Library Use of Materials by Young Adults and the School Year In-Library Use of Materials by Young Adults to find the ANNUAL IN-LIBRARY USE OF LIBRARY MATERIALS BY YOUNG ADULTS. Divide the ANNUAL IN-LIBRARY USE OF LIBRARY MATERIALS BY YOUNG ADULTS by the YOUNG ADULT POPULATION OF LEGAL SERVICE AREA to find the In-Library Use of Materials by Young Adults per Young Adult.

Interpreting and Using the Data

1. This measure is inclusive. Since it includes the in-library use of all materials, it subsumes **In-Library Use of Young Adult Materials per Young Adult.** If you trust the self-reporting of your young adult patrons, you could calculate the **In-Library Use of Young Adult Materials per Young Adult** from the Young Adult In-Library Use Tally Sheets by counting just the items labeled Young Adult from that form.

2. Because the data for this measure are collected by a very different technique than were data for **In-Library Use of Children's Materials per Child** as directed in *Output Measures for Public Library Service to Children* or **In-Library Materials Use per Capita** as directed in *Output Measures for Public Libraries,* second edition, you cannot compare it to either of them. It will be best used in com-

parison or in conjunction with statistics such as **Circulation of Materials per Young Adult.** You also can use it to compare in-library use of materials by young adults over time in your own library.

3. It may be helpful to look at this measure in relation to homework center measures.

Further Possibilities

1. Calculate in-library use rates for different kinds of materials, such as reference books.

2. Calculate in-library use rates by young adults for different time periods, such as after school or Saturdays.

APPENDIX G
Document Delivery

Output Measures: Document Delivery

Definition:	Percent of requested materials available within 7, 14, and 30 days, and longer.
Calculation:	Determine the percent of requests being tracked that are filled within 7, 14, and 30 days, or longer..
Data Collection:	Track one month's worth of requests for up to 30 days after they are placed.

Document Delivery measures the number of days required to get to users those materials not available at the time of their visits, either because the materials are not owned by the library, or because they are owned but are being used by someone else. Most libraries cannot have immediately available all the materials that their users request. This measure reflects how rapidly the library fills these requests.

> *Example:* A library tracked one month's worth of requests, for a total of 299. Of these, 72 (24%) were filled within 7 days, 20 percent between 8 and 14 days, 33 percent in 15 to 30 days, and 22 percent in more than 30 days.

Figure 22 is a log to be used in tracking requests. The source codes in figure 22 are suggested only: use the breakdown that makes the most sense for your library. Figure 22 categorizes sources into:

- Reserves: materials owned but temporarily unavailable (code R)
- Internal ILLs: materials borrowed from another branch of the same library (regard-

less of whether the requesting library owns the item) (code B)

- External ILLs: materials borrowed from another library (code I)
- Purchases: items not owned when requested but subsequently bought in response to the user's request, or items on order when the user requests them (code O)
- Other (code X).

Time counted is from the day the material is requested to the day it is physically available for borrowing, regardless of when the user picks it up.

Comparisons across libraries are best made using the results for all types of requests taken together (the bottom or "ALL" line of figure 24).

Analysis and Use of Data

Document Delivery measures how long users have to wait for requests. If **Document Delivery** is slower than you would like, you may want to study the various components of document delivery to deter-

Editor's note: Throughout this appendix, figure numbers have been changed to maintain the sequence within *Managing for Results.* Where feasible, cross references or sections irrelevant to this book were deleted.

From Nancy A. Van House and others, *Output Measures for Public Libraries: A Manual of Standardized Procedures,* 2d ed. (Chicago: American Library Assn., 1987), 62–5, 88–9.

FIGURE 22
Document Delivery Log

Library_____

Date Begun _____

Date Ended _____

Request No.	ID for Item	Date Requested Month/Day	Date Available Month/Day	Response Time (days)	Code[1]

1. Code for source of material; fill in after material arrives.
   R = Reserve (on your library's copy)
   B = Borrowed from another branch (intrasystem loans)
   I = Interlibrary loan
   O = Purchase
   X = Other (e.g., canceled, does not exist)

mine which aspect(s) needs attention. Some possible ways to reduce the wait:

- Consider whether your library is borrowing through ILL titles that it should own

- Buy more copies of high demand titles

- Make your ordering or processing more efficient

- Arrange for more frequent delivery between branches

- Improve your interlibrary and/or intralibrary loan procedures and/or delivery

- Change your library's policies about when you buy and when you borrow an item that is not owned
- Establish rush processing for urgent requests
- Consider buying heavily demanded titles locally rather than through your usual acquisitions process.

Collecting the Data

At least one month's worth of requests (i.e., all the requests placed by users over a period of one month) are needed. More requests will give a more precise estimate. These should total at least 100 requests. A library that handles fewer than 100 requests per month should probably record all requests for the entire year, or record requests over several periods during the year to a total of 100.

1. Pick a beginning day during a "typical" period. Using figure 22, Document Delivery Log, record every request during the next month. (Figure 23 is a partially filled-in example.)

2. Requests should be logged where the user picks up the material, usually the branch or circulation desk, *not* the central ILL unit. If, for example, all system ILLs go through a central ILL unit, but getting the material from there to the branch takes another day or two, measuring **Document Delivery** at the central ILL unit would underestimate the time that the branch patron had to wait. At the central library, log requests wherever the patron picks up the materials.

3. Mark each request in some way (for example, write its request number on it in a distinctive color of ink) so that when the material arrives, you know to update the Document Delivery Log.

   a. In a multibranch system, each unit or branch should track requests.

   b. Library-level results require a minimum of 400 requests, distributed among the

---

FIGURE 23

Worked Example of Figure 22: Document Delivery Log

Library __Main__

Date Begun __9/1/86__

Date Ended __9/30/86__

Request No.	ID for Item	Date Requested Month/Day	Date Available Month/Day	Response Time (days)	Code[1]
1	Birnham, J. Birnham's Theory	9/4	10/22	47	R
2	Onosko, Commodore 64	9/4	patron cancelled		
3	Angelou, All God's . . .	9/2	10/7	34	R
4	Beachley Q Clearance	9/4	10/17	42	O
5	Crane, Legacy of Lady Smith	9/4	10/7	32	I

branches in proportion to their circulation and/or their volume of requests. (The easiest approach is to have each branch track all its requests for a month, then add together the results for all the branches.)

4. Note on the log the source for each item as soon as it is known. With some items, that may be when the request is filled, with others it may be as soon as the request is placed.

5. As the items arrive, note on the log the source of the material (if necessary) and the date on which each becomes available for pickup (*not* the date on which the user did pick it up).

a. Count the actual days (including days the library was closed) between the date requested and the date available. Do not count the date of the request, but do count the date the item was finally available.

6. Use the Document Delivery Tally Sheet, figure 24, to calculate the **Document Delivery** figures. Calculate the percent of each type of request available within 7, 14, and 30 days, and more than 30 days, and those canceled (e.g., the user is no longer interested, the item does not exist, etc.) and those that never arrive.

Example: An item was requested on November 26 and the item was available on De-

---

FIGURE 24
Document Delivery Tally Sheet

Library _____

Date _____

No. of requests _____

Availability		Source of Material					
		Reserves	Interlibrary loans	Intrasystem loans	Purchases	Other	ALL
0–7 days	#						
	%						
8–14 days	#						
	%						
15–30 days	#						
	%						
More than 30 days	#						
	%						
Total[1]	#						
	%						

1. Totals may actually be a little more or less than 100% due to rounding.

cember 4. The Document Delivery Time was eight days.

Pointers/Special Considerations

- In some cases, a Document Delivery Log may not be practical, for example, where requests can go in many different directions and there is no convenient central place through which requests are processed. An alternative is to keep the needed information on each request form. For example, during the data collection every request slip may have the originating date written in a distinctive color ink. This would be the signal that when the item is available the date and source of material should be recorded and the request slip put aside to be counted. At some later time someone collects all the slips and fills out figure 22, Document Delivery Log.

- One caution about labeling the requests this way (or in an even more obvious way, like specially colored paper) is that it signals the staff that this request is being tracked. This could inadvertently result in special treatment. If the sample requests are given priority, the results will not be representative of the library's usual service. The advantage is that in some cases this will be easier than maintaining the log.

- The tracking ends when the item is available, not when the patron picks it up, because patron delays in coming to get it are not within the library's control. However, if you think that the library may contribute to patron delays (e.g., by inconvenient hours), you can easily add to figure 22 the pick-up date and analyze those delays.

Further Possibilities

- Calculate separate figures for different kinds of materials, for example, adults' versus young adults' and children's books versus periodicals.

- Determine **Document Delivery** for different sources, for example, within-state versus out-of-state interlibrary loans.

Materials Availability Measures

Output Measures: Materials Availability Measures

> Definition: Proportion of title and subject/author searches and of people browsing that are successful.
>
> Calculation: Number of successful searches divided by all searches, for each type of search.
>
> Data Collection: Materials Availability Survey, a survey of library users.

- **Title Fill Rate**
- **Subject and Author Fill Rate**
- **Browsers' Fill Rate**

These three measures reflect the degree to which library users were able to get the materials they were looking for during their visit. All three use data from the Materials Availability Survey (instructions below).

- **Title Fill Rate**

   The percentage of specific titles sought that were found in the library at the time of the request, including those requested by telephone.

   Calculation: NUMBER OF TITLES FOUND divided by NUMBER OF TITLES SOUGHT.

   Example: A user searching for *Dinner at the Homesick Restaurant* reports one title sought. If the user finds the book, that is one title found. One user may report more than one title sought.

- **Subject and Author Fill Rate**

   The percentage of requests for materials on a given subject or by a specific au-thor found at the time of the request. A request is considered "filled" if the user reports that she or he found something.

   Calculation: NUMBER OF SUBJECTS AND AUTHORS FOUND divided by NUMBER OF SUBJECTS AND AU-THORS SOUGHT.

   Example: anything by Ann Tyler; a book about restaurant management. Again, one user may report more than one search.

- **Browsers' Fill Rate**

   The percentage of users looking casually for something interesting (not for a specific title, subject, or author) who found something.

   Calculation: NUMBER OF BROWSERS FINDING SOMETHING divided by NUMBER OF BROWSERS.

   Example: Someone who comes in look-ing for "something good to read" is a browser.

Title and **Subject and Author Fill Rates** are the proportion of searches that are success-

---

Editor's note: Throughout this appendix, figure numbers have been changed to maintain the sequence within *Managing for Results.* Where feasible, cross references or sections irrelevant to this book were deleted.

From Nancy A. Van House and others, *Output Measures for Public Libraries: A Manual of Standardized Procedures,* 2d ed. (Chicago: American Library Assn., 1987), 50–9, 62, 81–7.

ful, not the proportion of users who were satisfied. A user may search for more than one title and/or subject on one visit. **Browsers' Fill Rate**, however, is the proportion of users who were satisfied.

> *Example:* During the sample period, one library counted 377 TITLES SOUGHT and 220 TITLES FOUND, for a **Title Fill Rate** of 58 percent (220/377). They counted 482 SUBJECTS AND AUTHORS SOUGHT and 287 SUBJECTS AND AUTHORS FOUND, for a **Subject and Author Fill Rate** of 60 percent (287/482). In addition, 280 users reported that they were BROWSERS, of whom 227 found something, for a **Browsers' Fill Rate** of 81 percent (227/280).

Analysis and Use of Data

Another way of looking at the **Fill Rates** is that each represents the probability that a search will be successful. A 60 percent **Title Fill Rate** means that the average user has a 60 percent chance of finding the title she or he is looking for.

The **Fill Rates** may reflect several things:

- The match between the library's collection and the users' wants

- The extent to which materials are owned and on the shelf when someone wants them

- How well users find things in the library.

The **Fill Rates** do not tell the library whether unsuccessful searches are due to the collection, the library's policies and procedures (longer loan periods may make it less likely that what people want will be on the shelf), or the user (such as users' ability to find materials on their own).

It is very important that these measures be looked at in the context of other measures, especially the Materials Use Measures: **Turnover Rate** and **Circulation per Capita.** The Materials Availability Measures indicate how successful users are, but not how much the library is used. If a library is rarely used, then the visitor's chance of finding materials on the shelf is quite high. When a library is very busy, however, some users are inevitably disappointed when what they are looking for is currently being used by someone else. The highest **Fill Rates** of all might occur in a library with a totally noncirculating collection.

A library with a low **Circulation per Capita** and/or a low **Turnover Rate** may have high **Fill Rates** because the collection is not being used. If a library increases its **Circulation per Capita** but not its **Fill Rates** from one year to the next, it is probably providing its users with more service. Although the **Fill Rates** haven't changed, the community is using the collection more and therefore getting more benefit from its library.

Other relationships to consider include:

- A high **Reference Transactions per Capita** and low **Subject and Author Fill Rate** may indicate the users are having trouble finding subject materials on their own and asking for help.

- A library with low **Fill Rates** and high **Circulation per Capita** may be exceptionally busy.

Generally, **Title Fill Rate** will be lower than **Subject and Author Fill Rate** because the library has more alternatives for filling subject/author requests. **Browsers' Fill Rate** is usually the highest of all.

Low **Fill Rates** may mean frustrated users. Ways to increase **Fill Rates** are:

- Examine your collection, especially in more popular areas, to see if you need to add titles, buy more duplicates, or shift purchasing from one area to another

- Speed up the reshelving of high-use materials

- Make it easier for users to find materials in the catalog and on the shelves

- Examine reserve, interlibrary loan, and reference requests to identify areas in which the collection needs improvement
- Shorten the circulation period for high-use materials
- Examine the responses to the Materials Availability Survey for ideas on ways to improve the collection.

Very high **Fill Rates** could indicate an underutilized collection. People have little trouble finding what they are looking for because materials aren't circulating, or because people are tailoring their searches to what they expect to find in the library. Possible ways to reduce **Fill Rates** include:

- Promote the library and its collection, inside and outside the library. Increasing **Circulation per Capita** may reduce the Fill Rates.
- Publicize the availability of reserves and interlibrary loan. Let people know that the library can get for them materials not on the shelf. This may encourage people to look for materials that they might not have expected the library to provide.

Collecting the Data

The data for these measures come from the Materials Availability Survey and a count of telephone requests, instructions for both of which follow. The Materials Availability Survey consists of giving a questionnaire to each person using the library during specified time periods, asking them to list what they looked for and whether or not they found it. The Telephone Request Tally adds in requests made over the telephone.

Pointers/Special Considerations

- Small libraries and others where most use is browsing may have difficulty collecting

enough title and subject and author searches for a reasonable sample. For them **Browsers' Fill Rate** may be the most appropriate **Fill Rate**. Generally, a library needs to be able to collect at least 100 searches within two weeks to be able to use the associated measure.

- It is very difficult for users to distinguish between reference transactions (discussed later in this chapter) and Subject and Author Searches. In the interests of simplicity, the Materials Availability Survey does not tackle the problem of distinguishing between these two. This means that some reference transactions will be included in calculating the **Subject and Author Fill Rate**.
- Because these measures are calculated from samples, they are estimates.

  The library's "true" **Fill Rates** may be a few percentage points lower or higher. Small differences among libraries or over time may be due to fluctuations in the measures rather than changes in library performance.

  Analysis of user's written comments and/or of the subject areas of failed searches may be particularly useful for diagnosing slight changes in service levels over time.

- **Fill Rates** depend not only on the library but also on users, including the variety of their requests and how adept they are at using the library. Differences in user communities should be considered in comparing **Fill Rates** across libraries and branches.

Further Possibilities

- Calculate separate children's, young adult, and adult **Title** and **Subject and Author Fill Rates** (ask age on the survey form). (Note that this would reflect each group's success in finding what they want, not people's success in finding children's, young adults', and adults' materials.)

- Follow up on materials not found to see why they weren't found. Were they not owned, owned but not available, available but not found by the user? This requires that the staff collect the forms quickly and trace the materials. See, for example, Paul B. Kantor, "Availability Analysis," *Journal of the American Society for Information Science* 27 (October 1976): 311–19.

- Analyze **Title** and **Subject and Author Fill Rates** by subject area.

- Read through the Materials Availability Survey responses and categorize the unfilled requests. Use this information for collection development.

Materials Availability Survey

Supplies Needed to Conduct Survey

Adequate copies of the MAS form (figure 29).

Pencils for users to borrow.

Sealed boxes for returning survey forms.

Signs for all entrances to library. Suggested text:
LIBRARY SURVEY TODAY. YOUR COOPERATION IS APPRECIATED.

Signs for all exits and the circulation desk. Suggested text:
HAVE YOU RETURNED YOUR SURVEY FORM? THANK YOU.

Copies of the Materials Availability Fact Sheet (figure 28) for everyone administering the survey and library service desks.

The Materials Availability Survey (MAS) is used to collect the data for the Materials Availability Measures: **Title Fill Rate, Subject and Author Fill Rate,** and **Browsers' Fill Rate.** The Materials Availability Survey asks users how successful they were during their current library visit at finding specific titles, at finding materials by an author or on a subject, and at browsing. At the same time, staff are tallying telephone requests to get a total view of user success.

This section provides step-by-step directions for scheduling and administering the Materials Availability Survey, keeping the Telephone Request Tally, and calculating the Materials Availability Measures.

Scheduling the Materials Availability Survey

Several decisions have to be made when scheduling the Materials Availability Survey (MAS):

- When during the year to do the MAS
- What goals to set for the numbers of questionnaires handed out and collected, and of searches reported: these determine for

how long a period of time the survey must be performed

- What days of the week and times of day during the sample period to administer the survey.

When to Do the MAS

1. Select a "typical" period when nothing unusual is happening that would affect library activities.
2. If you are also collecting data for **Reference Transactions per Capita** and/or **Reference Completion Rate,** you may or may not want to do the MAS at the same time.
   a. Both the MAS and the Reference Services Measures require the reference staff to keep tallies. It may confuse them to tally telephone requests for materials for the MAS and reference transactions for the Reference Services Measures at the same time.
   b. On the other hand, it is possible to modify the Reference Tally Sheet [not included] to incorporate the Telephone Request Tally Form (figure 30). This would avoid possible confusion over how to count telephone requests for materials while tallying reference transactions (requests for materials are not included in reference transactions).

How Many Questionnaires

The number of questionnaires to be handed out depends on how many questionnaires are needed to reach the target sample size of searches for the **Fill Rates.**

Example: A library distributed 1,000 MAS Forms to users. 690 were returned with usable responses for a response rate of 69 percent. (The remainder were never returned, or were unreadable.) Of the questionnaires returned, 30% reported one or more titles sought. (The rest reported no title searches.) 377 total TITLES SOUGHT were reported.

Figure 25, Calculating the MAS Sample, can be used to determine how many questionnaires to distribute and how long it will take. Figure 26 is a worked example.

1. Begin by determining your target number of TITLES SOUGHT. Enter on line 1 of figure 25.
   a. Because most libraries' users report fewer TITLES SOUGHT than SUBJECTS AND AUTHORS SOUGHT or BROWSING VISITS, a survey with enough TITLES SOUGHT will probably have enough responses for the other measures, too.
   b. To determine your target number of TITLES SOUGHT, either calculate your own sample size for **Title Fill Rate** or use the recommended sample size: preferably 400, but at least 100.
      1) A library that cannot get at least 100 TITLES SOUGHT and 100 SUBJECTS AND AUTHORS SOUGHT within two weeks should not use the Materials Availability Measures, or it should use *only* **Browsers' Fill Rate.** Many small libraries are used primarily for browsing, and so **Browsers' Fill Rate** is the most applicable of the Materials Availability Measures. In that case, the library needs at least 100 people checking the "browsing" question on the materials availability questionnaire within two weeks. While it may be useful for the staff to read through the answers to the other questions, the results for **Title** and **Subject and Author Fill Rates** probably won't be sufficiently accurate.
2. Enter on line 2 the average number of title searches that you expect on each questionnaire. This information can come from any of the following:
   a. The recommended MAS Pretest (described below)

FIGURE 25

Calculating the Materials Availability Survey Sample

	Your Library	OR	Default[1]
1. Desired number of title requests[2]			400
2. Title requests per questionnaire			.6
3. Target number of questionnaires (line 1 divided by line 2)			670
4. Response rate			.7
5. Number of questionnaires to hand out (line 3 divided by line 4)			960
6. Expected questionnaires distributed per hour[3]			no default value
7. Number of hours to distribute questionnaires (line 5 divided by line 6)			

1. If data are lacking for an individual library, use these recommendations.

2. Since most libraries receive fewer title requests than subject or browsing searches, basing the sample size on titles ensures an adequate size for all three.

3. Use your own library's data on visits, circulation, whatever is available.

FIGURE 26

Worked Example of Figure 25: Calculating the Materials Availability Survey Sample

	Your Library	OR	Default
1. Desired number of title requests	200		400
2. Title requests per questionnaire	.5		.6
3. Target number of questionnaires (line 1 divided by line 2)	400		670
4. Response rate	.8		.7
5. Number of questionnaires to hand out (line 3 divided by line 4)	500		960
6. Expected questionnaires distributed per hour	20		75
7. Number of hours to distribute questionnaires (line 5 divided by line 6)	25		15

b. Your library's past experience, if you have done the MAS before

c. A default assumption of .6 title searches per questionnaire returned. Note that this is based on other libraries' experiences: yours may be different.

3. Line 3 calculates the number of questionnaires that must be returned to get the required number of title searches.

4. Not all questionnaires come back, and not everyone follows instructions. The number of questionnaires to hand out (line 5) depends on the proportion of usable responses you expect to get back, that is, the response rate (line 4). This figure can come from the MAS Pretest or your library's past experience, where applicable. The default figure for line 4 is 70 percent.

5. The length of time needed to distribute the target number of questionnaires on line 5 of figure 25 depends on how many people use your library. You can determine this from the MAS Pretest or your past experience, or from whatever data you have on your library's use, such as number of visits per day or per hour (perhaps collected for **Library Visits per Capita,** or using a turnstile counter) or from your circulation figures. No default figure can be recommended.

Example: Using the default values for Figure 25, a library that needs 400 TITLES SOUGHT must get back 670 questionnaires (rounded up from 666). Given a response rate of 70 percent, it must hand out 960. This library expects to distribute 75 questionnaires per hour. It needs to administer the survey over 15 hours.

For simplicity, telephone requests are left out of these calculations.

All of these calculations are best done using your library's data rather than the default values. The MAS Pretest (described below) is useful for developing this information.

When to Hand Out Questionnaires

1. The number of hours during which a library distributes MAS questionnaires was determined above using figure 25.

2. The goal is to schedule the survey hours so that all the days of the week and times of day that the library is open are represented.

   - If a library were to simply start collecting questionnaires on Monday morning, for example, and stop when it reached its goal, it might be finished by Wednesday. If the people who use the library at the end of the week and on the weekend are looking for different kinds of materials from those at the beginning of the week (e.g., the homework crush comes Wednesday nights; the weekend home-repair crowd comes in on Saturday), the results will not represent all the kinds of uses that people make of the library.

3. The MAS should be distributed over the days of week and time periods that the library is open roughly in proportion to the library's schedule.

   Example: A library is open 60 hours a week, including:

   - 4 weekday mornings from 9 to 12, for a total of 12 morning hours, or 20 percent of its schedule
   - 5 weekday afternoons from 12 to 5, or 25 afternoon hours, 42 percent of its schedule
   - 4 weekday evenings from 5 to 9, for 16 evening hours, 25 percent of the total hours open
   - 8 hours on Saturday, 13 percent of the total

   This library's MAS is to run for at least 15 hours. Multiplying 15 by the percent of the hours open that each period of time accounts for, the MAS should run for 3 morning hours (20% of 15), 6 afternoon hours (42% of 15), 4 evening hours, and 2 hours on Saturday, for a total of 15 hours. The MAS is scheduled over the week as shown in figure 27.

FIGURE 27
Sample Materials Availability Survey Schedule

Time of Day	Mon.	Tues.	Wed.	Thur.	Fri.	Sat.	Sun.
9–10	(closed)	SURVEY					(closed)
10–11	(closed)				SURVEY		(closed)
11–12	(closed)				SURVEY		(closed)
12–1				SURVEY		SURVEY	(closed)
1–2				SURVEY		SURVEY	(closed)
2–3			SURVEY				
3–4	SURVEY		SURVEY				
4–5	SURVEY						
5–6	(closed)	SURVEY			(closed)	(closed)	(closed)
6–7	(closed)	SURVEY			(closed)	(closed)	(closed)
7–8	(closed)			SURVEY	(closed)	(closed)	(closed)
8–9	(closed)			SURVEY	(closed)	(closed)	(closed)

	= an hour the library is open
SURVEY	= an hour during which the MAS is conducted
(shaded)	= an hour the library is closed

There is no "formula" to this schedule: the hours were distributed to try to get an overall representation of days and hours that the library is open, avoiding the least busy periods (when few questionnaires could be collected). Some libraries have found that two-hour blocks work well for staffing.

This schedule is for a very busy library. Most libraries will distribute the survey times over two weeks, rather than one. In doing so, be sure that the schedules for the two weeks complement one another: for example, collect data on Tuesday morning one week, Tuesday afternoon the next.

Note that questionnaires are handed out to everyone *entering* the library during these periods. They will return the questionnaires when they leave, which may be after you have stopped distributing questionnaires for the day.

Administering the Materials Availability Survey

Staffing and Training

Select a survey coordinator responsible for materials, procedures, training, problem-solving, data analysis, and so forth. Generally, this will be the data coordinator.

The people handing out forms may be either staff members or volunteers. In some libraries, users respond better to people they can identify as staff members: but they may also ask the staff for help, directions, etc., that may interfere with the survey process. It helps if surveyors are easily identified as part of the library: a name tag or badge, for example. Some users are more willing to cooperate if they know that the library is doing the survey.

Surveyors need to be well-trained to ensure that they approach users in a friendly and nonthreatening way, can answer users' questions, and will politely but firmly ask people to turn in MAS forms as they leave. It helps to have some practice sessions for them to rehearse.

All staff members, regardless of whether they are directly involved in the MAS, should know the basics about the survey. People may ask them questions. Staff can answer questions about the form but must not influence people's responses in any way. The Materials Availability Fact Sheet (figure 28) will help them answer questions. Each person helping to conduct the survey should have a copy of the fact sheet. Additional copies for library staff members should be at all the service desks.

Pretest the MAS

Every new procedure has its problems. It is highly recommended that you do a short pretest before doing the MAS for the first time. The pretest is a one- or two-hour "rehearsal" of the MAS, best done during a moderately busy period. It is conducted exactly like the MAS itself, but the questionnaires are not tabulated as part of the full-scale MAS. The pretest serves two functions:

1. A test of all the procedures. A dry run can help the library to spot possible problems and fine-tune its training and procedures before the survey actually begins.

2. The pretest results can provide estimates of the response rate and the number of searches reported on each questionnaire, to be used in figure 25 (lines 2 and 4).

The Materials Availability Survey

1. Duplicate an ample number of MAS Survey forms (figure 29). If a large part of your clientele speaks a language other than English, you should translate this form into their language(s) as well. (This requires tabulators who can read these responses, too.)

2. Number the Materials Availability Survey forms (a number stamping machine helps) so that you will know how many were given out and how many came back, and so that during tabulation you can check back to the original form if questions arise.

3. During the sample periods, every user entering the library gets a form—no exceptions! Including children. All entrances must be covered.

4. If many of your clients have poor reading skills, or may otherwise have problems filling out the questionnaire, have additional staff available to help them. Children may need help, as well.

5. Users should fill out the questionnaire just before they leave the library, not as they enter.

6. Forms are collected at the exit.

   a. Have sealed boxes for the forms near all the exits, and at the Circulation Desk. Sealed boxes help to protect users' privacy, especially in small libraries.

   b. Someone should be at the exit reminding people to turn in their questionnaires. This can be the same person handing them out if the library is not too busy.

7. It is important that *everyone* returns a form. *The demeanor of the person collecting forms (and handing them out) can affect the number of forms that come back.* Because the response rate can affect the results, this is extremely important. Be assertive and friendly, not aggressive. This is no place for a shy person.

   a. All users who refuse to participate should be counted. Either (1) the surveyor marks

FIGURE 28
Materials Availability Fact Sheet

This survey measures how successfully people find the materials they are looking for in the library.

DIRECTIONS

1. During the survey time periods, *give a form to each person entering the library*. Explain that a survey is being taken today and the user's cooperation is appreciated. An appropriate comment would be "The library is doing a survey today. Please take one of these and fill it out just before you leave. Thank you." Do not ask in a manner that allows a simple "no" answer, such as "Will you please fill out this form today?"

2. Some terms used on the survey form:
   a. A TITLE search is for a specific book for which the user has all or part of the author or the title.
   b. A SUBJECT OR AUTHOR search is one where the user is looking for something (but not a specific item) on a subject, or anything by a certain author.
   c. BROWSING is looking for "something good to read," not something specific. A person can do a subject or title search and browse on the same visit.
   d. Someone who came into the library not to look for materials but *only* to do something else (use the copy machine, use the restroom, re-turn a book, etc.) should check the OTHER question at the bottom.

3. *EVERY person* (adult and child) *able to fill out the survey form, alone or assisted, must be given one*. Adults may fill out forms for children. You should help any users who need assistance.

4. *If a user is looking for too many items to write down,* ask how many subjects he or she was looking for and how many were found (ask the same for titles), and write those numbers on the survey form in the appropriate spaces. For example, if a user is looking for items on a bibliography, count the number of items on the bibliography and enter that number under "Title" on the survey form. Enter the number found under "yes" in the next column.

5. Ask each person to drop his or her form in the collection box.

6. *If a librarian identifies a specific title for a patron* as a result of a patron's question, this is a title search when the patron looks for the title.

7. *Answer questions about the form* but do not influence the responses in any way. The following answers to questions may prove helpful.

SOME STOCK ANSWERS TO QUESTIONS

1. *Why are you surveying me? Why don't you survey someone else?*
   "This survey period has been chosen to ensure that we get a representation of *all* our library users. It's important for the accuracy of the survey that everyone complete the survey form. Your answers are important."

2. *You gave my friend a questionnaire when he came in a little while ago: can I have one too?*
   "Thank you for being willing to help, but we are only surveying people who come into the library during specific time periods. This is to ensure that our findings are statistically correct."

3. *I really don't have time for this today!*
   "The survey only takes 5 minutes. You'll help us a lot if you can give your time, and your information is important to our study." If the respondent insists, mark the form "REFUSED" and put it in the collection box OR tally a refusal, whichever method your library is using.

4. *I already filled out a form the last time I was here.*
   "Thank you, but we do want you to fill out another one today."

5. *Who's doing the study?*
   "The _____ Library is doing this survey. I am a library staff member (or volunteer) helping with the survey."

6. *Do I write down only books, or records and magazines, too?*
   "All kinds of materials are included, not just books."

7. *Should I count materials I looked at in the library but didn't check out?*
   "Yes. This survey measures both things you use here and those you take home."

8. *Should I fill out the form for my children while we use the library today?*
   "Yes. It is important to us to know if they are finding what they want, too."

9. *I just came in to return a film.*
   "Fine, then you only have to check the 'Other' question at the bottom of the form and turn it in as you leave. But if you do end up looking for something else while you are here, please write that down."

FIGURE 29
Materials Availability Survey Form

Form number _____

LIBRARY SURVEY

Library _____   Date _____

PLEASE FILL OUT THIS SURVEY AND RETURN IT AS YOU LEAVE.

We want to know if you find what you look for in our libraries. Please list below what you looked for today. Mark "YES" if you found it, and "NO" if you did not find it.

TITLE

If you are looking for a specific book, record, cassette, newspaper, or issue of a magazine, please write the title below. Include any reserve material picked up.

NAME OF WORK   FOUND?
(Example)
• Gone with the Wind   YES NO

1. _____
2. _____
3. _____
4. _____
5. _____

SUBJECT OR AUTHOR

If you are looking for materials or information on a particular subject or a special author today, please note each subject or person below.

SUBJECT OR AUTHOR   DID YOU FIND
(Examples)   SOMETHING?
• how to repair a toaster
• any book by John D. MacDonald   YES NO

1. _____
2. _____
3. _____
4. _____
5. _____

BROWSING   If you were browsing and not looking for something specific, did you find something of interest?

YES _____   NO _____

OTHER   _____ Check here if your visit today did *not* include any of the above activities. (Example) using the photocopy machine.

COMMENTS   We would appreciate any comments on our service and collections on the back of this sheet.   **THANK YOU!**

a questionnaire "refused" and drops it in the return box, or (2) surveyors keep tallies of refusals. Decide ahead of time which method is most appropriate for your library and pick one.

The MAS can also be administered as an interview rather than a self-administered questionnaire.

Telephone Request Tally

During the same time periods that you administer the Materials Availability Survey, tally all the telephone requests for materials using figure 30, Telephone Request Tally Form. *Don't* tally requests all day long, only during the MAS sampling period.

1. Use a separate tally sheet for each sampling period (e.g., Monday morning, Tuesday afternoon, etc.).
2. You will need a form at each phone where such requests are received: for example, in a large library with subject departments you may need one at each department's reference desk.
3. Tally each request as either positive (item is currently available) or negative (item is not currently available, that is, not owned, not on the shelf, etc.).
4. At the end of the sampling period, gather all the tally forms and total the results.
5. These are added to the results of the MAS using figure 32, Materials Availability Survey Summary.

Tabulation

The MAS forms should be tabulated by staff members who are fairly well-acquainted with the library and the kinds of things that people are looking for. People don't always follow directions, so the staff should be able to recognize common titles and to distinguish between title and subject searches. In most libraries, this would be high-level support staff or professional staff.

If some questionnaires have been distributed in a language other than English, someone who knows this language is needed to tabulate these.

1. Use the Materials Availability Survey Tabulation Form, figure 31. You will need enough copies to record all the survey forms that you handed out. Enter the number of each survey form in the first column.
2. A person may report one or more title and/or subject searches and browse on the same visit; he or she may do some but not all of these searches; or he or she may do none of these.
3. *Titles:* For each survey form, on the line of the tabulation form with the survey form number, record the number of titles sought in column 1a, and the number found in 1b.
   a. A title search is a search for a specific item. It need not be a book, but may be a specific magazine (e.g., "current issue of *Time*"), movie, etc.
4. *Subjects or Authors:* Record the number of subjects and authors sought in column 2a, and the number found in column 2b.
   a. A subject/author search is a search for material on a subject or by an author.
      1) Include searches for particular genres of fiction (e.g., science fiction, romances).
      2) Do not count as subject searches the following responses: "novels" or "fiction" (unspecified); "new books"; type of material (e.g., magazines, movies); "nonfiction." If the user has listed one of these kinds of searches, this is considered a browsing search. Code and count the search as browsing.
5. *Browsing:* If the question about browsing was answered, put a "1" in column 3(a) "Browser."

FIGURE 30

Telephone Request Tally Form

Library _____

Date _____

Use one tally form for each day

TITLE REQUESTS:

On shelf	Not on shelf
TOTAL:	TOTAL:

SUBJECTS AND AUTHORS REQUESTS:

On shelf	Not on Shelf
TOTAL:	TOTAL:

Count all telephone calls asking whether specific materials (specific books, issues of magazines, film titles, etc.) are currently available. Count as "on shelf" materials that you find on the shelf, that the user could pick up immediately. Count as "not on shelf" materials that are not owned, on order, out in circulation, or otherwise currently unavailable.

a. If the answer to the browsing question is "Yes," also put a "1" in column 3(b).

b. If the answer is "no," enter a zero.

c. If the browsing question was not checked, put zeros in both 3(a) and 3(b).

6. *Other:* If the user checked *only* the "Other" question, put a "1" in column 4(a) and zeroes in all others. (The point of the "other" question is to allow all users to return a form, and to avoid confusion among users who did not search for materials.)

a. If they marked the "Other" question but also answered elsewhere, ignore the answer to the "Other" question.

7. Do *not* count (in either the "Sought" or "Found" columns) searches for which the user did not indicate whether the material was found. Counting these in the "Sought" column but not the "Found" column

FIGURE 31

Materials Availability Survey Tabulation Form

	(1) Title		(2) Subject/Author		(3) Browsing		(4) Other	
Form Number	(a) Number Sought	(b) Number Found	(a) Number Sought	(b) Number Found	(a) Browsers	(b) Found Something	(a) Other	(b) Refused, Blank, or Missing
TOTAL								
Enter on figure 32	line 7	line 10	line 13	line 16	line 19	line 20	line 3	line 5
	TITLES SOUGHT	TITLES FOUND	SUBJECTS/ AUTHORS SOUGHT	SUBJECTS/ AUTHORS FOUND	NUMBER OF BROWSERS	BROWSERS FINDING SOME-THING	OTHER	NOT USABLE

would erroneously treat them as failed searches, reducing the library's fill rate.

8. Any search for which the user's response is unclear or incomplete should not be counted at all. (On the questionnaire, write in red next to the answer "NC" for "not coded.") If the questionnaire is not codable (no questions were legibly answered, or the questionnaire is marked "refused" or is blank), put a "1" in column 4(b) and zeroes in all other columns.

9. In some cases, users may have clearly confused subject and title searches, or not followed directions. You may *correct* such clear mistakes, but *with caution:* only the user knows what she or he was looking for. *The coder is not to overrule the user except in clear cases. When in doubt, the user is right.*

a. Mark on the questionnaire in red any changes or interpretations that you make. For example, if the user has not marked the browsing question, but has listed under subject/author searches "novels," line through in red the answer under subjects, and check in red the browsing question. This is so that if you need to go back to the questionnaires you know how each question was coded.

10. Total the columns on each sheet, and add together the totals from all the MAS Tabulation Forms.

11. Turn to figure 32, Materials Availability Survey Summary, and follow the instructions on the form. It tells how to add together the results from figure 30, Telephone Request Tally, and figure 31, Materials Availability Survey Tabulation, to get your library's **Title, Subject and Author,** and **Browsers' Fill Rates.**

   a. Only the "unavailable" or "not on shelf" responses on the telephone tally are counted; presumably titles that were available were picked up later by the user and counted then.

12. All these measures need to be expressed as confidence intervals (+ or − 5%).

If too few of the people surveyed participate, the results may not be representative. A low participation rate on a survey usually means that there is something wrong with the survey: the questionnaire is too difficult, or the questions asked don't apply to the users, or the staff handing out and collecting the forms are not persuasive enough. Generally, a library should have a response rate of at least 60 percent for the results to be meaningful. Use figure 32 to calculate the response rate.

Example: A library distributed 400 Materials Availability Survey forms. 300 of them were returned with responses that could be coded using figure 32. Another 10 users answered the "Other" question, indicating that they had not come to the library looking for materials. Therefore a total of 310 people answered the questionnaire and followed instructions. Another 20 questionnaires were unintelligible, 5 had been marked "refused" by the staff distributing questionnaires, and 65 questionnaires just never turned up—apparently users had thrown them away or taken them home. The library's response rate is 78 percent (310 divided by 400).

FIGURE 32

Materials Availability Survey Summary

Response Rate	
1. Number of questionnaires handed out	
2. Questionnaires returned with usable title, subject and author, or browsing answers (total questionnaires minus the total of columns 4a and 4b, figure 31)	
3. Questionnaires with *only* "Other" question checked (total of column 4a, figure 31)	
4. Usable questionnaires (subtotal line 2 + line 3)	
5. Questionnaires marked "refused," with no usable responses, or never returned (total of column 4b, figure 31)	
6. Response rate (line 4 divided by line 1)	

(Continued)

FIGURE 32

Materials Availability Survey Summary (continued)

Title Fill Rate	
7. TITLES SOUGHT (total of column 1a, figure 31)	
8. Titles not available (Telephone Request Tally Form, figure 30)	
9. Total TITLES SOUGHT (line 7 + line 8)	
10. TITLES FOUND (total of column 1b, figure 31)	
11. **Title Fill Rate** (line 10 divided by line 9)	
12. Confidence interval for **Title Fill Rate** (+ or − 5%) LOW: HIGH:	

Subject Fill Rate	
13. SUBJECTS AND AUTHORS SOUGHT (total of column, 2a, figure 31)	
14. Subjects and Authors not available (Telephone Request Tally Form, figure 30)	
15. Total SUBJECTS AND AUTHORS SOUGHT (line 13 + line 14)	
16. SUBJECTS AND AUTHORS FOUND (total of column 2b, figure 31)	
17. **Subject and Author Fill Rate** (line 16 divided by line 15)	
18. Confidence interval for **Subject and Author Fill Rate** (+ or − 5%) LOW: HIGH:	

Browsers' Fill Rate	
19. NUMBER OF BROWSERS (total of column 3a, figure 31)	
20. NUMBER OF BROWSERS FINDING SOMETHING (total of column 3b, figure 31)	
21. **Browsers' Fill Rate** (line 20 divided by line 19)	
22. Confidence interval for **Browsers' Fill Rate** (+ or − 5%) LOW: HIGH:	

Output Measures for Children: Materials Availability Measures

These measures, all variants of Fill Rates, reflect the degree to which library users were able to get the materials they wanted during their visit. Therefore, the measures can give an indication of how well the library's collection meets the needs of its users. The data to calculate these measures are derived from surveys of library users. We have greatly simplified the survey forms used in *Output Measures for Public Libraries,* second edition, in order to make them easier for young people to fill out. We have sacrificed some of the detail of data, but we think the gain in user friendliness makes it worthwhile.

The basic measure is the **Children's Fill Rate.** For libraries with particular roles, such as Formal Education Support Center or Preschoolers' Door to Learning, we provide specialized fill rates—**Homework Fill Rate** and **Picture Book Fill Rate.** You may think of other fill rates that would be useful in your particular situation; the basic method should apply.

Children's Fill Rate

Definition:	The percentage of successful searches for library materials in any part of the library collection by users age 14 and under and adults acting on behalf of children.
Calculation:	Number of successful searches divided by all searches.
Data Collection:	A survey of library users age 14 and under and adults acting on behalf of users age 14 and under, taken during two sample periods, one in summer and one during the school year.
Example:	During the summer sample period, one library counted 145 items sought by the children and adults who filled out the library survey form. The library counted 112 items found, for a Summer Children's Fill Rate of 77 percent (112 divided by 145). During the school year sample period, the library counted 250 items sought, with a total of 180 found. The School Year Children's Fill Rate is 72 percent (180 divided by 250). To find the annual **Children's Fill Rate,** convert the percentages to decimals. Multiply the School Year Children's Fill Rate by 3. Add the Summer Children's Fill Rate to the weighted School Year Fill Rate, and divide by 4. For this library, the **Children's Fill Rate** is 73 percent. On average, there is a 73 percent chance that a person age 14 and under or an adult acting on behalf of a child has found something he or she wanted in the library during the past year.

$$\frac{112}{145} = .77 \quad \frac{180}{250} = .72 \quad \frac{.77 + (3 \times .72)}{4} = .73$$

From Virginia A. Walter, *Output Measures for Public Library Service to Children: A Manual of Standardized Procedures* (Chicago: American Library Assn., 1992), 42–4, 46–50, 85, 89, 91, 93, 97, 99.

Collecting the Data

Scheduling the Survey

1. You must be able to collect and count at least 100 surveys from library users who are 14 and under and adults acting on behalf of children who are 14 and under within a one- or two-week period in order to make valid assumptions about the data. Select typical periods in both summer and the school year to conduct the survey.

2. You will need to decide what days and hours during the sample week you will be handing out the survey forms. You may decide to target *every* child in order to reach the goal of at least 100 completed survey forms. We recommend this method.

   However, staffing considerations may dictate a sample. Then you will want to be sure that you distribute surveys during all times when children and their care givers are likely to be in the library. You will distort the results if you survey only the after-school crowd or if you over-sample the morning hours when parents and pre-schoolers are in the library. A sampling schedule for a library open Monday and Tuesday from 1:00 to 9:00, Wednesday, Thursday, and Friday from 10:00 to 6:00, and Saturday from 1:00 to 5:00 might be:

Monday:	1:00 to 3:00 and 6:00 to 9:00
Tuesday:	3:00 to 6:00
Wednesday:	10:00 to 12:00 and 3:00 to 6:00
Thursday:	1:00 to 3:00
Friday:	10:00 to 12:00 and 3:00 to 6:00
Saturday:	2:00 to 4:00

Administering the Children's Library Survey

1. One person should be responsible for the survey. This survey coordinator (usually the Children's Librarian) should train all staff and volunteers who will be involved in the survey, gather materials, collect the data, and so forth.

2. Be sure that *all* staff are aware that the survey is taking place and what its purpose is. All staff should be able to answer basic questions from the public and refer appropriate queries to the survey coordinator.

3. Pretesting your procedures is essential; this will help you identify unforeseen problems.

4. Duplicate enough Children's Library Survey forms (figure 33).

5. Number the forms so you will know how many were given out and how many came back. This also helps during tabulation if you need to refer to the original form.

6. Post signs announcing that a survey is being conducted of all library users who are age 14 and under or persons who are acting on behalf of people 14 and under.

7. Place clearly marked collection boxes for completed forms in strategic locations—the circulation desk, children's reference desk, and by the exits.

8. During the sample period, give a form to *every* library user under the age of 14 as well as to adults, such as parents or teachers, who are acting on behalf of children. It may be difficult to tell if an adult is looking for materials for a child or for his or her own use, even in the children's area of the library. If it is *probable* that the adult is acting on behalf of a child, give the adult a form. The adult can decide not to fill it out if it doesn't apply.

   It is not enough to simply have the forms available for people to take. Either a staff member or a volunteer should make contact with each library user. Much of

FIGURE 33

Children's Library Survey

Form # _____

1. How old are you? _____

   (If you are an adult looking for materials for a child, put down the child's age, not your own.)

2. Were you looking for anything special in the library?   YES   NO

   Please tell us what you were looking for:

   1. _____

   Did you find it?   YES   NO   Was it for school?   YES   NO

   2. _____

   Did you find it?   YES   NO   Was it for school?   YES   NO

   3. _____

   Did you find it?   YES   NO   Was it for school?   YES   NO

3. If you were just browsing and not looking for anything special, did you find anything interesting?   YES   NO

4. Did you come to the library for some completely different reason, such as attending a program or using the restroom?   YES   NO

5. Is there anything else you want to tell us about the library? You may write on the back of the page if you want to.

Thank you for answering our questions. Please leave this form with the librarian today.

the success of this process depends on how this person approaches the patrons. It can be very empowering for children to be asked for their input. The survey distributor may say something like, "The library wants to know if you are finding what you need here. Please fill this out and help us serve you better." Be assertive and friendly but not overbearing.

Cover all entrances to the library. This fill rate measures the success that children and adults acting on behalf of children have finding materials in any part of the library, not just children's materials.

9. Staff handing out the forms may need guidance in distinguishing patrons who are 14 from those who are 15 or 16. You shouldn't worry about this too much, because the form asks how old the patron is. You can discard forms filled out by patrons who are too old. If you have good signage announcing the survey, many people will self-select and offer to fill out the form before you have an opportunity to hand it to them.

10. Although the form is very simple, children under the age of 7 or 8 will need help filling it out. It is all right for a parent, staff member, or volunteer to interview the child and write in the information.

11. Parents and care givers of preschoolers and babies, or other adults acting on behalf of children, should be asked to fill out the survey on behalf of the children. They should give the age of the child, not their own age, and indicate the material sought for the child, not for their own use.

12. If a patron refuses to take a form, the survey distributor should mark it "refused" and drop it in the collection box.

13. Users should fill out the forms just before they leave the library, not as they enter.

Tabulating and Calculating the Data

1. Somebody who is familiar with children's library materials should do the tabulating. Some responses will require an informed eye to determine what was really meant; the tabulator should be able to recognize common children's book titles and frequently requested subjects.

2. Use the Children's Library Survey Log (figure 34). You will need enough copies to record all the survey forms that you distributed. Write the number of each form in the first column.

3. In column (1), enter information drawn from the question "Were you looking for anything special in the library?"

4. Column (2) records information about browsing searches.

5. Column (3) is for recording other uses of the library and forms that were blank or refused.

6. Add up the total for each column and enter on the bottom line of the form. Add the column totals for each page of the log that you have filled out.

7. Turn to the Children's Library Survey Summary (figure 35). Follow the directions to calculate **Children's Fill Rate**. You will also be able to calculate the **Homework Fill Rate** on this form from the data collected if you have used the forms exactly as we have provided them.

Interpreting and Using the Data

1. The fill rates don't tell you *why* any particular patron search is unsuccessful. All they tell you is the probability that a search will be successful. In other words, a 75 percent **Children's Fill Rate** means that a young patron or an adult acting on behalf of a young person age 14 and under has a 75 percent chance of finding something that he or she is looking for.

2. Before trying to interpret what the fill rates mean in your particular situation, it is important to look at them in the context of the library's mission and role and in reference to other output measures. The Materials Use Measures provide some particularly interesting points of reference with fill rates. A very busy library with a high **Circulation of Children's Materials per Child** and/or **Turnover Rate of Children's Materials** might have a low **Children's Fill Rate** because the collection is

FIGURE 34
Children's Library Survey Log

Form Number	(1) Title, subject, author				(2) Browsing		(3) Other	
	(a) Sought for school		(b) Not for school		(a) Browsers	(b) Found something	(a) Other	(b) Refused, blank, or missing
	(c) Found	(d) Not found	(e) Found	(f) Not found				
TOTAL								
	School items found	School items not found	Nonschool items found	Nonschool items not found	Number of browsers	Browsers finding something	Other	Not usable

FIGURE 35
Children's Library Survey Summary

1. Number of questionnaires handed out _____

2. Questionnaires returned with usable title/subject/author or browsing answers (total of questions minus the total of columns 3a and 3b) _____

3. Questionnaires with *only* "other" question checked (total of column 3a) _____

4. Usable questionnaires (subtotal of lines 2 and 3) _____

5. Questionnaires marked "refused," with no usable responses, or never returned (total of 3b) _____

6. Response rate (line 4 divided by line 1) _____

Children's Fill Rate

7. Title/subject/authors sought (total of columns 1c, d, e, and f) _____

8. Title/subject/authors found (total of columns 1c and 1e) _____

9. Title/subject/authors fill rate (line 8 divided by line 7) _____

10. Number of browsers (total of column 2a) _____

11. Number of browsers finding something (total of column 2b) _____

12. Browsing fill rate (line 11 divided by line 10) _____

13. **Children's Fill Rate** (total of line 8 and line 11 divided by total of line 7 and line 10) _____

Homework Fill Rate

14. Title/subject/authors sought for school (total of column 1c and 1d) _____

15. Title/subject/authors sought for school and found (total of column 1c) _____

16. **Homework Fill Rate** (line 11 divided by line 12) _____

so heavily used. Both a library with a large noncirculating collection or an underused library might have high **Children's Fill Rates.**

3. Focus groups might help you understand **Children's Fill Rates** that are particularly high or low.

4. If you want to increase **Children's Fill Rates:**

   • Reexamine your collection development policy; perhaps you need to add more duplicate copies of popular titles or work harder to determine and meet user needs in your community.

- Make your collection easier to use by arranging it differently or adding better signage.

- Offer more effective assistance in using the collection. Perhaps the staff needs some additional training in providing readers' advisory service to young library users or perhaps the staff needs to be more visible.

- Speed up the process of reshelving popular materials.

Further Possibilities

1. As described here, the **Children's Fill Rate** measures access to all library materials by young people under the age of 14 and adults who are acting on behalf of young people. You might want to structure a fill rate that measures access to only children's library materials.

2. The following output measures are examples of ways to customize the **Children's Fill Rate** to provide a specialized fill rate for a particular purpose.

Homework Fill Rate

Definition:	Proportion of searches for information and/or library materials to assist with homework by library users age 14 and under and adults acting on their behalf that are successful.
Calculation:	Number of successful searches for library materials divided by all searches.
Data Collection:	A survey of library users 14 and under and adults acting on behalf of people 14 and under, taken during a sample period.
Example:	During a typical week during the school year, one library found that juvenile library users and their care givers sought 143 items for school use; 95 of those items were found. The **Homework Fill Rate** was calculated to be 66 percent (95 divided by 143). There is a 66 percent chance that a patron age 14 and under or an adult acting on behalf of a child is able to find library materials needed for homework purposes. $$\frac{95}{143} = .66$$

Collecting the Data and Calculating the Measure

1. See the data collection section for the previous measure, **Children's Fill Rate.** You will probably need to schedule only one sample period, during the school year, for this measure. Otherwise, use the forms and methods described for the more general **Children's Fill Rate.**

2. Calculate the data as indicated on the Children's Library Survey Summary form (figure 35).

Interpreting and Using the Data

1. This measure is particularly meaningful to libraries who have selected the role of Formal Education Support Center. It indicates

specifically how successfully the collection supports curriculum needs. A library with a strong educational mission would be looking for relatively high **Homework Fill Rates.**

2. A low **Homework Fill Rate** may be entirely appropriate in a community where school libraries are well developed or where the public library is consciously trying to fill other information and reading needs of its young users.

3. This measure may also give valuable information to libraries who are still looking around, analyzing the community and current patterns of library use.

Picture Book Fill Rate

Definition:	The percentage of successful searches for picture books by all library users.
Calculation:	Number of successful searches divided by all searches.
Data Collection:	A survey of users of the picture book collection, taken during a sample period.
Example:	During the sample period, one library counted 225 searches of its picture book collection. Patrons indicated that 195 of those searches were successful. The **Picture Book Fill Rate** is 87 percent (195 divided by 225). There is an 87 percent chance that a patron will be able to find a desired picture book.

$$\frac{195}{225} = .87$$

Collecting the Data

1. Decide whether you want to sample both school year and summer use. If you have any reason to think that school year and summer use vary, you should schedule two sample periods, one during a typical week in summer and one for a typical week during the school year. (See the data collection section for **Children's Fill Rate** for directions for averaging if you decide to use the two sample periods.)

2. You must be able to collect at least 100 surveys from users of your picture book collection during the sample period for the results to be valid. If you are unable to do this in a one- or two-week period, this may not be an appropriate measure for your library to use.

3. We recommend that you survey *every* qualifying library user, that is, every person who looks for a picture book during your sample period. However, if staffing constraints make it impossible to hand out the Picture Book Use Survey form during every hour that the library is open, then you will have to designate particular times during the week that you will target every potential user. Be sure that you designate hours that capture typical users of the collection. A typical sampling schedule for a library open from 10:00 to 9:00

Monday through Thursday, from 10:00 to 6:00 on Friday and Saturday, and from 1:00 to 5:00 on Sunday might be

Monday, Wednesday, and Friday: 10:00 to 12:00 and 2:00 to 4:00

Tuesday and Thursday: 3:00 to 5:00 and 7:00 to 9:00

All day Saturday and Sunday

4. Duplicate enough Picture Book Survey forms (figure 36).

5. Post signs announcing that you are conducting a survey of the use of the picture book collection.

6. Place a box labeled "Completed Picture Book Use Survey Forms" in a conspicuous place in the picture book area. Put another one at the circulation desk and another one at each exit.

7. Number the blank forms. During the sample period, give a Picture Book Use Survey form to each person using the picture book section. A staff member or volunteer must be available to do this at all times during the survey; this person must be able to observe and approach all persons in the picture book area.

FIGURE 36

Picture Book Use Survey

Form # _____

1. How old are you? _____

(If you are an adult looking for materials for a child, put down the child's age, not your own.)

2. Were you looking for any particular picture books today?   YES   NO

What were they? Please tell us the name of the book you were looking for, or the author, or the subject.

Did you find what you wanted? Please circle YES or NO for each item.

1. _____

Found?   YES   NO

2. _____

Found?   YES   NO

3. _____

Found?   YES   NO

3. If you were just browsing and not looking for anything special, did you find anything interesting? YES   NO

Thank you for answering our questions. Please leave this form with the librarian today.

8. Adults should be asked to fill in the form on behalf of children in their care who are too young to fill in the form themselves. People who serve as survey distributors should be trained to approach adults in an assertive but friendly way, asking for their help in conducting a survey that will help the library evaluate use of the picture book collection.

9. Unaccompanied children who have difficulty with the form may be "interviewed"; the staff member or volunteer can ask them the questions and fill out the form for them. Children should be approached with respect, asking for the same information. The survey distributor should then say to children who may not be able to fill in the form, "Would you like me to fill in the form for you or would you rather do it yourself?"

10. If a patron refuses to fill in a form, the survey distributor should mark the form "refused" and put it in the collection box.

Tabulating and Calculating the Data

1. Use the Picture Book Survey Log (figure 37). You will need enough copies to record all the survey forms that you handed out. Write the number of each form in the first column.

2. In column 1, enter information drawn from question 2 on the Picture Book Use Survey form. Count the number of items found and not found on each form and enter the totals in the appropriate spaces under columns 1a and 1b.

3. In column 2, record information about browsing searches. In 2a, make a check if the form had either *Yes* or *No* circled for question 3. Check 2b if *Yes* was circled.

4. Make a check in column 3 only if the form was unusable for some reason. If it is unusable, do not mark anything in columns 1 or 2.

5. Add up the total for each column and enter on the bottom line of the form. Add the column totals for each page of the log that you have filled out.

6. Turn to the Picture Book Survey Summary (figure 38). Follow the directions to calculate the **Picture Book Fill Rate.** If you plan to conduct the survey twice during the year, in summer and during the school year, you would follow the directions for the general **Children's Fill Rate** to find the yearly figure.

Interpreting and Using the Data

1. Although this survey measures use of the picture book collection by users of all ages, it would nonetheless be a useful indicator for libraries emphasizing service to preschoolers.

2. Analyze the **Picture Book Fill Rate** in connection with other specialized measures, such as Picture Book Circulation per Preschool Child.

Further Possibilities

1. Use the Picture Book Use Survey forms with parents whose children attend Preschool Story Hour over a period of several weeks or for the time that a particular story hour series lasts. Calculate a **Picture Book Fill Rate** based on just that market segment.

2. Look at the author/title/subject data on individual survey forms to gain a better understanding of specific needs of your picture book users. Use in collection development.

FIGURE 37

Picture Book Survey Log

Form Number	(1) Title, subject, author		(2) Browsing		(3) Other
	(a) Found	*(b)* Not found	*(a)* Browsers	*(b)* Found something	
TOTAL					
	Found	Not found	Number of browsers	Browsers finding something	Other

FIGURE 38

Picture Book Survey Summary

1. Number of questionnaires handed out

2. Total of column 3 ("other")

3. Questionnaires returned with usable title/subject/author or browsing answers (total number of questions minus the total of column 3)

4. Response rate (line 3 divided by line 1)

5. Title/subject/authors sought (total of columns 1a and 1b)

6. Title/subject/authors found (total of column 1b)

7. Title/subject/authors fill rate (line 6 divided by line 5)

8. Browsing materials sought (total of columns 2a and 2b)

9. Browsing materials found (total of column 2b)

10. Browsing fill rate (line 9 divided by line 8)

11. **Picture Book Fill Rate** (total of line 6 and line 9 divided by total of line 5 and line 8)

Output Measures for Young Adults: Materials Availability Measures

The materials availability measures are variants of the fill rates presented in *Output Measures for Public Libraries,* second edition. They indicate the degree to which young adult patrons are able to find the materials they are looking for when they come to the library. The measures are expressed as the percentage of searches for particular items that are successful.

The data for calculating the fill rates are taken from user surveys. The survey form in this book has been tested with many young adults, and it works very well. Teenagers seem agreeable to filling it out, even eager in some cases. In field tests, there were only a few cases of obvious scams, when groups of young adults suddenly found great amusement in filling in the form with "made up" information.

Young Adult Fill Rate

Definition: The percentage of successful searches by young adults for library materials in any part of the library collection.

Calculation: Number of successful searches divided by all searches.

Data Collection: A survey of young adult library users taken during two sample periods, one in summer and one during the school year.

Example: During the summer sample period, one library counted 102 items sought by the young adults who filled out the library survey forms. The library counted 89 items found, for a Summer Young Adult Fill Rate of 87 percent (89 divided by 102). During the school year sample period, the library counted 200 items sought, and a total of 142 found. The School Year Young Adult Fill Rate is 71 percent (142 divided by 200). To find the annual **Young Adult Fill Rate,** convert the percentages to decimals. Multiply the School Year Young Adult Fill Rate by 3; the figure is 2.13. Add the Summer Young Adult Fill Rate to the weighted School Year Fill Rate; the figure is 3.0. Divide by 4. For this library, the **Young Adult Fill Rate** is .75 or 75 percent. On average, there was a 75 percent chance that a young adult's search for a particular item in the library was successful during the past year.

$$\frac{89}{102} = .87 \qquad \frac{142}{200} = .71 \qquad \frac{.87 + (3 \times .71)}{4} = .75$$

From Virginia A. Walter, *Output Measures and More: Planning and Evaluating Public Library Services for Young Adults* (Chicago: American Library Assn., 1995), 61–2, 64, 67, 102, 104–5.

Collecting the Data

Scheduling the Survey

1. Select a typical week during the summer and a typical week during the school year to collect your data.

2. You must be able to collect and count at least 100 usable surveys from young adult library patrons during the sample period to make valid assumptions about the data. If you cannot collect 100 surveys in a one-week period, you will need to extend the time to two weeks.

3. Administer the survey during all hours that the library is open, targeting *every* young adult library user during the sample period, if possible. However, if staffing constraints dictate a sampling approach, then be sure that you distribute surveys during representative hours that young adults are in the library. You will distort the results if you survey only after school or if you oversample during the mornings, when most young adults are in school.

Administering the Survey

1. One person should be responsible for the survey. The survey coordinator should train all staff who will be involved in the survey, prepare materials, schedule data collectors, and collect the survey forms.

2. Be sure that *all* staff are aware that the survey is taking place and that they know its purpose. All staff should be able to answer basic questions about the survey from the public and refer appropriate queries to the survey coordinator.

3. Pretesting your procedures is essential; this pretest will help you to identify unforeseen problems.

4. Duplicate enough copies of figure 39, Young Adult Library Survey, to be able to give one to *every* young adult entering the library during the sample period.

5. Number the forms so you will know how many were given out and how many came back.

6. Post signs indicating that a young adult library survey is being taken. The wording could be something like: "Attention, young adults! We are taking a library survey this week. Please fill out the Young Adult Library Survey forms before you leave today. Thank you!"

7. During the sample period, give a form to all young adult library users, preferably as they enter the library. It is not enough to simply have the forms available for the young adults to take. You must make a friendly, nonaggressive personal contact with all young adult users and ask them to fill out the form. The data collector should ask the young adult to leave the completed form in the marked box at the circulation desk or exit on the way out.

8. Survey distributors may need some guidance in identifying young adults. During training, provide information that may assist them, but don't worry about it too much. The age line on the survey will enable you to eliminate any forms from patrons who are too young or too old. If the survey distributor is standing next to the sign that announces a young adult survey in progress, some people may volunteer or offer the information that they are too old or too young.

9. If a young adult refuses to take a form, the survey distributor should mark it "refused" and drop it in the collection box.

Calculating the Data

1. A staff member who is familiar with young adult library materials should do the tabulating. Some responses will require an

FIGURE 39
Young Adult Library Survey

Form # _____

1. How many items (books, magazines, tapes, etc.) did you check out today? _____

2. Were you looking for anything in particular in the library?   YES   NO
   If you were just browsing, skip down to question 3.

   If you were looking for particular things, please list them here:

   a. _____

       Did you find it?   YES   NO

       Was it for school?   YES   NO

   b. _____

       Did you find it?   YES   NO

       Was it for school?   YES   NO

   c. _____

       Did you find it?   YES   NO

       Was it for school?   YES   NO

   (If you were looking for more than three things, please list them on the back.)

3. If you were just browsing and not looking for anything special, did you find
   anything interesting?   YES   NO

4. Did you come to the library for some competely different reason, such as attending a program or
   meeting a friend or using the restroom?   YES   NO

5. How old are you? _____

6. Is there anything else you want to tell us about the library? You may write on the back of the page if you
   want to.

Thank you for answering our questions today! Please leave this form in the marked box when you leave the
library.

informed eye to determine what was really meant.

2. Use the Young Adult Library Survey Log (figure 40). You will need enough copies to record all the survey forms that were distributed. Write the number of each form in the first column.

3. In column (1), enter information drawn from the question "Were you looking for anything special in the library?"

FIGURE 40
Young Adult Library Survey Log

Form Number	(1) Title, subject, author				(2) Browsing		(3) Other	
	(a) Sought for school		(b) Not for school		(a) Browsers	(b) Found something	(a) Other	(b) Refused, blank, or missing
	(c) Found	(d) Not found	(e) Found	(f) Not found				
TOTAL								
	School items found	School items not found	Nonschool items found	Nonschool items not found	Number of browsers	Browsers finding something	Other	Not usable

4. Column (2) records information about browsing searches.

5. Column (3) is for recording other uses of the library and forms that were blank or refused.

6. Add up each column and enter the totals on the bottom line of the form. Then add the column totals for each page of the log that you have filled out.

7. Now turn to the Young Adult Library Survey Summary (figure 41). Follow the directions to calculate the **Young Adult Fill Rate.** You also will be able to calculate the **Homework Fill Rate** on the form from

---

FIGURE 41
Young Adult Library Survey Summary

1. Number of questionnaires handed out .... (1) _____

2. Questionnaires returned with usable title/subject/author or browsing answers (total of questions minus the total of columns 3a and 3b) .... (2) _____

3. Questionnaires with only "other" question checked (total of column 3a) .... (3) _____

4. Usable questionnaires (subtotal of lines 2 and 3) .... (4) _____

5. Questionnaires marked "refused," with no usable responses, or never returned (total of 3b) .... (5) _____

6. Response rate (line 4 divided by line 1) .... (6) _____

Young Adult Fill Rate

7. Title/subject/authors sought (total of columns 1c, d, e, and f) .... (7) _____

8. Title/subject/authors found (total of columns 1c and 1e) .... (8) _____

9. Title/subject/authors fill rate (line 8 divided by line 7) .... (9) _____

10. Number of browsers (total of column 2a) .... (10) _____

11. Number of browsers finding something (total of column 2b) .... (11) _____

12. Browsing fill rate (line 11 divided by line 10) .... (12) _____

13. **Young Adult Fill Rate**

 (13a) total of line 8 and line 11 .... (13a) _____

 (13b) total of line 7 and line 10 .... (13b) _____

 (13c) 13a divided by 13b .... (13c) _____

Homework Fill Rate

14. Title/subject/authors sought for school (total of column 1c and 1d) .... (14) _____

15. Title/subject/authors sought for school and found (total of column 1c) .... (15) _____

16. **Homework Fill Rate** (line 15 divided by line 14) .... (16) _____

the data collected if you have used the forms exactly as described.

8. The form also provides data about circulation of library materials to young adults, data that are often unavailable through normal circulation reporting systems.

Interpreting and Using the Data

1. The fill rates don't tell why a patron's search was unsuccessful. They simply indicate the probability that a search by a young adult will be successful.

2. Some libraries have added an additional line that asks, "Did a librarian assist you today?" The answer to this question may provide a little more evidence to help in interpreting the results.

3. It is sometimes enlightening to examine Materials Use measures along with Materials Availability measures. You might find that your **Circulation of Materials per Young Adult** is very high, while the **Young Adult Fill Rate** is quite low. This discrepancy might indicate a very busy library in which the collection is so heavily used that individual patrons are sometimes frustrated in their searches for specific items. On the other hand, an underused library might have very high fill rates. In this library a few patrons are able to find much of what they want.

4. The information on the Young Adult Library Survey forms may give you some clues about why your fill rates are high or low because the young adult has a space to write in what he or she was looking for, as well as whether it was found.

5. If you want to increase **Young Adult Fill Rates:**
   - Reevaluate your collection development policy to see if it meets the needs of your current young adult patrons.
   - Make your collection easier to use by putting up more effective signs or arranging it differently.
   - Offer more effective reference and readers' advisory services to young adults.

6. If you are concerned about what seem to be low fill rates and are unable to figure out their cause, try conducting some focus groups with young adult library users to find out more about their experiences when they try to find something in the library.

Further Possibilities

1. **Young Adult Fill Rate** measures the probability of a young adult having success finding an item anywhere in the collection. You might want to structure a survey that measures search success in only the young adult collection.

2. The following output measure, **Homework Fill Rate,** is an example of a specialized fill rate. You might think of others that you would like to design.

Homework Fill Rate

Definition:	Proportion of successful searches by young adults for information and/or library materials to use with homework assignments.
Calculation:	Number of successful searches for homework materials divided by all searches for homework materials.
Data Collection:	A survey of young adult users taken during one typical week during the school year.
Example:	During a typical week during the school year, one library found that young adults searched for 267 items for school use. Of these, 180 searches were successful. Divide 180 by 267 to find the **Homework Fill Rate.** The figure is .67, or 67 percent. There is a 67 percent chance that a young adult's search for a library item needed for homework use was successful during the year.

$$\frac{180}{267} = .67$$

Collecting the Data and Calculating the Measure

1. See the previous measure, **Young Adult Fill Rate,** for directions on administering the survey and calculating the measure. You may calculate this measure from the data from one typical week during the school year; it is not necessary to collect data during the summer months when school is not in session.

2. Calculate the measure from data on the Young Adult Library Survey Summary (figure 41), as directed.

Interpreting and Using the Data

1. If your library has adopted Formal Education Support Services as one of its roles, you will be interested in the results from this output measure. It tells you how well your collection and services support the curriculum needs of your young adult patrons.

2. If the middle schools and high schools in your community have excellent school library media centers, you may find that you do not need to be as aggressive about meeting curriculum needs of young adults. You may find that you have low **Homework Fill Rates** because you have not really tried to meet the needs of the few young adults who come to you instead of their school libraries for homework materials.

3. You may want to work with the school library media centers in your community to develop collections and services that are complementary to each other to meet the needs of the young people in your community.

Index

359

Sandra Nelson is a consultant, speaker, trainer, and writer specializing in public library planning and management issues. She has presented hundreds of training programs in more than 35 states during the past two decades. During her career, Nelson has worked in both large and small public libraries and in state library agencies. She chaired the Public Library Association committee that developed the PLA planning process, *Planning for Results: A Public Library Transformation Process,* and is coauthor of *Wired for the Future: Developing Your Library Technology Plan* (ALA, 1999).

Ellen Altman was Visiting Professor, Department of Library and Information Studies, Victoria University of Wellington, New Zealand, until July 1997. She has been a faculty member at the Universities of Kentucky and Toronto and at Indiana University. She was Professor and Director of the Graduate Library School at the University of Arizona. She has been Feature Editor of *Public Libraries,* the official publication of the Public Library Association of the United States, since 1992. Dr. Altman is co-editor of "The JAL Guide to the Professional Literature" in the *Journal of Academic Librarianship* and a member of *Library Quarterly*'s Editorial Board. Professor Altman was one of the coauthors of *Performance Measures for Public Libraries* published in 1973. She has served on many professional and governmental committees. She received the Distinguished Alumni Award from Rutgers School of Communication, Information and Library Studies in 1983 and has been included in *Who's Who in America* since 1981.

Diane Mayo is vice president of Information Partners, Inc., an information technology and library automation consulting firm that specializes in assisting libraries with planning and implementing a wide range of technologies. She is a professional librarian, with more than twenty years' experience in the field of library automation, who speaks frequently on managing technology in public libraries. In addition to her consulting work, Mayo has managed both technical services and public services operations in multibranch public libraries as well as having worked for a vendor of automated library systems. Mayo is coauthor of *Wired for the Future: Developing Your Library Technology Plan.*